PMP® Exam Practice Tests

600 Questions with Explanations
with complete reference to the
PMBOK® Guide Sixth Edition

Daud Nasir, PMP

Daud Nasir (author) and GetXSolution Inc. (publisher) reserve all rights in and to this copyrighted work. Except the right to store and retrieve one copy of the work, you may not decompile, disassemble, reverse engineer, reproduce, modify, create derivative works based upon, transmit, distribute, disseminate, sell, publish or sublicense the work or any part of it without publisher's prior consent. You may use the work for your own non-commercial and personal use; any other use of the work is strictly prohibited. Your right to use the work may be terminated if you fail to comply with these terms.

This work is provided "AS IS." The author and the publisher make no guarantees or warranties as to the accuracy, adequacy, suitability, completeness of or results to be obtained from using this book. This includes any information or work that can be obtained through a hyperlink or otherwise provided through this book. They also expressly disclaim any warranty express or implied, including but not limited to implied warranties of merchantability or fitness for a particular purpose. The author and the publisher do not warranty that the information and functions contained in the work will meet your requirements. Neither the author and the publisher shall be liable to you or anyone else for any inaccuracy, error or omission, regardless of cause, in the work or for any damages resulting therefrom nor will they be liable for any indirect, incidental, special, punitive, consequential or similar damages that result from the use of or inability to use the work, even if any of them has been advised of the possibility of such damages. This limitation of liability shall apply to any claim or cause whatsoever whether such claim or cause arises in contract, tort or otherwise.

Copyright © 2019 GetxSolution Inc.

All rights reserved.

ISBN: 978-1-7950-7530-5

Please note that all trademarks are the trademarks of their respective owners. Trademarked names do not show trademark symbol after every occurrence but there is no intention of infringement of the trademark. Each use of trademarked name is for the benefit of that trademark owner.

CONTENTS

1	Instructions	1
2	PMP Mock Test 1	3
3	PMP Mock Test 2	47
4	PMP Mock Test 3	93
5	Answers & Explanations Test 1	137
6	Answers & Explanations Test 2	181
7	Answers & Explanations Test 3	223
8	An Additional Offer	263
9	About the Author	265

1 INSTRUCTIONS

The following tips will enhance your learning experience and help boost your chances of success in the actual PMP® exam.

Take each of the tests as a whole by setting aside 4 hours. The actual test is 4 hours long. The time does not stop once it starts. However, you can take breaks, if you like, but the clock keeps ticking.

Have a few blank sheets of paper and pencil ready before you start the test. You will receive the same when taking the actual test. You can use these sheets to perform calculations or take notes to analyze the choices.

You are to look for the best choice as the answer to each of the questions. It means there can be one or more choices that are valid and correct but may not be the best choice.

Target about 50 questions per hour if you continue to attempt and answer all questions. Slower than this rate means you may not be able to complete the test in the given time. If you are marking a significant number of questions for later review, you need to target a higher number per hour than this in the first 2-3 hours.

Review your answers after completing each test. Look at the explanations for the ones you got wrong and also for the ones you got right. To improve your understanding, you have to analyze each of your answers to see why the best choice is the best. Did you come up with the same reason to mark the correct choice or was it a fluke? Each explanation provides a reference to the relevant section and page of the PMBOK guide. You can review these references for further reading.

All the three tests are very similar to each other and the actual exam considering distribution and difficulty of questions. So to observe an improvement, your score should go up as you take the next mock tests.

Good luck!

Daud Nasir, PMP

2 - PMP MOCK TEST 1

200 Questions - Time Limit: 4 Hours

1. The project management office advised the project manager to perform a procurement audit. A procurement audit is a tool and technique that is used in the _____ process.
    A) Conduct Procurements
    B) Audit Procurements
    C) Control Procurements
    D) Close Project or Phase

2. A project manager completed the perform integrated change control process. What is the next piece of work done?
    A) Preventive actions are published
    B) Approved change is implemented
    C) Corrective actions are recommended
    D) The change request is closed

3. You have been assigned to a project because the previous project manager left the company. You have found that the morale of the team is pretty low and team members seemed a bit reserved. The team finds it difficult to complete deliverables. There were several other small issues too. What can you do to bring the team morale up and resolve other problems?
    A) Rebuild the team by redoing WBS and involving the team in re-planning of the project. This will boost the morale of the project team.
    B) Perform individual and team assessment and activate the reward

system
- C) Inform management that the previous project manager had failed to go through team development phases and ask for extra time
- D) Replace key team members and bring fresh enthusiastic resources

4. A project management student you are mentoring is confused about the benefits of work breakdown structure. You explained how the work breakdown structure is an input to many project management processes. Then you mentioned all of the following processes as examples EXCEPT _____.
   A) Define Activities
   B) Plan Quality Management
   C) Acquire Resources
   D) Estimate Costs

5. You have successfully handed over the final deliverable of your project to the customer as part of the Close Project or Phase process. As part of project closeout, you analyzed the interrelationships between various project variables to understand their contribution to project results so that future projects' performance can be improved. Which data analysis technique have you used?
   A) Document analysis
   B) Regression analysis
   C) Trend analysis
   D) Variance analysis

6. What is incorrect about the Identify Stakeholders process?
   A) This process cannot occur before the project charter is written
   B) This process should occur when a significant change in the organization happens
   C) This process may be repeated as many times as needed
   D) This process should occur at the start of each phase

7. Which of the following processes best facilitates lessons learned document?
   A) Identify Stakeholders
   B) Plan Quality Management
   C) Plan Communications Management
   D) Manage Quality

8. You are the project manager of a new human resources training system project. The project is currently behind schedule due to several

reasons. You are updating the assumptions log with a newly identified resource constraint that is contributing to the delay. Which of the following is a resource constraint on the project?
   A) A tester's per day cost was higher than expected
   B) Report specifications were not clear that resulted in rework
   C) A programmer was less experienced than expected
   D) A developer was absent for 5 days due to sickness

9. When ranking the risks in Perform Qualitative Risk Analysis process, many risk parameters can be considered. One of those parameters is to compare the degree to which a risk is perceived to matter by one or more stakeholders. What is this parameter called?
   A) Dormancy
   B) Connectivity
   C) Propinquity
   D) Controllability

10. A project's current Schedule Performance Index (SPI) is 1.05. What is the project's schedule status?
    A) Behind schedule
    B) On schedule
    C) Ahead of schedule
    D) Cannot be determined from SPI alone

11. How is success measured in the case of portfolio management?
    A) Deliver on time, within budget, and with quality
    B) Aggregate investment performance
    C) Deliver intended business benefits and the efficiency with which these are delivered
    D) Continue efficiently with optimal resource usage

12. There are two recommended ways a schedule can be compressed. These are _____.
    A) Crashing and Schedule Networking
    B) Crashing and Fast Tracking
    C) Resource Leveling and Crashing
    D) Resource Leveling and Scheduling

13. A project implemented several steps to improve customer satisfaction, but the results from the next survey remained the same as before. How can the results be analyzed to find out why the steps did not make any improvement?
    A) Use a fishbone diagram to find out what is still causing customer

dissatisfaction
B) Perform a quality audit to verify the quality measurements
C) Draw a control chart to see how many survey results are outside the limits
D) Create an affinity diagram to see what the biggest dissatisfaction customer is having

14. Project constraints can be all of the following EXCEPT _____.
    A) Schedule
    B) Quality
    C) Cost
    D) Template

15. How will you differentiate between the project management plan and the project baselines?
    A) The project management plan can be changed at regular intervals while project baselines can be changed anytime
    B) The project management plan and project baselines are the same. There is no difference.
    C) Project management plan changes as project progresses while project baselines are frozen once created
    D) Project management plan describes how the project will be executed, monitored, controlled, and closed while project baselines are used for measuring performance.

16. You are the project manager of a business process improvement project whose customer has rejected the final deliverable. The team has identified a fix to the deliverable and is now working on it. The plan is to resubmit the deliverable to the customer for acceptance. Which of the following process will you start when the customer accepts the deliverable on resubmission?
    A) Validate scope
    B) Close Project or Phase
    C) Control Communications
    D) Monitor and Control Project Work

17. PESTLE is a common strategic framework used for the identification of overall project risks. What does PESTLE represent?
    A) Political, engineering, social, technological, legal, and environmental
    B) Project, engineering, social, technical, labor, and environment
    C) Political, economic, social, technological, legal, and environmental

D) Project, engineering, scope, time, labor, and expenses

18. You were invited to a project management class at a community college as a project management practitioner. One student asked a question about the level of effort and wanted to know which process usually has the highest level of effort involved. What was your reply?
    A) Executing process group usually has the highest level of effort involved
    B) Each process has approximately the same level of effort involved
    C) It depends on the type of project
    D) Monitoring and controlling group usually has the highest level of effort involved

19. After performing risk analysis, you find that close to 50% of the risks are technology risks. What will you do next?
    A) Develop a risk response strategy for all the technology risks that require a response according to plan
    B) Develop a risk response strategy for all the technology risks
    C) Develop a risk response strategy for all the risks that require a response according to the plan
    D) Acquire subject matter experts and highly qualified resources

20. Which of the following is NOT a typical characteristic of a project management office (PMO)?
    A) Coaching and training project managers
    B) Coordinating communication across projects
    C) Developing and managing project management methodology and standards
    D) Managing project resources and assigning project tasks

21. A project planned 3 resources to work on the design for 6 hours/day each for twelve days. What will be the planned value of work on design at the end of the eighth day?
    A) 576 hours
    B) 216 hours
    C) 48 hours
    D) 144 hours

22. A project manager has invited proposals from a list of qualified sellers to accomplish few deliverables of her project. She has created evaluation criteria to compare those proposals and select the best one. In which process is she engaged?
    A) Initiate Procurements

B) Plan Procurement Management
C) Conduct Procurements
D) Control Procurements

23. It is your dream to work on a space exploration project. You found out that a large contract, worth several hundred million dollars to work on a deep space exploration project, has been awarded to your company. This project is part of the next-generation spaceship development program. The project is, obviously, an agile project that will require significant research before any development can happen. Which of the following can help you the most in researching and running experiments?
    A) Continuous integration
    B) Test-driven development
    C) Kanban board
    D) Spikes

24. You are the project manager for a system upgrade project. The practice at your company is to estimate project costs based on historical data and statistical analysis. This cost estimation technique is called _____.
    A) Bottom-Up estimating
    B) Risk-based estimating
    C) Analogous estimating
    D) Parametric estimating

25. Which of the following is not an objective of the Control Schedule process?
    A) Influence factors that may have an impact on the project schedule
    B) Find out if there is a change in the project schedule
    C) Analyzing activity durations to produce the project schedule
    D) Manage changes to schedule baseline of the project

26. You are the project manager of a network replacement project for a 40-floor office building. You plan to hire a contractor to pull the old cables out and then install the new cables. The work has to be done in such a way to minimize disruption to the tenant organizations during business hours, hence you need to hire a well experienced reputed firm. You contacted the procurement department to develop a list of firms that have the capability to do the work. What are you referring?
    A) Negotiating a contract
    B) Prequalified sellers list

C) Develop evaluation criteria
D) Solicitation package to be sent out to prospective sellers

27. Which one of the following is NOT an output of the Monitor Communications process?
    A) Evaluate communication effectiveness
    B) Identify new procedures to eliminate communication bottlenecks
    C) Revise the stakeholders' information distribution method
    D) Analyze stakeholders' interest and involvement in the project

28. Which of the following is INCORRECT about the Control Scope process?
    A) It is the process of managing changes to the scope baseline
    B) It is the process of ensuring all scope changes get processed through the integrated change control process
    C) It clarifies scope to stop scope creep and disallow scope changes
    D) It evaluates the scope changes to understand the impact on the project scope

29. As the project manager for a new software development project, you are in the middle of identifying stakeholders. Which process group are you carrying out?
    A) Initiating process group
    B) Stakeholders process group
    C) Executing process group
    D) Planning process group

30. A project's approved budget is 250,000 and planned budget to date is 150,000. What will be the Schedule Variance when Schedule Performance Index is 0.8?
    A) 30,000
    B) -30,000
    C) 50,000
    D) -50,000

31. A project manager was asked by the project management office to make a presentation on project management to company employees in attendance. He made an incorrect statement about projects. Which one is it?
    A) Projects are a way to create value and benefits in organizations
    B) Projects that do not get a project manager assigned formally may succeed
    C) Current projects may have an impact on future projects in the

same organization
D) Completing projects on time and within budget always satisfies project stakeholders

32. You, being the project manager, are going through a method that involves six steps, in order, as identify, define, investigate, analyze, solve, and check. What is this method called?
    A) Project management method
    B) Problem-solving method
    C) Decision-making method
    D) Decision tree method

33. The project charter identifies the key stakeholders of the project. Which of the following information about key stakeholders the project charter includes?
    A) Key stakeholders engagement level on the project
    B) Key stakeholders influence on the project
    C) Key stakeholders interest in the project
    D) Key stakeholders responsibilities on the project

34. You are about to complete a project with resources in a matrix environment. One of the activities you will be doing is to release the project resources. Which of the following is NOT an example of releasing the resources?
    A) Return of the rental equipment
    B) Transfer of individuals to various departments
    C) Engaging resources on another project
    D) Writing performance report of individual resources

35. A project team consisted of six team members during the requirement gathering phase, but the number increased to eleven in the design phase. How many additional channels of communication were added in the design phase?
    A) 15
    B) 55
    C) 40
    D) 25

36. Project stakeholders should be classified according to their interest, influence, and involvement in the project because _____.
    A) It helps in relationship building with stakeholders
    B) Stakeholders usually have very little time to spend on the project
    C) Such a classification makes it easier to assign responsibilities to

stakeholders

D) Stakeholders need to know which group they belong to in terms of interest, influence, and involvement in the project

37. What is the monitoring and controlling process of project stakeholder management knowledge area called?
    A) Monitor and Control Stakeholders
    B) Monitor and Control Stakeholder Engagement
    C) Control Stakeholder Engagement
    D) Monitor Stakeholder Engagement

38. As a project manager, you can use a template to create _____.
    A) Risk management policy
    B) Resource training procedure
    C) Project Scope statement
    D) Requirements gathering

39. Which document contains the information that describes how will the formal verification and acceptance of the project deliverables be obtained?
    A) Scope verification document
    B) Statement of work
    C) Scope management plan
    D) Communications management plan

40. Uncertainties on an activity can be represented by probability distributions. Which of the following is not a probability distribution used for this purpose?
    A) Uniform
    B) Discrete
    C) Beta
    D) S-curve

41. Make or buy decision is an implicit input to which process group?
    A) Monitoring and Controlling
    B) Executing
    C) Planning
    D) Initiating

42. Which of the following is CORRECT about the product scope?
    A) Product scope is a combination of project scopes of components
    B) Product scope and project scope are the same concepts. It is called the project scope by the project team and product scope

by the customer.
C) Product scope is sometimes considered the subset of the project scope
D) Product scope is the work needed to deliver the product on time, within budget and within the scope

43. For effective risk management, project risks _____.
    A) Acceptance is the best strategy
    B) Should continue to be tracked even after they have occurred
    C) Should be identified whether they are expected to have a positive or negative outcome
    D) Should be identified, analyzed and responded to

44. A risk was identified and analyzed and then a risk response was created and recorded on the risk response plan. The risk has occurred and the project manager has implemented the risk response plan but it is not producing the desired results. Which of the following can help the project manager the most to improve risk response?
    A) Change request
    B) Expert judgment
    C) Interpersonal and team skills
    D) Risk audit

45. A SIPOC diagram can be drawn to represent data related to processes. What does S stand for in SIPOC?
    A) Stakeholder
    B) Scope
    C) Schedule
    D) Supplier

46. What is the name of the technique that examines the problems experienced within the project, limitations faced, and the feeling of non-value-added work?
    A) Quality audit
    B) Quality assurance
    C) Scatter diagram
    D) Process analysis

47. A project manager is managing a project under a contract for a client. Due to certain delays, the project will be late for three weeks. According to the contract, each full week of delay will cost a penalty of 10,000 deducted from the payment with a maximum penalty of 60,000. However, the project manager has the option of hiring an additional

crew to speed up the work. The crew will work 5 days per week. What is the maximum cost of the crew that will make hiring the crew a better option financially than paying the penalty?
A) 2,000 per day
B) 2,500 per day
C) 3,000 per day
D) Not enough information provided to make a decision

48. Which two processes are parts of the Initiating process group?
A) Initiation and Develop Project Charter
B) Develop Project Charter and Collect Requirements
C) Develop Project Charter and Approve Project Charter
D) Develop Project Charter and Identify Stakeholders

49. All of the following are incorrect about the Validate Scope process EXCEPT _____.
A) It ensures that the project completes on time and within budget
B) It is concerned with the completion of change requests
C) It is concerned with the acceptance of completed project deliverables
D) It is concerned with meeting requirements to deliver business benefits

50. In the part of the network diagram shown, what is the lag between activity B and activity E?

FS = Finish-to-Start

A) 1 day
B) 2 days
C) 3 days
D) 5 days

51. For a medical research project running in two different regions, in which process are the human resources engaged?
    A) Acquire Resources
    B) Engage Resources
    C) Storming
    D) Develop Team

52. Disputes may arise between the buyer and seller on a contract. There are several techniques that can be used to resolve such disputes. Which of the following is the most preferred method for alternative dispute resolution?
    A) Negotiation
    B) Arbitration
    C) Litigation
    D) Mediation

53. When will the parametric estimating be considered most reliable?
    A) When the expert judgment is used
    B) When estimating is done at a higher level and distributed down to activities
    C) When considerable historical data is taken into account
    D) When estimating is done at activity level and then summed up for the project

54. A large enterprise software development project requires that requirements documentation be produced for each of the 18 departments. The project team created a checklist to manage the quality of these documents. The checklist is filled out for each of the documents produced and is approved before sending it to the design team. The design team has identified issues with all 4 documents created till now. Which of the following is an appropriate action that should be taken?
    A) Review the quality plan, the completed checklist, and the issues identified by the design team
    B) Share the completed checklists with the design team to show that the quality standards set by the project were met
    C) Inform the design team that it is too late for an objection since the documents have already been approved
    D) Reproduce the requirements documents so that the issues may not get repeated

55. What do you call the difficulties that can hinder the project team's ability to achieve project goals?

A) Risks
B) Issues
C) Assumptions
D) Constraints

56. In order to calculate the Estimate at Completion (EAC), the following is typically needed _____.
    A) Actual Cost (AC) and the Estimate to Complete (ETC) the unfinished work
    B) Cost Performance Index (CPI), Actual Cost (AC), and the Earned Value (EV)
    C) Cost Performance Index (CPI) and the Actual Cost (AC)
    D) Earned Value (EV) and the Actual Cost (AC)

57. The following are the goals of manage quality process EXCEPT _____.
    A) Increase chances of achieving project quality goals
    B) Identify the causes of poor quality
    C) Confirm that the project quality activities conform to quality policies and procedures
    D) Verify that the project results comply with relevant quality standards

58. Which one of the following is NOT an input to the Develop Project Charter process?
    A) Expert judgment
    B) Agreements
    C) Enterprise environmental factors
    D) Business case

59. A team goes through various stages of team development. In which stage the team members begin to work together and adjust their behaviors and work styles?
    A) Storming
    B) Norming
    C) Performing
    D) Adjusting

60. After a detailed meeting with the sponsor regarding the downward trend of the project's progress, the project manager created a change request by examining three different approaches to select the corrective action. What type of analysis was done for the change request?

A) Cost-benefit analysis
B) Alternatives analysis
C) Trend analysis
D) Variance analysis

61. Right after you received final deliverable approval from the sponsor of your project, you were assigned to a new project and were asked to skip the closing process for the current project. For which kind of projects can you skip the closing processes?
    A) Completed projects
    B) Abandoned projects
    C) Canceled projects
    D) Closing process should not be skipped for any kind of project

62. A new project manager in your organization is performing administrative closure activities. The management terminated her project so now she is preparing project closure documents. What is she expected to have in that formal documentation?
    A) A formalized procedure of transferring complete and incomplete deliverables
    B) A formalized procedure of transferring complete deliverables only
    C) The lessons learned register
    D) The documents for the organization to maintain and operate the product or service delivered

63. Which process addresses the actions and activities required to satisfy exit criteria for the project or the phase?
    A) Close Project or Phase
    B) Develop Project Charter
    C) Define Scope
    D) Validate Scope

64. All of the following are required to establish cost baseline EXCEPT _____.
    A) Control Costs
    B) Determine Budget
    C) Create WBS
    D) Estimate Costs

65. A change has been requested by the project team to fix a problem by bringing the future performance of the project in line with the project management plan. Such a change request is called _____.

A) Corrective action
B) Submitted change request
C) Supportive action
D) Preventive action

66. You are the project manager working on a project for an external customer. Which of the following will you NOT use to develop the Project Charter?
    A) Signed Contract
    B) Business Case
    C) Benefits management plan
    D) Project performance baselines

67. Which of the following is NOT an objective of the Monitor Risks process?
    A) Analyze if contingency reserve requires a change
    B) Check if risk management policies are followed
    C) Develop a risk mitigation strategy
    D) Determine if implemented risk responses are effective

68. As a project manager you have to consider _____ which are factors that are believed to represent reality, considered to be certain and taken as truth.
    A) Assumptions
    B) Deadlines
    C) Constraints
    D) Risks

69. What happens when a project manager involves the project team members in project planning?
    A) It takes too long to plan the project
    B) A more realistic achievable plan is developed
    C) Project team becomes more committed to the project
    D) The result is a clear scope definition with an aggressive schedule to deliver

70. On a product development project, which is taking a totally new approach to product development unprecedented in the industry, what would be the BEST way to develop the quality management plan?
    A) Take the old plan and add the continuous improvement tool, stakeholder's required tests, and the project team's preferred tests
    B) Delay the quality management plan until execution to ensure all requirements are fully defined

C) Use the quality management plan from last product development project that was completed successfully
D) Create the plan from scratch with input from subject matter experts using brainstorming

71. What do you call the process that provides the seller with formal written notice of completion of a legal agreement?
    A) Close Project or Phase
    B) Control Procurements
    C) Close Procurements
    D) Legal settlement

72. A project manager is managing three projects simultaneously. These three projects, A, B, and C are related to each other. Project A is to customize a software application X, project B is to deploy X to the whole organization and C is to train users according to their roles in X. How would you describe the situation?
    A) He is managing one project which has three phases
    B) He is managing a program with three inter-related projects
    C) This is an operational work and should not be considered a project
    D) Project B should start after project A and Project C after Project B

73. You are managing a project to design and build a new ship. There are several outsourcing contracts in place with sellers to provide various parts needed for the project. One supplier has to provide 2 million rivets over a period of one year. In the third month of receiving the supplies, your team has informed you that they suspect the rivets measurements have deviated from the required size. What is your course of action?
    A) Create a change request to repair the defects and remove the deviation
    B) Reject the supply and return it to the seller
    C) Check quality control measurements to verify if there actually is a deviation
    D) Ask the seller to provide an explanation of why there is a deviation

74. Your project has completed its 50% deliverables and is in the middle of execution. You created a stakeholder register during the initiating process which was then used to create the stakeholder management strategy. You have been managing stakeholders according to this

strategy. Now you have recently become aware of a highly influential stakeholder that has not been identified on the stakeholder register. What is the BEST course of action?
   A) Send a request to the senior management asking for direction
   B) Inform the stakeholder that it is too late for him to be involved in the project as the stakeholder register was completed during the initiating process
   C) Ask the project sponsor if this person can be included in the stakeholder register
   D) Update the stakeholder register and stakeholder management strategy with the new information

75. You are working on creating the project charter for standard PC image development project. You have identified that the image must be ready for deployment by end of the year and the project can only use internal resources. You will capture these conditions under _____.
   A) Assumptions
   B) Scope of work
   C) Constraints
   D) Deliverables

76. A project manager suddenly resigned and left the agile project in the middle of execution. A new project manager assigned to the project found that most team members were I-shaped people and very few were T-shaped people. There were too many roadblocks that the team was facing and work efficiency was low. What is meant by I-shaped and T-shaped people?
   A) I-shaped people are working part-time on the project while T-shaped people are working full time on the project
   B) I-shaped people require constant coaching while T-shaped are self-organized
   C) I-shaped people have low skills in project domains while T-shaped people have high skills in project domains
   D) I-shaped are specialists in one domain only while T-shaped are specialists in one domain and generalists in many others

77. At the end of each phase of a business process streamlining project, a lessons learned review is held by the project team. The results of the lessons learned review are _____.
   A) Distributed to each and every stakeholder for their information and feedback
   B) Kept confidential until the project is closed

C) Published in the organization-wide newsletter for the benefit of all employees
D) Put into records of each team member to be used as part of their performance review

78. You are a project manager on a highway construction project. The project is on hold for the last five days because of continuous rain and high winds but you are not worried at all about the project delay because you insured your project against delay due to inclement weather. How have you managed this risk?
A) Accept
B) Transfer
C) Mitigate
D) Avoid

79. Which process identifies the ways to eliminate causes of unsatisfactory performance?
A) Plan Quality Management
B) Control Quality
C) Perform Quality Performance
D) Project Quality Management

80. Which of the following change management activity is NOT performed as part of the Perform Integrated Change Control process?
A) Identifying that a change has occurred
B) Reviewing the requested changes
C) Implementing the approved changes
D) Approving the requested changes

81. You are the project manager of a clinical trial project. In project planning processes, what will you consider to understand how the costs will be managed?
A) Reporting formats and control thresholds
B) Quality checklists and work performance data
C) Work performance data and the project charter
D) Business case and earned value measurements

82. As a project manager on a software development project for a customer, you have received a piece of advice from the customer that they want deliverable based invoices. This means you will have to track the costs by each piece of work done. The system within your organization is setup to capture costs by resources which means the total cost of the project at a certain instance is derived from costs

booked against the project for the resources. What should you do?
A) Follow internal procedures and refuse the customer
B) Evaluate to find out the cost of complying with customer's demand
C) Only track costs as requested by the customer
D) Track costs both ways to fulfill internal and external requirements

83. A project manager wants to determine how his project is performing at the end of the sixth month. The actual total expense of the project is 720,000. The planned budget for this length of time was 600,000. He finds that _____.
A) There is not enough information to determine how the project is doing
B) The project is on track
C) The project is over-budget
D) The project is ahead of schedule

84. What is NOT an objective of controlling the costs of a project?
A) Establish the cost baseline by including estimates
B) Monitor completion of the work and the money spent
C) Understand the cost variances from the baseline cost
D) Inform relevant stakeholders of all the costs including the change related cost

85. Which of the following factors in terms of use of the communication technology CANNOT generally affect the project?
A) Ease of use
B) Project environment
C) The urgency of the need for information
D) Sender/receiver communication model

86. As the project manager, you have provided a unique and verifiable product to your customer. This product has been worked on and prepared by your project team and accepted by the customer previously. Now you are looking forward to starting the next phase of your project. What is this unique and verifiable product called?
A) A plan
B) A project
C) A template
D) A deliverable

87. In order to close a project or a phase, exit criteria must have been

defined and later used to verify that the criteria have been met. The criteria can vary from one organization to another or even between types of projects within an organization. It is addressed in several documents. In which document is the exit criteria defined the first time?

A) Scope statement
B) Business case
C) Project charter
D) Project management plan

88. While writing the cost management plan, you were to decide the level of precision required in the cost estimates. Using expert judgment by reviewing previous similar projects you have decided to round up the estimates to nearest 100. One of your team members is asking how to round up 9,701.34. What will you say?

A) To 9,800
B) To 10,000
C) To 9,700
D) To 9,000

89. Which of the following is not a tool and technique of Manage Stakeholder Engagement process?

A) Feedback
B) Political awareness
C) Stakeholder engagement assessment matrix
D) Ground rules

90. A bridge construction project needs rivets installers to install 400,000 rivets. If a skilled installer can install 40 rivets per day. How many installers will be needed to install all the rivets in 500 days?

A) 5 installers
B) 10 installers
C) 20 installers
D) 40 installers

91. In which process do you analyze and document the influence and potential impact of the stakeholders on the project success?

A) Identify Stakeholders process
B) Manage Stakeholders Engagement process
C) Monitor Stakeholders Engagement process
D) Analyze Stakeholders process

92. Only one of the following statements is CORRECT about the work

breakdown structure (WBS). Which one is it?
- A) WBS is a hierarchical decomposition of the total scope of work to be carried out by the project team
- B) WBS is a hierarchical list of project activities shown under each department
- C) WBS is a method to distribute work to various resources so that the project can be completed successfully
- D) WBS is the list of project deliverables that must be agreed on, in writing, by the sponsor to move the project forward

93. _____ process uses earned value management to help understand performance variances in a project.
- A) Control Schedule
- B) Monitor Risks
- C) Manage Communications
- D) Direct and Manage Project Work

94. All of the following are input to the Control Quality process EXCEPT _____.
- A) Project management plan
- B) Quality metrics
- C) Deliverables
- D) Issue log

95. Which interpersonal or team skill a project manager will use to encourage nominated risk owners to take necessary actions when required?
- A) Influencing
- B) Active listening
- C) Emotional intelligence
- D) Focus groups

96. You are managing an office space refurbish project. You are in the middle of negotiating the contract with a prospective seller. What is the primary objective of contract negotiation?
- A) Pressurize the seller to do more work for the same price
- B) Develop a good working relationship and a better understanding
- C) Push the seller to reduce the price
- D) Negotiate for better terms and conditions for the buyer

97. Why is the change request an output of the Validate Scope process?
- A) If a completed deliverable is rejected, a change request can be created to repair the defect

B) Each change request has to be validated because it is considered complete
C) Change requests are the result of the acceptance of deliverables by the customer in order to align scope with customer requirements
D) To ensure that all requested changes and recommended corrective actions are completed

98. During the Define Activities process, constraints and assumptions are explicitly considered. What is considered implicitly?
    A) Defining activities
    B) Deliverables
    C) Critical path
    D) All information is considered explicitly

99. A project manager for a global business expansion project lost a key resource on the project due to sudden illness. The resource is expected to recover in three weeks. Luckily the resource needs to start working on a deliverable exactly after three weeks. What is the BEST option for the project manager?
    A) Immediately ask for a replacement resource
    B) Call the resource and let him know the importance of getting back on time
    C) Add a three-week contingency to the project schedule to cover up for the absence
    D) Take no action. Just keep in touch with the resource

100. One of the following tasks is NOT part of the Control Procurements process. Which one is it?
    A) Answering questions of prospective sellers
    B) Review performance of the contract
    C) Review payment requests by the seller
    D) Resolve dispute occurring between the buyer and seller

101. Which of the following is a best practice in the Plan Procurement Management process?
    A) Sellers who have failed to deliver in the past should be disqualified
    B) Prefer fixed-price contracts as these are less risky for the buyer
    C) Procurement planning should start only after project management planning has been completed
    D) Go through make-or-buy decision to analyze the risks involved

102. Your close friend, who is a project manager of a software development project that has the whole team co-located in one office, is having problems identifying a technique to use for team building. Which of the following will you recommend?
    A) Install the instant messaging application on each team member's computer
    B) Distribute contact information of project team members to the whole team
    C) Send the technical team lead for training on 'working together in teams'
    D) Arrange for all team members to participate in an offsite event

103. A project manager working for a government department is in the source selection process. He had advertised in the widely circulated newspaper at a much higher cost than just inviting the six sellers of good reputation who have previously worked for his department. What can be the reason?
    A) The project manager is unaware of a cheaper solution of advertising through the internet
    B) Government regulation requires a public invitation to sellers for certain types of contracts
    C) Get the best seller available in the market
    D) Delay the process of awarding the contract to a seller

104. During a regular project team meeting, one team member recommends a change to the product design that will make the product look more appealing, but would not add to its functionality. The product is for internal use by the customer. The team agrees that if the customer is convinced of this change, it will not only enhance the product but it will also increase the project scope, budget and time. Thus, a secondary benefit is that the project organization will make more profit from this project and everyone on the project will be engaged for longer. One team member said, "It is a win-win situation." Your company encourages upselling so this seems to be a good opportunity. What will be your response?
    A) Refuse to upsell something that does not add value in reality
    B) Evaluate budget and schedule impact before speaking with customer
    C) This is scope creep. You cannot allow this to happen to your project
    D) Setup a meeting with the customer to upsell the product

105. The table contains work performance data from a project.

Which activity has the best performance considering both schedule and budget?

Activity	Planned Value (PV)	Actual Cost (AC)	Earned Value (EV)
A	1,200	1,000	1,100
B	600	500	600
C	300	300	300
D	1,800	2,000	1,800

A) Activity D
B) Activity C
C) Activity B
D) Activity A

106. What is the output of a decision tree analysis?
A) Expected monetary value for each option
B) Cost of managing the risk that was analyzed
C) List of decisions that can be made
D) Recommended corrective actions

107. You are working on a project. You want to find out which projects are closely related to your project and should be managed together along with your project. You can find this information from _____.
A) Program planning
B) Project planning
C) Portfolio planning
D) Strategic planning

108. What is the impact of noise on communication?
A) Noise interferes with the understanding of the message by the receiver
B) Noise makes it hard to hear the communication since it is too loud
C) Noise changes the message while being delivered
D) Noise impacts only if it is persistent

109. Sonia has just completed the project management plan for her new product launch project. She is having problems finding the project team members with required competencies. Now she is looking for alternative resources. What is true about alternative resources?
A) Alternative resources must have the required competencies
B) Alternative resources must be available as per the training plan

C) Alternative resources must have the same overall cost
D) Alternative resources must meet the mandatory criteria

110. One process in the Executing process group is where performance of a team member is tracked, appropriate feedback is provided and issues are resolved. This process is called _____.
    A) Develop Team
    B) Manage Team
    C) Manage Stakeholder Engagement
    D) Monitoring and Controlling

111. All of the following are tools and techniques of Acquire Resources process EXCEPT _____.
    A) Pre-assignment
    B) Multi-criteria decision analysis
    C) Negotiation
    D) Networking

112. Which of the following should a project team be least focused on while managing engagement of stakeholders?
    A) Negotiate stakeholder expectations
    B) Resolve stakeholder engagement issues
    C) Address stakeholder management risks
    D) Exceed stakeholder expectations

113. A project manager works with various stakeholders, including negative stakeholders, mainly to meet the needs and expectations of the stakeholders, and foster appropriate stakeholder involvement. He used all of the following skills except _____.
    A) Negotiation
    B) Observation
    C) Political awareness
    D) Decision making

114. You are the project manager for employee time management project. You are considering four different resources with different skill levels located in various regions. Which of the following will you use as a supporting documentation to provide a clear understanding of how you estimated the resource?
    A) The method you used for the estimate
    B) The software you used for the estimate
    C) Resource breakdown structure
    D) Scope baseline

115. You are managing a project as seller's project manager when you receive a request to add some work to the scope. Which type of communication is the optimum choice in this circumstance?
    A) Formal written communication
    B) Formal verbal communication
    C) Informal written communication
    D) Instant messaging communication

116. The project team has decided that a preventive action must be taken to solve an issue. What are they referring to?
    A) They are referring to an activity that can help lessen the chances of negative outcomes of the actions
    B) They are referring to an activity that can help improve the performance back to the desired state
    C) They are referring to an activity that can help eliminate the performance of the desired state
    D) They are referring to an activity that can help repair the chances of the negative impacts

117. You, as the project manager, are transferring lessons learned to the lessons learned repository. Which process are you in?
    A) Direct and Manage Project Work process
    B) Monitor and Control Project Work process
    C) Manage Project Knowledge process
    D) Close Project or Phase process

118. You are the project manager for a technology implementation project. A change has been identified and needs to be presented to the Change Control Board (CCB). What do you know about the role and responsibilities of the change control board?
    A) Should be clearly defined and documented in the change management plan
    B) Should be available on intranet site for all stakeholders
    C) Should have detailed contact information of all CCB members
    D) Should be clearly stated as part of project manager's role and responsibility

119. A project manager working on a project is identifying which project deliverables could be achieved from procurement through sellers. This project manager is in _____ process.
    A) Plan Procurement Management
    B) Conduct Procurements

C) Control Procurements
D) Seller Procurements

120. Which of the following is NOT a voting technique?
    A) Autocratic
    B) Unanimity
    C) Plurality
    D) Majority

121. The following four activities with identical durations have their early finish and late finish given. Which activity is a critical activity?
    A) Activity X: early finish = 3, late finish = 7
    B) Activity T: early finish = 5, late finish = 11
    C) Activity F: early finish = 9, late finish = 12
    D) Activity M: early finish = 6, late finish = 6

122. You are starting a new project as a project manager. While talking to various resources being acquired for the project you found out that one full-time resource will be away on vacation for four weeks during project execution. What will you do?
    A) Update the resource calendar with the information
    B) Inform the resource that he cannot go away for four weeks in the middle of the project
    C) Update Activity attributes of activities for which this person is a resource
    D) Modify the schedule baseline and the critical path

123. What type of time constraints impact schedule development and need to be considered in the Develop Schedule process?
    A) Scope and cost
    B) Explicit and implicit
    C) Forced milestones and external deadlines
    D) Lead time and lag time

124. You are the project manager of a technology project and currently going through risk identification exercise. What does the Identify Risks process actually identify?
    A) It identifies what might happen on the project
    B) It identifies what will happen on the project
    C) It identifies what has happened in previous projects and still can happen
    D) It identifies risks that are a risk to the project

125. The project quality management knowledge area explains quality that conforms to the concept given in all of the following EXCEPT _____.
    A) Total Quality Management
    B) Lean Six Sigma
    C) Management by walking around
    D) PDCA by Shewhart

126. Thinking of communications planning for a global project with resources in different continents, which of the following is an example that BEST represents an assumption?
    A) Team members are acquired in various geographical locations
    B) The entire team is fluent in the English language
    C) All resources are technically competent
    D) Costs in all countries are within budget

127. A project manager on a software development project used the quality management plan from his previous similar highly successful project. What will be your advice to him?
    A) Create a new plan for this project. Remember each project is unique.
    B) Reuse the plan as it has proved to be adequate for this type of project.
    C) It is the customer's responsibility to provide the plan as they are the ones who know what quality is acceptable.
    D) Update the previous quality management plan keeping in view the uniqueness of this project, the customer's requirements, and expectations.

128. Which of the following is an output of the bid solicitation process in a project?
    A) Prospective sellers' proposals
    B) Advertisement
    C) Award of contract to a seller
    D) Create qualified seller list

129. Which of the following is LEAST challenging for virtual team members on a product design project?
    A) Communication
    B) Conflicts
    C) Reports
    D) Team building

130. An office renovation project is well underway. The sponsor being co-located makes frequent visits to the work area. About 300 out of the total 400 desk areas have been renovated when the sponsor asks if another electric outlet could be placed on the right side of the desk in addition to the left side outlet. This is an example of _____.
    A) Micro-management
    B) Schedule delay
    C) Scope creep
    D) Cost overrun

131. Which of the following is not a product analysis technique?
    A) Systems engineering
    B) Value engineering
    C) Product breakdown
    D) Affinity diagrams

132. Which tool & technique of the Collect Requirements process includes mind mapping and affinity diagrams?
    A) Data gathering
    B) Data analysis
    C) Data representation
    D) Interpersonal and team skills

133. What is a procurement statement of work?
    A) It is the same as project statement of work
    B) Work as defined in the project charter
    C) A detailed description of the procurement items
    D) The terms and conditions of the procurement

134. Which of the following tools and techniques is MOST valuable while performing probability and impact analysis when the customer is part of the team?
    A) Risk register
    B) Expert judgment
    C) Detailed risk mitigation plans
    D) Customer's experience

135. The project manager just received a report that identifies two instances where the project plan is not following the organization's standards. Which report is it?
    A) Project performance report
    B) Executive report
    C) Project problems report

D) Project quality report

136. You are the project manager for a manufacturing process improvement project for an automotive parts manufacturing plant. The hole size on one of the part was a big quality problem. The project identified the causes and fixes were put in place. Now you want to inspect the parts being produced to see if the fixes put in place have been successful and the parts being produced are within acceptable limits. Which of the following tools will you use?
    A) Fishbone diagram
    B) Scatter diagram
    C) Control chart
    D) Pareto chart

137. What is true about the project kick-off meeting in large projects?
    A) Project manager plans most of the project and kick-off meeting is done before initiating the project
    B) Project management team plans most of the project and kick-off meeting is done at the start of executing
    C) The whole project team plans the project and kick-off meeting is done at the start of planning
    D) Project manager plans most of the project and kick-off meeting is done whenever stakeholders are available

138. Can you calculate the cost variance (CV) of a project if, at a certain point in time, the actual cost (AC) is 19,500 and the earned value (EV) is 24,000? If yes, what is it?
    A) Yes. CV is 1.23
    B) Yes. CV is 4,500
    C) Yes. CV is -4,500
    D) No. CV cannot be calculated from the information given

139. You are the senior project manager on a new product development project. Your project management team includes a resource manager, reporting manager, and a scheduler. You have advised the scheduler to build the schedule with the most common activity to activity relationship. Which relationship among the following are you referring to?
    A) Start-to-Finish
    B) Finish-to-Finish
    C) Start-to-Start
    D) Finish-to-Start

140. There are several methods of forecasting project cost at completion. Which of the following is NOT a forecasting method used on projects?
   A) Work will be performed as per three-point estimate
   B) Work will be performed at the budgeted rate
   C) Work will continue at the current cost performance
   D) Work will continue at the current cost and schedule performance

141. If you were to explain the difference between control quality and manage quality. Which example explains it the BEST?
   A) **Control quality:** Control the spelling errors in the manuscript. **Manage quality:** Assure that the spelling errors have been controlled
   B) **Control quality:** count nuts being produced. **Manage quality:** count nuts being produced with defects
   C) **Control quality:** measure the diameter of the wheel to see if it is within limits. **Manage quality:** Verify limits for wheel diameter are set correctly
   D) **Manage quality:** count number of books printed with the reverse title. **Control quality:** count the number of books printed with the correct title

142. What is the name of the technique that represents data by visually organizing information about stakeholders and their relationships with each other and the organization?
   A) Salience model
   B) Mind mapping
   C) Stakeholder engagement assessment matrix
   D) Stakeholder cube

143. The project schedule that you had submitted to the customer is not acceptable because the product delivery date is two months farther out than what the customer wants. Your company has deep expertise in the subject area and several more resources are available that can be engaged by the project. What will you do?
   A) Fast track the project schedule
   B) Level the resources
   C) Crash the project schedule
   D) Estimate activity resources

144. Meeting minutes and memos belong to which of the following tools?
   A) Project deliverables
   B) Project internal communication

C) Information management system
D) Project records

145. Which of the following will have the BIGGEST impact on the project team's performance?
    A) When individual authority and responsibilities match
    B) Highly experienced project manager
    C) Expert level technical knowledge
    D) Co-located project team

146. Another project manager comes to you and asks for your opinion about a discipline problem he is having on his project. One of his team members is continuously being late to meetings and this is affecting the project's progress. Your advice is to talk to the person in private and find out what is wrong. What type of power explains this scenario?
    A) Formal power
    B) Relational power
    C) Expert power
    D) Ingratiating power

147. A project deliverable has been formally accepted by the customer in the Validate Scope process. In which process this acceptance is documented?
    A) Close Project or Phase
    B) Manage quality
    C) Validate Scope
    D) Control Procurements

148. Which of the following is the BEST action to increase acceptance of deliverables?
    A) Involve stakeholders during initiating
    B) Ask stakeholders to define deliverables
    C) Offer a discount on fees if deliverables are accepted quickly
    D) Send a written request to accept deliverables

149. Which of the following is an input to Manage Team process?
    A) Work performance data
    B) Work performance standards
    C) Work performance reports
    D) Work performance information

150. For a technology project, in which process the project or a project phase is authorized to proceed?

A) Conduct Procurements
B) Project Planning Process
C) Initiating Process group
D) Develop Project Charter

151. As the project manager, you are going through the Conduct Procurements process of a project. The solicited prospective sellers' proposals have a significant price difference. What should you do?
    A) Award the contract to the best supplier
    B) Cancel the bid and re-advertise to solicit more bids
    C) Verify if the statement of work and terms of the contract are clearly defined and unambiguous
    D) Award the contract to the lowest bidder to get the best value for the money

152. One of your team members is frustrated because he is unable to find relevant information about a problem through web searches. What is true about this situation?
    A) The team member lacks web search skills
    B) It will be quicker to ask for help than trying various search terms unsuccessfully
    C) He should first find the keywords and then search to find the information
    D) The team member should use lessons learned register instead of web search

153. Tools and techniques that connect people to information can be enhanced by adding an element of interaction. Which of the following will be an example of such interaction?
    A) Circulating a monthly subscribed journal among the team members
    B) A white paper based on lessons learned along with the name and contact information of the project manager
    C) Sign up project team members for a web-based learning course
    D) Archiving lessons learned in the organization's lessons learned repository

154. In which process is the bidder's conference held?
    A) Close Procurements
    B) Plan Procurement Management
    C) Conduct Procurements
    D) Control Procurements

155. An organization is highly reputed for deliverables quality. What would be an appropriate statement that BEST represents this situation?
    A) The organization uses a standard quality management plan for all projects
    B) The organization has a high cost of quality
    C) The organization has a low cost of quality
    D) The organization's project schedules are highly robust

156. A project manager who joined a new organization was asked to take over a project because the previous project manager has resigned and left the organization. On taking over, she reviewed all the project documentation and uncovered several facts. The consolidated meeting minutes revealed that very few meetings were held to update stakeholders on the project's progress. The issue log showed several open stakeholder issues which had no status update. She could clearly see that the stakeholders were dissatisfied and disengaged. What can she do to make things right?
    A) Send an email to all stakeholders asking them to update the issue log as soon as possible
    B) Invite all stakeholders to a meeting and explain what has been missing
    C) Review and update the stakeholder engagement assessment matrix
    D) Perform a quality audit of the project to determine why such lack of information has happened on the project

157. A customer has asked you that he wants to review the completed deliverable before the project moves to the next phase. What will your response be?
    A) You cannot allow this until the project closing when the customer has to validate completion of project work
    B) The deliverables should have been reviewed by the customer as these were completed
    C) Completed deliverables should be validated at the end of each phase before the project moves to the next phase
    D) You can allow this only if the sponsor approves the customer's request

158. Which of the following is the project manager always responsible for?
    A) Prioritizing projects based on business need
    B) Lead project team to achieve the project's objectives
    C) Meeting the project's profit margin
    D) Writing performance reports for project resources

159. A project manager working on a highway extension project finds out that noise barriers are required, for approval by the provincial highway authority, before the work can proceed. The company has a defined process and forms to go through the approval process. What is this defined process called?
    A) Organizational process assets
    B) A program
    C) Enterprise environmental factor
    D) Government requirement

160. Impact/Influence grid is a tool and technique used in _____.
    A) Monitor Stakeholder Engagement process
    B) Manage Stakeholder Engagement process
    C) Plan Stakeholder Management process
    D) Identify Stakeholders process

161. A project manager uses all of the following technical project management skills to coordinate work towards accomplishing a goal EXCEPT _____.
    A) Plan thoroughly and prioritize diligently
    B) Tailor techniques and methods for each project
    C) Implement strategy in a way to maximize the value
    D) Make issue log readily available

162. Which of the following is a tool and technique for the Monitor Risks process?
    A) Audits
    B) Corrective action
    C) Contingent response strategies
    D) Risk register updates

163. You are managing a project that is near closing. The project team first went through the _____ stage and quickly moved into _____ stage, then passed through _____ stage to reach the _____ stage and stayed there for most of the project. Now since the project is closing the team will go through _____ stage.
    A) forming, storming, norming, performing, adjourning
    B) forming, storming, norming, performing, adjusting
    C) forming, norming, storming, performing, adjourning
    D) forming, norming, storming, performing, adjusting

164. You are managing a gas pipeline river crossing project. The project involves drilling piles in the river bed to build a bridge to cross the gas pipeline over the river. The biggest risk, you have identified and planned the response for, was the delay in shipping and import of steel piles from abroad. There were two shipments planned a few months apart. The first shipment was received at the docks on time. Three large trailers took off from the docks to the site, carrying enough piles for three weeks of work. It will take them one week to reach the site from the docks. All the teams and installation equipment was ready on south bank of the river on the day the shipment was to arrive. The shipment reached the site on time but on the north side of the river. It would take a whole week to bring it to south side as the bridge which can accommodate the large trailers was very far from the site. The risk response plan for the potential delay did not cover this aspect. What do you think will be the BEST way to handle this situation?
    A) This should be handled as an issue and not as a risk
    B) Analyze this risk and use contingency reserve which is for unplanned risks
    C) Add this to risk register, analyze and develop risk response, then communicate to make sure no more trailers get sent to the north side
    D) Evaluate impact of this issue on project performance baselines

165. You are the project manager of a web development project. A seller was awarded a contract to build the dashboard to be integrated with the other web development work. Under the terms of the contract, the seller was required to produce a schedule of interviews with stakeholders for the clarification of requirements. The schedule was to be approved by the buyer before the seller could proceed with the dashboard development. The seller instead had some informal discussions with few of the stakeholders that he knew really well from before. What should be your approach?
    A) Cancel the contract and award to the second best bidder
    B) Create a schedule and provide to the seller to move things along
    C) Issue a warning to the seller that if the schedule is not submitted immediately, the contract will be canceled
    D) Ask the seller in writing to stop the work and submit the schedule for approval

166. An organization uses a desktop scheduling software for project scheduling. What will you call this software?
    A) Enterprise environmental factor
    B) Integrated change control system

C) Project management office
   D) Organizational process asset

167. Which process includes identifying new risks and monitoring residual risks?
   A) Plan Risk Management
   B) Monitor Risks
   C) Identify Risks
   D) Residual Risk Management

168. The products or services acquired through seller under a contract must meet the needs of the project. Who is responsible to ensure this compliance?
   A) The seller
   B) Procurement department
   C) Project team
   D) Project sponsor

169. With _____, potential problems are linked to various factors.
   A) Quality assurance
   B) Pareto chart
   C) Cause-and-effect diagram
   D) Process analysis

170. Which of the following cannot be an output of the Plan Schedule Management process?
   A) Development approach
   B) Reporting format
   C) Control thresholds
   D) Release and iteration length

171. A project manager wants to exceed the expectations of his management. To achieve that, he has built aggressive schedules and tight budgets. What is his risk approach?
   A) He is accepting risks
   B) He is seeking risks
   C) He is avoiding risks
   D) He is transferring risks

172. Which of the following is the right tool to implement a quality assurance activity to supplement existing quality control activities?
   A) Control chart
   B) Statistical sampling

C) Benchmarking
D) Problem Solving

173. You are a new project manager and have been assigned to estimate a project's costs. You ask a senior project manager, who has been working in the company for 10 years, for his advice. He asks you to increase your cost estimate by 25% since the management always cuts the project budget by 25% before approving the project. What will you do?
    A) Present the actual cost estimate along with a brief explanation of the impact of a budget cut on the project
    B) Present the actual cost estimate along with a note that you will not manage the project if the budget is not approved as is
    C) Inflate each task's cost estimate by 25%
    D) Add contingency reserve equal to 25% of the costs

174. When most of the team members of a project are working remotely, the benefits of colocation are lost. Which one of the following is the BEST way to build social relations among such team members?
    A) Bring all team members together for an offsite team building event
    B) Ask everyone to come in once a week to get some benefits of colocation
    C) Use instant messaging for real-time discussions
    D) Plan daily conference calls with the team

175. Which of the following normally provides the summary milestone schedule?
    A) Business case
    B) Project charter
    C) Project requirements document
    D) Project scope statement

176. A hospital wants to build a clinical information system (CIS) so a senior project manager was assigned to the three years long CIS project. It has several smaller projects starting and completing at different times. This is an example of _____.
    A) Phases of the project life cycle
    B) An Operational endeavor with multiple projects
    C) A large project with multiple sub-projects
    D) A large program with multiple projects

177. While managing a project you have a dispute with the seller about

some changes. The seller believes these changes are constructive changes while you believe these are part of the original scope. What type of changes are these?
A) Enterprise environmental factors
B) Contested changes
C) Preventive changes
D) Corrective changes

178. A technology company is looking into four projects but can only execute one at this time. These are as follows:
1) An application enhancement project with an internal rate of return (IRR) of 10 percent
2) A system upgrade project with an internal rate of return (IRR) of 15 percent
3) A new marketing project with an IRR of 20 percent, and
4) A new product development project with an IRR of 25 percent.
Which project should the company select?
A) Application enhancement project
B) System upgrade project
C) New product development project
D) New marketing project

179. A project schedule has activities and milestones. What do you know about milestones?
A) Milestones mark significant events in the project and are required to create a valid schedule
B) Milestones mark significant events in the project and can be requested by the sponsor
C) Activities are summed up into milestones which makes them significant events
D) WBS work packages are also known as milestones

180. A project manager will select the appropriate technology to ensure that communications between the project team and stakeholders are efficient and effective. Which of the following factors is least likely to impact a change in the technology being used for this purpose?
A) A colocated team has two new members who are located in a different country
B) A new government regulation regarding privacy of data has come into effect
C) The number of stakeholders has almost doubled since the project started
D) The organization has deployed a new document management

system

181. Which statement is INCORRECT about the level of authority of the project manager?
    A) A project manager has little or no authority in a weak organization
    B) A project manager has little or no authority in a multi-divisional organization
    C) A project manager has little or no authority in a functional organization
    D) A project manager has little or no authority in an organic organization

182. Who cannot authorize a project?
    A) Project manager
    B) Project management office
    C) Project Sponsor
    D) Portfolio manager

183. A project manager on a large scale laptop deployment project is doing reserve analysis. What is she comparing?
    A) How much contingency reserve has been spent compared to how much is remaining
    B) How much contingency reserve is still remaining compared to how much is the amount of remaining risk
    C) How much contingency reserve has been spent compared to how much management reserve has been spent
    D) How much contingency reserve was spent on risks compared to how much was spent on other items

184. Which one of the following is the main tool and technique used in the Control Procurements process?
    A) Contract negotiation
    B) Litigation
    C) Inspection
    D) Proposal evaluation criteria

185. The table shows crashing data for a schedule. Calculate the cost of crashing the schedule by seven days?

Activity	Duration	Predecessor	Cost of Activity	Cost of Crashing (per day)	Max Days it can be Crashed
A	7		2,000	200	0
B	9	A	3,000	200	2
C	8	B	2,000	300	2
D	9	C	4,000	300	3
E	5	C	3,000	500	3
F	4	D,E	1,000	100	0

A) The cost is 9,000
B) The cost is 1,900
C) The cost is 2,500
D) The cost is 1,600

186. A project manager has been assigned to an agile project that is in trouble. The project has a high technical debt resulting in too many user complaints. Which of the following can help in this regard?
    A) Burn-down chart
    B) Refactoring
    C) Timeboxing
    D) User stories

187. You are the project manager of a building construction project. One of the routine meetings you have is a weekly meeting with the project team where each team member reports how much work has been completed on assigned tasks and what are the measurements from quality tests. What are these examples of?
    A) Earned value analysis
    B) Work performance data
    C) Time and cost estimating
    D) Perform quality audits

188. Which one, among the following, is the MOST useful place to see Estimate At Completion (EAC) and Estimate To Complete (ETC) information?
    A) Schedule performance data
    B) Forecast
    C) Cost performance data
    D) Lessons learned

189. Which of the following is an example of ambiguity risks?
    A) Upcoming regulations changes may complicate approval of the

flying car design
B) Developer coding rate may be higher or lower than the planned rate
C) Organizational transformation may result in a varying number of working hours per week at times
D) Change in weather pattern may cause period of a dry spell and/or rainfall

190. You have realized that you have to crash a few tasks in order to meet the external deadline. What is going to be your approach?
A) Crash as many tasks as possible to reduce overall effort
B) Crash non-critical tasks to remove wasted time
C) Crash tasks on the critical path
D) Crash tasks that have the highest cost associated with them

191. Which of the following is NOT a tool and technique for the Control Schedule process?
A) Resource optimization
B) What-if scenario analysis
C) Three point estimation
D) Schedule compression

192. There are many documents that are input to the Monitor and Control Project Work process. Which of the following is not an input to Monitor and Control Project Work process?
A) Issue log
B) Work performance report
C) Schedule forecast
D) Quality reports

193. The optimistic and the pessimistic estimates for a major task are 12 and 24 days respectively. What is the standard deviation of this task?
A) 2
B) 4
C) 1
D) 12

194. You are in the Control Procurements process for your project. What is the Control Procurements process responsible for?
A) Control the bidders' conference with appropriate controls
B) Create and manage the statement of work
C) Define contract terms for optimum performance by the seller
D) Manage the contractual relationship between the buyer and seller

195. As the project manager working for a seller of application development services, you prepared a response to a bid invitation for executing a statement of work. The schedule and cost estimate was based on the premise that certain expert resources will be acquired and engaged for the project. After award of the contract, when you started to acquire the team, you ended up engaging resources with very little experience. The buyer had a serious objection to that. What should be the FIRST thing you should do?
    A) Engage additional resources to cover up for low capability and to help the schedule stay on track
    B) Evaluate the impact of resource capability on project cost and schedule
    C) Submit a change request to update cost and schedule baselines to reflect reduced cost and delayed deliverables
    D) Discuss with the buyer what his concern is, and assure that the project will be completed within budget and on time

196. Which Project Communications Management knowledge area process is part of the Monitoring and Controlling process group?
    A) Manage Communications
    B) Monitor and Control Communications
    C) Control Communications
    D) Monitor Communications

197. You are the project manager for an application enhancement project. One of your designers is working very closely with the customer to ensure that the design meets all the customer requirements. During one session, the two of them changed the design of one deliverable that resulted in another deliverable being eliminated. This resulted in significant savings for the customer. You were not happy when you found out about this saving plan. Why?
    A) Deliverables cannot be changed once baselined
    B) The savings will result in reduced profit for your company
    C) Scope control process was not followed
    D) You were not included in the decision making

198. You are mentoring a new project manager who recently started her career in project management. She wants to know which deliverable will provide her with the criteria and guidelines to create and manage the project schedule. What will be your reply?
    A) Schedule baseline
    B) Schedule management plan

C) Resource management plan
D) Activity management plan

199. Which of the following is the BEST example of the use of coercive power by the project manager?
    A) Project manager talking to a resource "I want you to complete this report by end of tomorrow."
    B) Project manager asks a resource "Should I meet in person or just send her an email. Which is the right approach?"
    C) Project manager asks a resource "Come on. You know you owe me. Get me the report by tomorrow."
    D) Project manager says to a resource "If I do not get the document from you within two days, I will speak with your manager."

200. In a typical project, which of the following costs should be fully included in the budget?
    A) All payments made to the vendors
    B) All equipment used on the project
    C) All resources working on the project
    D) All project resources that are being charged to the project

3 - PMP MOCK TEST 2

200 Questions - Time Limit: 4 Hours

201. There are four kinds of dependencies when sequencing activities. These are called, mandatory, discretionary, internal, and external. Which type of dependencies are fully documented since they can create arbitrary float values and can later limit scheduling options?
    A) Preferential logic
    B) Fixed logic
    C) Floating logic
    D) Environmental logic

202. A buyer has rejected a deliverable that was submitted for acceptance by the seller. The buyer has cited the specific term of the contract under which the deliverable has been rejected. On a closer review, the seller's project manager agrees with the buyer. Which is the BEST option for sellers' project manager among the following choices?
    A) Submit a change request to change the relevant term of the contract
    B) Identify team member responsible for the error and take disciplinary action
    C) Review the requirements and submit a change request for defect repair
    D) Review the relevant term of the contract with the legal counsel

203. One of the following is neither an input to nor an output of the Develop Project Charter process. Which one is it?
    A) A project charter

B) Project management plan
C) Business case
D) Agreements

204. What is the impact on the project team development in a functional organization when the whole team reports to one functional manager?
    A) There is no need for team development in a functional organization since everyone in the team already works in the same group
    B) There is no impact on team development because team development is the same process no matter what the organizational structure is
    C) Team development is tedious and difficult to manage
    D) Team development is a much simpler ongoing process

205. Which of the following is not a type of risk attitude of organizations?
    A) Risk appetite
    B) Risk tolerance
    C) Risk threshold
    D) Risk response

206. What type of contract is most commonly used when the product specifications are very detailed, precise and well-defined?
    A) Time and material
    B) Fixed-price
    C) Cost-reimbursable
    D) Time lapsed

207. If a project manager finds himself in a position where an external team is about to start the quality audit of the project but the internal team is against such an audit in the middle of the project, what should be his approach?
    A) Request the audit team to delay the audit until the end of the project so that the project team can focus on completing work on time
    B) Inform sponsor about team's concern and ask for direction
    C) Inform the team that quality audit will help identify inefficient and ineffective policies and procedures
    D) Inform the team that quality audit will verify the time sheets submitted by the team members to ensure compliance with company policies

208. You are managing a building construction project. The project is at a

stage where you are spending most of the budget and managing the maximum number of resources. The level of influence stakeholders can exert in this phase compared to earlier phases has _____.
A) Reduced
B) Increased
C) Stayed the same
D) Reduced for project sponsor and increased for the rest of the stakeholders

209. Out of the following four, which statement is true about the scope management plan and requirements management plan?
A) Scope management plan details how the work breakdown structure will be created while the requirements management plan describes which traceability structure will be used
B) Requirements management plan details how the work breakdown structure will be created while the scope management plan describes which traceability structure will be used
C) Scope management plan explains the prioritization process while the requirements management plan lists techniques that will be used to collect user needs
D) Requirements management plan shows how deliverables will be accepted while the scope management plan discusses how the scope baseline will be approved

210. What is the relevance of team performance assessments for project team members?
A) Specific training can be identified to improve team performance
B) Individuals collective performance is project performance
C) The team that performs well is praised well
D) Project performance as appraised by a third party impacts how project team members are valued outside the project

211. Which of the following is NOT considered a characteristic of team building?
A) Team building activities can be done formally as an agenda item
B) Team building activities should be work related
C) Team building activities can be done for the virtual team
D) Team building activities should continue throughout the project

212. You may use a resource management software to monitor resource utilization on your project. What is meant by that?
A) Ensure all resource problems are tracked and solved
B) Ensure resources are acquired for the right cost at the right time

C) Ensure the right resources are identified for the right activities
D) Ensure the right resources are working on the right activities at the right time and place

213. You are working on an HR process streamlining project. The subject matter expert (SME) that was supposed to work on your project was reassigned to a high visibility project which has the Chief Information Officer as the sponsor. What action will you take?
A) Track and manage this issue on the issue log
B) Put in a request to hire a consultant to fill the SME role
C) Demand that the resource is allocated back to your project since the resource was assigned first to your project
D) Compress schedule so that you can manage the project without this resource

214. If a project's actual total cost is 300,000 against a total budget of 400,000 and the project is 75% complete, then what is the earned value?
A) Earned value is 0.75
B) Earned value is 100,000
C) Cannot be determined from the information given
D) Earned value is 300,000

215. A project manager is starting a new project. Which of the following he must do FIRST before proceeding with the project?
A) Create the project scope statement
B) Develop stakeholder assessment matrix
C) Gather detailed requirements
D) Get the project charter approved

216. On-demand scheduling is an emerging practice in project schedule management. What is this approach based on?
A) Demand and supply
B) Theory of Constraints
C) Precedence Diagramming Method
D) Monte Carlo simulation

217. During a negotiation with the customer about the work to be performed and effort involved, the customer objects to the effort being proposed to manage quality and control quality processes. As the project manager, which one of the following concepts you will explain to the customer to remove the objection?
A) CMMI audit requirements

B) Continuous improvement focus
C) Cost of conformance vs. cost of nonconformance
D) Quality assurance and quality control

218. How does quality relate to the project scope?
    A) Quality meets the scope by completing the needs whether stated or implied
    B) Quality exists to satisfy project scope
    C) Quality, whether stated or implied, is to meet the needs whether stated or implied by completing the scope
    D) Quality is the measuring of the scope of a project

219. A project can have stakeholders from inside and outside of the executing organization. One of the following is not a stakeholder on a software development project. Which one is it?
    A) The programmer writing code during the development phase
    B) The vendor performing third-party testing of the code
    C) The workplace manager responsible for allocating office space to project team members
    D) The seller responsible for fixing a broken chair and desk in the office

220. A project manager issued a purchase order to a seller to provide catering service during a major event. The event is a three-day meeting to be held for requirements gathering. The project manager is in which of the following processes?
    A) Deliver Procurements
    B) Control Procurements
    C) Plan Procurement Management
    D) Conduct Procurements

221. You are the project manager on an RFID research project. The project is in the planning process and you are estimating the project costs. The team has come up with an estimate of 750,000 using the parametric estimating technique. A senior project manager in the company gives his opinion that the project should not cost more than 500,000. Which estimate will you use?
    A) Total estimate of 500,000
    B) Total estimate of 1,250,000
    C) Total estimate of 750,000
    D) Total estimate of 625,000

222. You are managing your first project at a company. This is a system

upgrade project that happens every 2-3 years for the last 10 years. In order to estimate costs, you are consulting the cost performance baselines and lessons learned from those projects. Which technique are you using?
A) Parametric estimating
B) Bottom-Up estimating
C) Ball Park estimating
D) Analogous estimating

223. Which of the following is an attribute of project scope management?
A) Project scope management defines the processes to enable the project to include all the work that is required and only the work that is required to achieve the project's objectives
B) Project scope management is the management of scope so that the project can be completed on time, within budget and with high quality
C) Project scope management is the same as project management, as both deal with managing the project to success
D) Project scope management defines the scope, gathers the requirements and creates the deliverables of the project

224. You are working as a seller's project manager for a buyer on a cost reimbursable contract. The buyer wants to add scope to the current statement of work and also wants to change the contract to a fixed price one. You have all of the following options available EXCEPT _____.
A) Negotiate a new fixed price contract for the additional scope but stay on the cost-reimbursable for the original statement of work
B) Refuse to do the additional work but complete the original work under the cost-reimbursable contract
C) Since the buyer wants a fixed-price contract, negotiate one that includes all the work that is still to be performed
D) Negotiate with the buyer to restart the whole project with a fixed-price contract so that a dispute can be avoided

225. What does corrective action mean in regards to risk response?
A) It means a resulting corrective action change request when putting the planned risk response into action
B) It means creating a risk response that suggests corrective action
C) These are two different things. Corrective action is related to change while risk response is to risk
D) It means correcting the risk response on a continuous basis

226. A new project of computer deployment to the large global workforce in 90 countries received an approved budget in US dollars because the company's headquarters are in the United States. The cost of deployment in each country is different and has to be estimated independently. Which of the following challenges best represents this scenario?
    A) Scope creep
    B) Fast track schedule
    C) Budget constraint
    D) Cost estimation

227. Though all of the following techniques are used to solve problems in projects, which one do you consider to be the BEST?
    A) Collaborating
    B) Reconciling
    C) Smoothing
    D) Directing

228. All of the following are the tools used in the Control Quality process EXCEPT _____.
    A) Scatter diagrams
    B) Histogram
    C) Control charts
    D) Gantt chart

229. A work breakdown structure was created for the auto parts plant manufacturing project. The team reached a point where they were able to identify 75 work packages. The work package information was sent to various departments for review. All the departments were content with the level of detail for their work package but the store department objected that the work packages were too high level and should be sub-divided into smaller manageable packages so that accurate estimate can be prepared and a detailed schedule can be developed. The team identified a technique that will be used to fulfill this request. Which technique is it?
    A) Rolling wave planning
    B) Analogous estimating followed by parametric estimating
    C) Work packaging by the type of resources instead of by the departments
    D) Discretionary planning

230. In which process, advertising is generally used as a tool?
    A) Conduct Procurements

B) Plan Procurement Management
C) Control Procurements
D) Manage Procurements

231. A project manager is having problems with attendance in the team meeting. One member is too busy with the project work and another member dislikes meetings. Both of them never bother to show up. A highly experienced senior project manager is asked to help the project manager identify a solution. The senior project manager recommends that a meeting notification should be sent out in advance identifying that attendance is mandatory and leave of absence must be taken in advance from the project manager. Which power is the senior project manager referring to?
    A) Referent
    B) Coercive
    C) Expert
    D) Formal

232. What is still left to be done when the final product has been transitioned to the customer?
    A) Obtain formal acceptance by the customer
    B) Submit the final change request
    C) Close the procurement
    D) Update the lessons learned register

233. An environmental clean-up project has been completed. There are strict requirements imposed by the government as environmental issues are very sensitive. To make sure all of the requirements are met and an audit is cleared without a hitch, you want to engage environmental experts that are luckily available within your company. You are considering _____ for closing the project.
    A) Enterprise environmental factors
    B) Expert judgment
    C) Organizational process assets
    D) Scope Validation

234. A market demand, new technology, or a legal requirement commonly results in which of the following?
    A) Hiring a project manager
    B) Initiating a project
    C) Engaging a stakeholder
    D) Resourcing a project

235. You are the project manager of documentation project which is part of an enterprise program. Currently, you are developing the criteria of source selection for your contract. Source selection happens in which process?
   A) Plan Procurement Management
   B) Control Procurements
   C) Request Seller Responses
   D) Conduct Procurements

236. _____ is responsible for the quality of the project deliverables for a building construction project.
   A) The sponsor
   B) The project team
   C) The seller
   D) The quality assurance team

237. Which of the following is an output of the Manage Stakeholder Engagement process?
   A) Assumption log
   B) Risk register
   C) RACI chart
   D) Issue log

238. In which process group will you create a list of all of the people who will be directly affected by the project?
   A) Initiating
   B) Planning
   C) Executing
   D) Closing

239. If you were to find out the longest time between the planned start and finish dates of a project, which tool will you use?
   A) Work Breakdown Structure
   B) Network diagram
   C) Business case
   D) Project charter

240. You have been assigned as project manager for a human resources process improvement project. While performing stakeholder analysis, you identified one stakeholder who is an expert in domain knowledge which has been marked risky for the project. This stakeholder has high interest in the project but very low influence due to his position in the organization. Which would be the best approach?

A) Manage this stakeholder closely
B) Keep him satisfied by sending him regular project performance reports
C) Keep him informed and solicit his feedback on risks and issues
D) Monitor him so that he could be managed closely if he becomes influential

241. A project manager created a simple status report for his project. The report was in a dashboard format showing performance information including percent complete, above, at or below planned. What is this information for?
    A) It shows the schedule, budget, and scope. Their % complete and status of where actual stands vs. planned
    B) It shows the project manager's performance vs. other team members' performance
    C) It shows how much work each project resource has completed and how is the performance against the expected performance
    D) It shows % completed work by the seller and the actual rating against the expected rating

242. What is the main objective of the Validate Scope process?
    A) Acceptance of work
    B) Complete project on time and within budget
    C) Receive customer feedback
    D) Start Project Close process

243. A project manager is concerned about the performance of a team member. The team member has completed all of the assigned tasks later than the planned date and has not been able to provide a valid reason for that. The project manager sends him a notice of a meeting to discuss his performance in the presence of the company's human resource representative. This is an example of what type of communication?
    A) Informal written
    B) Formal written
    C) Informal oral
    D) Formal oral

244. While managing a project with resources working in two countries, a project manager receives two resumes for an open position in the other country. One candidate is the team leader's son who barely meets the requirement and another person who is well experienced. The preferred practice in the country is to hire immediate family

members before hiring from outside. What should the project manager do?
- A) Hire the team leader's son if every other criterion is met
- B) Hire the experienced resource to get maximum productivity out of this role
- C) Replace the team leader before hiring the experienced resource
- D) Leave the decision to the team leader because he is ultimately responsible for getting the work done

245. You are managing a corporate training system project. You have to present monthly the project performance report to the senior management stakeholders including the project sponsor. Which of the following will NOT be part of the information presented?
- A) Forecast of when the project will be completed
- B) Contract performance information
- C) Issues that need management attention
- D) A team member's performance issues

246. You are the project manager of a simple technology deployment project. The project is expected to be completed in one year by deploying the technology on all the computers in the company. How often are you going to perform risk identification?
- A) At the start of the project only since it is a simple project
- B) At the start, middle and end of the project as it is a simple project but a bit long
- C) At a regular frequency throughout the project
- D) At the start of the project and just before deployment as that is the most critical time when the whole company becomes stakeholders

247. As a project manager, you will record and track issues on an issue log. Which piece of information will you not record on an issue log?
- A) Priority
- B) Probability
- C) Status
- D) Type

248. Which data gathering technique can be very helpful when planning to involve stakeholders at the desired engagement level?
- A) Cultural awareness
- B) Benchmarking
- C) Political awareness
- D) Checklists

249. The project you have been managing has run into problems lately. During code testing, several issues have been identified that require significant amount of work to fix. You need additional resources to stay on track and complete the project on time. Your formal request to add more resources has been approved by the sponsor. What will be your next step?
    A) Modify the schedule baseline
    B) Close the identified risk
    C) Review project scope to identify changes
    D) Request funds from management reserves to pay for the additional resources

250. If one has to estimate the intended cost of the project for the purpose of comparing with cost estimates so that significant anomalies can be identified, which tool would be the BEST?
    A) Bottom-up estimating
    B) Bidders' conference
    C) Independent cost estimate
    D) Procurement audit

251. What is the concept of watch list in risk management context?
    A) List of resources whose performance is being watched for corrective action
    B) List of identified risks that are watched to see if their probability or impact changes to warrant a response
    C) List of identified risks that have risk response planned and watched to see if it actually occurs
    D) List of scope items from the project scope that are risky

252. If there is an approved change to a project that affects the project's cost, what will you update to reflect the change?
    A) Project charter
    B) Project's cost baseline
    C) Integrated change control system
    D) Project's Earned value

253. As a project manager, you will be doing an assessment of individuals and the team during the Develop Team process. Which of the following tool is not used for that assessment?
    A) Structured interview
    B) Ability test
    C) Focus group

D) Mind mapping

254. A project team was trying its best but was unable to meet the specification of the product. Project manager decided to analyze the variance and decide a proper course of action. Which process will that be in?
    A) Define Scope
    B) Control Scope
    C) Control Quality
    D) Perform Integrated Change Control

255. Out of the following four, which can be a reason to update the project performance baselines of a tunnel boring project?
    A) A change request to increase the overall cost of the project by 50,000, due to a change in the price of drill bits, has been approved
    B) The supplier is adding more resources to the project on a fixed price contract
    C) Some rework was done which cost the supplier an additional 40,000
    D) Electrical contractors just bought a new machine for 500,000 to use on the project

256. Disputes occurring in a project that is being executed under a contract are common. These disputes can be related to the scope, price, schedule, quality, resources, etc. Which of the following is the preferred method of resolving these disputes?
    A) Arbitration
    B) Small claims court
    C) Mediation
    D) Negotiation

257. An output of Manage Quality process is _____.
    A) Quality metrics
    B) Quality control measurement
    C) Quality management plan
    D) Change requests

258. A medical research project usually has a very fuzzy scope and a high degree of uncertainty. The BEST approach for such a project is _____.
    A) Detailed work breakdown structure
    B) Predictive life cycle

C) Rolling wave planning
D) A well-defined scope statement

259. In a typical project, which process from the project schedule management knowledge area takes most of the effort?
    A) Control Schedule process
    B) Estimate Activity Durations process
    C) Define Activities process
    D) Develop Schedule process

260. Which of the following statements is incorrect when thinking about the identification of stakeholders for a project?
    A) Stakeholders with a positive approach help project manager succeed
    B) Demands of positive stakeholders should have a higher priority than the negative stakeholders
    C) A project may get into trouble if negative stakeholders are ignored
    D) Various stakeholders may have opposing views on a project

261. You were managing a pharmaceutical project when suddenly the project sponsor, who was the head of the laboratory, resigned from the company. The management immediately assigned his duties to another person who became the new head of the laboratory and, by default, became the project sponsor. What is the MOST effective thing you can do?
    A) Arrange a meeting and introduce yourself then do a detailed review of the project
    B) Send him the project schedule, budget, and scope details along with the latest progress report
    C) Understand the communication needs of the new sponsor and update the communication management plan
    D) Provide him access to project repository and send him access information so that he may review the project records on his own schedule

262. The Close Project or Phase process can be affected by various Organizational Process Assets. Which one of the following is NOT an Organizational Process Asset that can affect the Close Project or Phase process?
    A) Project audit requirements
    B) Acceptance criteria
    C) Team performance appraisal guidelines

D) Marketplace conditions

263. Which technique will you use to engage a very hard to find and an expensive resource so that you can maximize the value?
    A) What-If scenario
    B) Pareto
    C) Leveling
    D) Fast Tracking

264. Which of the following is the most effective way to build trust which helps in managing knowledge?
    A) Active listening
    B) Face-to-face interaction
    C) Virtual interaction
    D) Meetings

265. Several meetings will take place during project closeout process. Which of the following is not a type of meeting you will use as part of project closeout process?
    A) Celebration
    B) Daily stand up
    C) Customer wrap-up
    D) Lessons learned

266. Your latest report says that by the end of last week your project had Earned Value (EV) of 127,200 and Planned Value (PV) of 143,000. You are going to present that report later today. How will you explain in simple terms how is your project doing?
    A) Ahead of Schedule
    B) Exactly On schedule
    C) Cannot be determined from the information given
    D) Behind Schedule

267. As the project manager for a new product development project, you read a report on hot consumer trends for the next decade. You realize that your product lacks most of those aspects. After review and discussion with the business and the marketing department, you have established that the project will have a high degree of change throughout its lifecycle and the project has to deliver frequently. Which lifecycle best suits this situation?
    A) Incremental
    B) Predictive
    C) Agile

D) Iterative

268. A project manager was managing the intercontinental high-pressure gas pipeline construction project. The project was being executed using the company's internal resources but needed to be fast tracked now. He looked at options and decided to quickly bring in a contractor to do the work. Since there is no time to issue a tender, he invited the contractor who had recently replaced plumbing in head office and had done a really good job, to sign the contract. What did he miss?
    A) Request for proposal
    B) Qualification of the seller
    C) Independent estimate
    D) Bidders' conference

269. Why a risk has a very low score when its probability of occurrence is very high?
    A) A calculation error
    B) Impact has low value
    C) Impact has high value
    D) Impact has not been assigned yet

270. What is the most common problem in project risk management when it comes to implementing risk responses?
    A) A documented risk response is not audited
    B) A risk response is not fully documented
    C) A documented risk response is not executed when the risk occurs
    D) A risk owner is not assigned to a documented risk response

271. There are many personality traits of a project manager. The ability to make things happen is called _____ trait.
    A) Intellectual
    B) Social
    C) Systemic
    D) Political

272. Monitoring the stakeholders is essential to adjust the engagement strategies in order to improve stakeholder engagement throughout the project. What is used for this purpose?
    A) Stakeholder engagement plan
    B) Stakeholder register
    C) Stakeholder engagement assessment matrix
    D) Communications management plan

273. You have just been hired by Company X as project manager for their X31 project. You do not know the organization because you are new, but you do need to start developing the project charter immediately. What will be most helpful at this stage while creating the project charter?
    A) Organizational Process Assets
    B) Project management plan
    C) Meeting management
    D) Project team development

274. You are a project manager working on a new product development project. You have a long-term contract with a reputed seller. Under the contract, the seller is charging you 50 per hour per resource engaged on your project and 200 per week as overhead charges. You have a _____ contract with the seller.
    A) Fixed price
    B) Cost plus fixed fee
    C) Cost reimbursable
    D) Time and material

275. As the project manager, you have gone through risk identification exercise with the project team and other stakeholders. The result was a comprehensive list of identified risks recorded on the risk register. Next, you created an online survey with the identified risks as questions, requiring answers in the form of probability and impact. You asked all stakeholders to go online and fill the survey. The responses are confidential so no one knows who else filled the survey and no one can see others' responses. Which of the following techniques have you used?
    A) Risk probability and impact assessment
    B) Probability and impact matrix
    C) Risk analysis
    D) Risk categorization

276. Your colleague has been working as the project manager on Human Resource Information System project. From the first month, the project schedule started to slip and this has been the trend for the last 6 months. Almost all deliverables have been late and the sponsor and end users are all disappointed. He told you, over a cup of coffee, that his reputation is on the line and does not know what to do. You worked with him and used what-if scenario analysis to identify the factors that had impacted the schedule. After that, you recommended him to _____.

A) Redevelop project schedule with ample float to manage the identified factors
B) Send the list of factors to the sponsor and end-users with an explanatory note
C) Add new activities into the schedule to cover for identified factors
D) Create a change request to update the schedule baseline

277. The difference between the project life cycle and product life cycle is that _____.
A) Project life cycle can be sequential while product life cycle cannot be sequential
B) Project life cycle can have varying duration while product life cycle has a fixed duration
C) Project life cycle can span multiple product life cycles while product life cycle has only one project life cycle
D) Project life cycle provides the basic framework for managing the project while product life cycle represents the evolution of the product

278. During the Conduct Procurements process, who generally takes the lead role negotiating contracts for project work?
A) Procurement specialist
B) Functional manager
C) Project manager
D) Project sponsor

279. The project manager received a letter from the vendor's representative. Who is the decoder?
A) Project manager
B) Vendor's representative
C) No one
D) Letter

280. The final project performance report of a project that was completed 6 months late shows Cost Performance Index (CPI) as 0.83. What is this project's Schedule Performance Index (SPI)?
A) SPI = 0.50
B) SPI = 0.83
C) SPI = 1.00
D) Cannot be determined from the information given

281. What will you tell a sponsor who wants to know the current value of

expected return of 500,000 in 5 years when the discount rate is expected to be a steady 6%?
A) 670,000 approximately
B) 500,000 approximately
C) 470,000 approximately
D) 370,000 approximately

282. Which term best represents the type of process Manage Quality is?
A) Management
B) Controlling
C) Measurement
D) Inspection

283. In which type of organization the following resource problem can occur? A project manager is unable to get his resource request accepted by the infrastructure manager because all resources are engaged in other projects. The only way he can get resources is to escalate and discuss the issue with the director of the infrastructure manager.
A) Functional
B) Weak matrix
C) Strong matrix
D) Project-oriented

284. Library services, web searches, and reading published articles are examples of _____.
A) Organizational process assets
B) Information management
C) Lessons learned repository
D) Knowledge management

285. A project manager has used affinity diagram method to review and group a large number of errors being reported on the project. He is planning to further analyze and identify the root cause of errors. What is he doing?
A) Performing integrated change control
B) Making a decision
C) Brainstorming
D) Managing quality

286. You are the project manager of a large construction project where over 200 resources are working. The project accountant is unsure about the cost center of one particular resource. Which of the

following is the BEST tool that can help in this situation?
A) Resource leveling
B) Work Breakdown Structure Dictionary
C) Bottom-Up estimating
D) Scope Validation

287. There are various activity attributes associated with a defined activity. Which attribute will be defined during the initial activity definition?
A) Duration
B) Start date
C) WBS ID
D) Predecessor activities

288. How will you explain the concept of SWOT?
A) It is a specialized workers official team to handle complex issues
B) An analysis of strengths, weaknesses, opportunities, and threats
C) A devil's advocate in sheep's clothing
D) Expressed from 0 to 100 and converted to 0 to 1 for later calculations

289. A structured review of the procurement process is performed by reviewing procurement from the Plan Procurement Management through the Control Procurements to identify what went well and what did not. What do you call such a review?
A) Audits
B) Performance review
C) Negotiated settlement
D) Procurement review

290. You are managing an intranet development project for your company. During the design phase, one designer found a cool application that shows the stock value of the company in real time. As most of the employees own shares of the company, the team believed that this will be an extra value-add which will be appreciated by the employees. What is going on?
A) Gold plating
B) Exceeding expectations
C) Ensuring business benefits
D) Nothing is going on

291. What is a configuration management system?
A) A System that describes the process of controlling the project management processes and methods to actually control these

processes
B) A System that describes items requiring formal change control and provides the process for controlling changes to these items
C) A system that configures the project for better management and provides management reports for such configuration
D) An encompassing system that includes integrated change control and project management information systems

292. The project cost baseline should include all of the following EXCEPT _____.

    A) Management costs
    B) Labor costs
    C) Material costs
    D) Equipment costs

293. A project manager finds two of his team members in disagreement over the testing approach. The project manager met with the team members and _____.
    A) Told them that arguing on petty matters can derail the project
    B) Advised them to discuss in private as their disagreement is damaging the team spirit
    C) Asked them to write a change request so that a formal decision can be made
    D) Tried to understand the cause of the disagreement so that a solution can be developed collaboratively

294. Is Work Performance Information an input, an output or a tool and technique of the Monitor Communications process?
    A) Output
    B) None of these
    C) Input
    D) Tool and Technique

295. Direct and Manage Project Work process has various inputs, outputs, and tools and techniques. Which of the following is none of those?
    A) Project management information system, work performance data, project management plan updates
    B) Deliverables, issue log, change requests
    C) Approved change requests, project charter, and project management information system
    D) Approved corrective actions, approved preventive actions, and expert judgment

296. You are the project manager of an enterprise application time tracking project. Your project requires several changes to meet customer needs, stay on schedule and within budget. You have a system to manage and control these project changes. Each of the proposed change goes through an analysis of the impact of that change on the project scope, deliverables, cost, and schedule. A change is approved, rejected, or deferred and stakeholders may be notified if needed. What helps you achieve all that?
   A) Control chart
   B) Configuration control and Change control
   C) Configuration chart and Cost control
   D) Change control and Control board

297. The project team is working on estimating activity durations for the Next Generation Tablet Development project. The team has a mix of resources, some without experience and others with expert level experience. The estimates provided for tablet assembly range from 3 hours to 12 hours. There seems to be a consensus that most likely it will take 10 hours to assemble the tablet. In this situation, you have no choice but to use the three-point estimation using triangular distribution to determine how long it will take to assemble the tablet. You found out that it will take approximately _____ hours.
   A) 9
   B) 18
   C) 8
   D) 4

298. Your project is in the middle of executing processes. You were in a meeting with the sponsor when he mentions a concern. This is a risk that has not been identified before and recorded on the risk register. What are you going to do?
   A) Explore this risk further with the sponsor and alleviate his concerns
   B) The risk identification process was already over so this concern can be ignored
   C) Inform the project team what this risk is about
   D) Record on the risk register and analyze that risk

299. You being the project manager of Fertilizer Plant Extension project are reviewing the schedule developed for your project. Your goal is to determine the project end date based on schedule analysis of the least flexible activities. Which tool are you using to perform this analysis?
   A) Precedence Diagramming Method (PDM)

B) Three-point analysis
C) Ishikawa diagram
D) Critical Path Method

300. A project management office (PMO) in a fast-paced company is looking into establishing the practice of mandatory project gate reviews and audit and also planning to centralize project reporting through PMO but does not want to manage the projects. What type of PMO will provide this level of control and influence?
    A) Supportive
    B) Managerial
    C) Controlling
    D) Directing

301. Which of the following is NOT a piece of advice you would give to your project team members in regards to managing project stakeholders?
    A) Focus on project work and let the project manager take care of stakeholder engagement
    B) Whenever a stakeholder is identified, the stakeholder register should be updated
    C) Understand stakeholders' needs and expectations
    D) Understand the influence stakeholders can exert on the project

302. You are a project manager of an airport construction project. You have analyzed risks and found that a risk has changed its probability and impact. Which process are you performing?
    A) Identify risks
    B) Perform qualitative risk analysis
    C) Perform quantitative risk analysis
    D) Monitor risks

303. What will be the cost contingency reserve for a project with the following quantified risks? An opportunity with a 40% chance of speeding up the work that can result in 10,000 savings. There is a 70% chance of labor strike that could cost project 13,000 and a 20% chance of inclement weather that has a cost of 5,000.
    A) Contingency reserve is 14,100
    B) Contingency reserve is 7,100
    C) Contingency reserve is zero.
    D) Contingency reserve is 4,100

304. How will you differentiate between Direct and Manage Project Work

process and Monitor and Control Project Work process?
A) Both processes are the same
B) Direct and Manage Project Work process is concerned with the performance of work while the Monitor and Control Project Work process reviews the project performance
C) Monitor and Control Project Work process is part of the Direct and Manage Project Work process
D) Direct and Manage Project Work process reviews the project performance while the Monitor and Control Project Work process is concerned with the performance of work

305. You are the project manager of a design-build project that has an approved budget of 1,000,000. The project started eight months ago and has a total actual cost of 650,000 till now. The 650,000 is the _____.
A) Earned value
B) Cost variance
C) Design cost
D) Sunk cost

306. If a scatter diagram shows a majority of points around the diagonal line on the chart, what does this tell you?
A) The variable trend is increasing as time progresses
B) Factors affecting the chart are resulting in a straight line relationship which is an indication of nonconformance
C) Variables are closely related to each other
D) Variables are independent of each other

307. All of the following statements are correct about portfolio management EXCEPT _____.
A) The success of portfolio cannot be determined from success or failure of just one of many projects and programs within it
B) A portfolio can have projects, programs, subsidiary portfolios, and operations
C) A portfolio serves strategic goals of an organization or department
D) A portfolio has a fixed scope that ends with the completion of the portfolio

308. Which one of the following confirms that a communication has occurred?
A) The project manager emailed the issue details to the sponsor
B) The team member's performance improved after he came back

from training
C) The project manager has consolidated minutes of meeting document
D) The project progress report was published in the company newsletter

309. Which of the following is not an input to determine the project budget?
A) Scope baseline
B) Reserve analysis
C) Cost estimates
D) Agreements

310. As the project manager of an application development project, you were in a meeting with the customer where your developer was displaying the newly developed report. The report showed the names of the employees who have not completed their mandatory training. You also saw the date of start of employment displayed against the name of the employee, which you knew was not part of the requirements. The customer was happy with this new information and believed this will help with the purpose of the report. What happened here?
A) Scope creep
B) Exceeding expectation
C) Benefit realization
D) Project success

311. The figure shows a network diagram with values given as per the legend in the diagram. What is the late start (LS) of activity C, the duration of activity A, and the late finish (LF) of activity B?

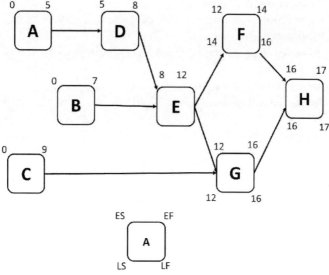

A) The LS of C is 3, the duration of A is 5, and the LF of B is 8
B) The LS of C is 1, the duration of A is 0, and the LF of B is 7
C) The LS of C is 5, the duration of A is 5, and the LF of B is 8
D) The LS of C is 4, the duration of A is 3, and the LF of B is 7

312. A project manager prepared the statement of work and developed the procurement management plan. He also has the bid package ready for distribution to the sellers. Which process does the project manager go through next?
A) Control Procurements
B) Procure Seller
C) Plan Procurement Management
D) Conduct Procurements

313. You are the project manager of an inner-city development project. You are to ensure that resource utilization on the project is optimized. You have the following information about two cranes. Which one will you select if the estimated work is 400 hours?

Crane A: Rent 400 per 8-hr work day, initial fee 6,000, Operating cost 100 per hour
Crane B: Rent 80 per hour, initial fee 2,000, operating cost 80 per hour
A) Crane A
B) Crane B
C) Crane A or crane B

D) Neither crane A nor crane B

314. What is the difference between residual risks and secondary risks?
    A) Residual risks are the risks that cannot have a response plan while secondary risks are the risks that need a fallback plan
    B) Residual risks are the risks for which contingency reserve is used while secondary risks are the risks for which management reserve is used
    C) Secondary risks are the left-over risks after the implementation of risk response while residual risks are the risks that arise due to the implementation of risk response
    D) Residual risks are the left-over risks after the implementation of risk response while secondary risks are the risks that arise due to the implementation of risk response

315. A project is terminated in the middle of execution when half of the deliverables are already complete. If you are the project manager of this project, what will you do?
    A) Hand over the completed and/or incomplete deliverables
    B) Send a detailed project status report to the sponsor on how well the project was performing
    C) Discuss with the sponsor of what can be done to keep the project running
    D) Stop the work immediately and release project resources

316. Which of the following is NOT part of the project scope statement?
    A) List of activities that must be completed to achieve the project's objectives
    B) Set of conditions to accept deliverables
    C) Out of scope items
    D) List of deliverables that must be produced by the project

317. Risk register can be BEST described as _____.
    A) A document that contains all of the outcomes of risk management processes
    B) A document that contains a list of identified risks
    C) A register that is used to check-in and check-out risks for response planning
    D) A document that identifies risks so that responses can be planned

318. During a Joint Application Development session, who works with the business subject matter experts to gather requirements and improve

the software development process?
A) Development team
B) Project sponsor
C) Project manager
D) Business analyst

319. What is the key benefit of the schedule control process?
A) Apply approved changes to the schedule baseline
B) Maintain the schedule baseline
C) Measure schedule variances from the schedule baseline
D) Minimize changes to the project schedule

320. Which option is NOT an objective of the kick-off meeting?
A) Gathering the requirements
B) Communicating the project objectives
C) Clarifying the roles & responsibilities
D) Gaining commitment of the project team

321. A customer rejected a deliverable, which was submitted by the project team for acceptance, with the objection that it does not meet requirements. The team believes that the deliverable fully meets the requirements. What is the FIRST thing the project manager should do?
A) Review the acceptance criteria and the deliverable then consider arguments presented by both customer and project team
B) The customer is always right. Ask the team to make the change
C) The issue requires a confronting approach followed by a forcing technique to resolve the problem
D) Submit a change request to resolve the discrepancy

322. One of the resources on your project asks you that she has been assigned two tasks that have a 5 days lag between them and have a start-to-start relationship. What does that mean?
A) Successor task will start 5 days before the predecessor task starts
B) Successor task will start 5 days before the predecessor task finishes
C) Successor task will start 5 days after the predecessor task finishes
D) Successor task will start 5 days after the predecessor task starts

323. Which of the following is NOT a characteristic of the performance measurement baseline?
A) It is used to monitor and control cost performance of the project
B) It is derived from the schedule baseline

C) It shows the cumulative cost of control accounts
D) It can be displayed in the form of an S-curve

324. When is the BEST time to do a lessons-learned identification exercise?
A) At the end of the project
B) At the end of each issue or failure
C) Throughout the project life cycle
D) As soon as a lesson is learned

325. The sponsor is not happy with the project communication and has asked for a weekly progress update instead of the monthly one. Also, he wants the update presented to him in a meeting rather than sent through the email. What should the project manager do?
A) Accept sponsor requirement and assign a project team member to present the progress report to sponsor in-person every week
B) Assess impact and if approved, update project communication plan by changing the monthly email to a weekly in-person meeting
C) Inform sponsor that a weekly in-person meeting is not possible since you also have to do the work
D) Invite a team meeting to discuss this new requirement from the sponsor

326. You have been assigned to a project that is expected to have a large number of stakeholders but you do not know who they are. What would be the BEST way to start to identify all those stakeholders?
A) Use the stakeholder analysis matrix
B) Use the business case
C) Use the project management plan
D) Use the salience model

327. Which of the following is true about constructive changes?
A) Formal or informal change that can be implemented, without going through the integrated change control process, once the other party agrees
B) Specific action oriented approved changes
C) Uniquely identified and documented through project formal communication
D) Submitted by the seller to the buyer to improve the quality of bid

328. Which of the following is NOT a type of cost-reimbursable contract?
A) Cost plus fixed fee
B) Cost plus incentive fee

C) Cost plus award fee
D) Cost plus material fee

329. You are planning to engage three welders on your oil pipeline project which has a deadline to be completed in one year that equals about 250 working days. There are 20,000 joints to be welded and each welder can weld, on average, 30 joints per day. Do you think the number of welders is too many, too less, or just about right to finish the job before the deadline?
    A) Too many
    B) Too less
    C) Just about right
    D) Cannot be determined from the information given

330. A project manager is considering risks that can generally have both positive and negative outcomes. These risks are called _____.
    A) Overall project risk
    B) Fire and theft
    C) Injury
    D) Life risks

331. A project manager was struggling with managing team meetings. Some issues he noticed were: late to the meetings, leaving the meeting room without any indication, missing a meeting without notice, taking mobile phone calls during meetings, and occasional texting. What can the project manager do to improve the situation?
    A) Request sponsor to join a meeting and motivate the team
    B) Advise members of serious consequences if they do not behave
    C) Set new ground rules that address the attendance, behavior and distractions issues
    D) Get the team out on a team-building exercise to develop the team spirit

332. When managing a medical research project, what will not be part of your work during the Direct and Manage Project Work process?
    A) Implement approved changes
    B) Report project progress
    C) Collect work performance data
    D) Manage technical and organizational interfaces

333. After performing the Quantitative Risk Analysis process, what particularly happens to the risk register?
    A) Risks on the risk register get prioritized

B) Risk register is archived as a historical record
C) Risk register gets updated with risk response plans
D) It is continuously updated to reflect the changes

334. Which of the following would be the LEAST preferable way to classify stakeholders?
    A) Power, influence, interest
    B) Power, legitimacy, urgency
    C) Upward influence, sideward influence, outward influence
    D) Executives, managers, staff

335. If the scope is being added to a project that is already executing, additional risks must be identified. Correct this statement.
    A) If the scope is being withdrawn from a project that is already executing, additional risks must be identified
    B) If the scope is being added to a project that is already executing, risk identification should be performed
    C) If the scope is being added to a project that is already monitoring and controlling, additional risks must be identified
    D) If the scope is being added to a project that is already executing, new risks will occur

336. According to Manage Project Knowledge process, the knowledge that can be readily recorded using words, pictures, and numbers is called _____ knowledge.
    A) recorded
    B) explicit
    C) tacit
    D) real

337. _____ is a structured, independent review to determine whether the project activities comply with the organizational and project policies, processes, and procedures.
    A) An organizational audit
    B) Senior management review
    C) Customer audit
    D) A quality audit

338. The material resources needed for the project should be allocated and released for use so that the project can continue without any stoppage or delay. One of the following will not impact the release of material resources for this purpose. Which one is it?
    A) The right time

B) The right cost
C) The right place
D) The right amount

339. A project manager finds that the reason for a sponsor's worried communications about the project work is because there are several issues that were recorded in the issue log were not updated since last month. No one seems to be working on those as there is no update shown. What should the project manager do FIRST?
    A) Review open issues, update the issue log and take steps to get those resolved
    B) Send an apology note to the sponsor and assure that issue log will be regularly updated from now on
    C) Increase the frequency of communication to stakeholders especially sponsor
    D) Perform a performance review of the team member responsible for the delay

340. As a project manager, you will have to manage conflicts as these are natural and can occur at any time in a project. Which of the following is the least likely to be a source of conflict on a project?
    A) Personal work styles
    B) Shortage of resources
    C) Scheduling priorities
    D) Cost estimates

341. What is true about agile projects when it comes to cost management?
    A) High-level estimation is usually done which can be adjusted later
    B) Detailed estimation is usually done which can be adjusted later
    C) There is no need to estimate costs for an agile project as changes are always occurring
    D) Agile project costs are fixed in the beginning since iterations are timeboxed and so no other estimation is required

342. Two of your project team members are arguing about who is responsible to manage quality on the project. One says that the project manager is responsible to manage quality but the other member says that the project team and the project manager are responsible to manage quality on the project. What will you tell them?
    A) Project manager
    B) Project team
    C) Project manager and the project team
    D) Project manager, project team, sponsor, and customer

343. Which of the following is an example of trend analysis when it comes to the Monitor and Control Project Work process? Cost performance index for the last three months, in order, is 0.96, 1.02, and 1.05.
    A) The project is under-budget
    B) The project cost performance is improving
    C) The project cost performance is declining
    D) The project is over-budget

344. Which of the following is an input to the Manage Stakeholder Engagement process?
    A) Change requests
    B) Work performance data
    C) Schedule management plan
    D) Change log

345. You work at a fast-paced product development company. One of the requirements set out by the project management office at your company is that each project should create a lessons-learned document. In which process will you record the accuracy of the business case in the lessons-learned register?
    A) Close Project or Phase process
    B) Develop Project Charter process
    C) Control Costs process
    D) Never as this is not the purpose of lessons learned register

346. You are managing a tunnel boring project in a remote area. You have a choice to either buy or rent a mole (boring machine). If you buy it, you will pay 150,000 lump sum price but also incur 5,000 per month for its maintenance. If you rent it, you will pay 10,000 per month and an additional one-time administration fee of 5,000. How many minimum months you have to use it to justify buying it rather than renting it?
    A) 30 months
    B) 16 months
    C) 15 months
    D) 29 months

347. Total Quality Management can be explained as _____.
    A) A quality improvement initiative to find methods that will continuously improve products, services, and business practices
    B) Quality management planning that results in an end to end quality product from the project results
    C) The planning that results in reducing the defects to one part per

million or less
D) The process to ensure the Plan-Do-Check-Act process is carried out

348. Which one of the following is an example of "halo effect?"
A) Project manager with strong technical knowledge was the reason for the technical team's success
B) A very successful programmer on projects was promoted as project manager
C) Project manager received an award for project success although the whole team worked hard
D) Project manager creates such an environment that team members produce genuinely creative results

349. You joined a new company where projects are assigned to each project manager at the start of the fiscal year. The project manager is responsible for completing all projects by the end of the year. It is his/her responsibility to prioritize the project execution. You were assigned four projects, A, B, C, and D project. You started working on project A and while it was in the executing processes, you initiated project B. Both projects were running concurrently. Project A was a small system upgrade project but the scope of project B has been expanding since initiation. So you find it difficult to manage project B. While going through project repositories you found a similar project executed two years ago. What will be your line of action?
A) Put project B on hold until project A is completed
B) Review project documents of the previous project and discuss challenges with its project manager
C) Complete project A as soon as possible and do not get engaged in project C or D until project B is done
D) It is important to define the requirements completely. There is no need to feel overwhelmed.

350. One of your friends has recently become a PMP certified and has now joined an organization where he will be managing a new project. He tells you that he will be a transformational leader of his project team because he truly believes in this way of leadership. What exactly is he talking about?
A) He will allow the team to make their own decisions and set goals
B) He will focus on his team's growth and development, collaboration, and relationships
C) He will inspire and motivate his team, encourage idealized behavior and innovation

D) He will focus on goals, feedback, and accomplishment to determine rewards

351. Which of the following rules for effective meetings helps the MOST in order to stop everyone talking at the same time, being non-participative, and discussing random points?
    A) Reduce the number of people at the meeting. Invite only those that are participating.
    B) Make participation mandatory when inviting participants for the meeting
    C) Advise all in attendance to discuss one topic at a time
    D) Publish an agenda before the meeting stating the objectives of the meeting

352. A project manager, who is working on a custom house project, has been asked by the customer to make a change to the dining room size. What is the BEST way of communicating with the customer on this issue?
    A) Informal written
    B) Formal verbal
    C) Formal written
    D) First Informal written then formal verbal

353. Job shadowing is a technique used for collecting requirements. What type of technique is this?
    A) Observation/conversation
    B) Interviewing
    C) Facilitation
    D) Nominal group technique

354. A software development project has teams defined by project phases. There is a requirement team, a design team, a development team, and a testing and deployment team. Each of these teams is responsible for work in a separate phase. What will identify the transition from one phase to another within the project's life cycle?
    A) Handoff
    B) Deliverables
    C) Milestones
    D) Project reports

355. A project manager on a large project submitted the project charter to the sponsor for approval and stated that the project will be divided into three phases. Each phase will start with the initiating processes.

The project manager plans to use the initiating processes in subsequent phases to _____.
A) Fulfill the requirement to go through all the project process groups on the project
B) Close the previous phase and start the next phase
C) Ensure all approved changes get implemented
D) Help keep the project aligned to meet the business needs

356. The quality audit team came back with their last month audit report. The report shows an increase in the number of non-conformances month over month. What steps can you take as the project manager to find out the reason for this increase?
A) Use a fishbone diagram to explore the root cause of the issue
B) Send for training the project team member responsible for quality control measurements
C) Review the impact on the deliverable acceptance by the customer
D) Recommend corrective action to improve the quality

357. A project manager who is working on a retail banking project for a large financial institution has developed the project management plan. He believes it is a realistic plan and thus should be formally approved. Which of the following organizational assets will not have impacted the development of the plan?
A) Project management plan template
B) Lessons learned from a previous project
C) Organization's change management policies
D) The business case for the project

358. An internal application deployment project is running into trouble. Too many errors have been reported by the users. Which of the following tools should the project manager use to see the frequency and types of issues being reported?
A) Affinity diagram
B) Matrix diagram
C) Histogram
D) Scatter diagram

359. Which of the following is the most likely reason for submitting a change request during Direct and Manage Project Work process?
A) Project performance report shows cost overruns
B) An issue is prohibiting the completion of planned work
C) Technical testing of completed deliverable shows several defects
D) The customer has identified defects and has rejected the

deliverable

360. All of the following are attributes of the control charts EXCEPT _____.
    A) Stability of a process can be observed
    B) Results of a process can be monitored
    C) Relationship between two factors or objectives can be shown
    D) Cost and schedule variances can be monitored

361. What is the difference between quality and grade?
    A) Quality and grade are one and the same
    B) Grade is how many features are in the product while quality is how much the features of the product perform to the specifications
    C) Quality is how many features are in the product while grade is how much the features of the product perform to the specifications
    D) Quality is what is measured in the Quality Control process and grade is what is measured as part of quality assurance

362. Which of the following is a characteristic of a project team in a project-oriented organization?
    A) Each team member has multiple reporting relationships
    B) Team members report to the project manager
    C) Team members report to functional managers
    D) Team members may work as full-time or part-time on the project

363. If someone asks you what a program is; what will be your response?
    A) A program is a set of projects running concurrently
    B) A program is a way to meet business needs by coordinating and controlling multiple related projects
    C) A program consists of projects from one department trying to achieve the strategic goals of the department
    D) A program is a result of a government mandate to comply with legislation

364. Resource Calendars are an output of Acquire Resources process. Which of the following information is NOT provided by a resource calendar?
    A) Vacation time of the resources
    B) Engagement period of the resources
    C) Location and contact information of the resources
    D) Resource schedule conflicts

365. One of the stakeholders on your project has been identified as having high power, low urgency, and appropriate legitimacy (involvement in the project). Which classification method did you use?
   A) Stakeholder cube
   B) Prioritization
   C) Power/influence grid
   D) Salience model

366. A phase end review identified that the deliverables completed as per plan do not meet the business need and are unacceptable by the customer. The next step can be _____.
   A) Review if the project should be killed
   B) Inform customer that the deliverables are as per plan and must be accepted
   C) Identify that change in business need is outside the control of the project and hence cannot be presented as an excuse to reject deliverables
   D) Contact other stakeholders and ask for help

367. A project manager who is working on a project to design a new concept vehicle was asked by the design team to advise on an issue they are facing. They are concerned with the reliability of the new innovative braking system prototype that is being tested. Usability and safety of the braking system are also under review. Which of the following tools the project manager should ask them to use to optimize the design for various factors including reliability, usability, and safety?
   A) Checklists
   B) Quality audit
   C) Design for X
   D) Benchmarking

368. A project manager is in the process of gathering sellers' responses, selecting a seller and then awarding the contract. This process is called Conduct Procurements and is part of the _____ process group.
   A) Monitoring and Controlling
   B) Control Procurements
   C) Planning
   D) Executing

369. Due to resource shortage in the market and within the organization, a

project manager has fewer resources available than what he estimated for his project. Due to this reason he decided to use the three point estimation technique to estimate the duration of a few impacted activities. Activity Y has been estimated as follows. If he is able to engage highly skilled resources the estimate is 10 days but if he is unable to hire skilled resources, the learning curve will be steep and he expects many defects to occur, the estimate is 28 days. However, he expects a combination of skilled and novice resources which will result in 16 days duration. What should be the expected duration for this activity if the beta distribution is used?
   A) 15 days
   B) 16 days
   C) 17 days
   D) 18 days

370. You are a project manager working on a global project with project team members distributed in four continents. Which of the following can help you the MOST to be successful?
   A) Instant messaging & email
   B) Responsibility assignment matrix
   C) Knowledge of local languages and customs
   D) Well developed communication plan

371. Kaizen method is the same as _____.
   A) Just In Time
   B) Marginal analysis
   C) ISO9000 method
   D) Continuous improvement

372. A project has a Cost Performance Index of 0.6. All activities were completed on time except one work package. This work package was for design work and could not be done because the expert resource was unavailable till now. Now the project manager has to calculate the estimate to complete for the remaining project work. Which approach will he take?
   A) Use the current rate of progress
   B) Create a totally new estimate
   C) Use the originally planned rate of progress
   D) Use current rate of progress for design work package and planned rate of progress for rest of the work

373. Which of the following is the MOST important point to understand an argument between two individuals?

A) What time of the day, early morning or close to the end of the day
B) Expertise level of the individuals on the subject matter of argument
C) Facts and fiction in the arguments
D) Gestures, the tone of voices, and facial expressions

374. For a multi-year project dealing with multiple currencies, which of the following enterprise environmental factor, in addition to currency exchange rates, will you consider during Estimate Costs process?
A) Cost of quality
B) Lessons learned repository
C) Inflation
D) Cost estimation policy

375. You, as the project manager, are discussing with management that a project management methodology should be used since it helps the project succeed. As a first step you told them that you will create a project charter because you believe it will help you _____.
A) Create a strong business case
B) Identify all the stakeholders
C) Get more authority as a project manager
D) Get the project charter approved

376. Which of the following is NOT a tool used in the Monitor Communications process?
A) Stakeholder engagement assessment matrix
B) Forecasting methods
C) Meetings
D) Project management information system

377. You were invited to a meeting with the manager. When you entered the room you saw sitting there the key user working on your project. The manager informed you that she has discussed with the key user a change to the functionality being developed by your project: they both agree that it should be changed from manual data entry to system generated data entry. He then asks you to fill out the required form and get it signed. The manager has used his positional power to direct you. What would be the related leadership trait in this situation?
A) Focus on the long-range vision
B) Do the right things
C) Guide and collaborate using relational power
D) Do things right

378. Which of the following is not an engagement level of a stakeholder?
    A) Unaware
    B) Managing
    C) Neutral
    D) Leading

379. As a project manager of a mission-critical project for your organization, you are holding a coaching session for your team. While explaining the importance of knowledge management, you mentioned two key purposes for managing both tacit and explicit knowledge. These two key purposes are _____.
    A) Integrating existing knowledge and sharing new knowledge
    B) Reusing existing knowledge and creating new knowledge
    C) Conducting lessons learned sessions and updating project documents
    D) Information management and knowledge management

380. What is Earned Value Analysis (EVA) commonly used for?
    A) Analyzing the actual costs of the project incurred to date
    B) Measuring the earned income by resources on the project to date
    C) Measuring project performance
    D) Measuring the expenses incurred by the project at a certain point in time

381. What is the advantage the Precedence Diagramming Method has over other network techniques?
    A) It is the most commonly used technique
    B) It shows project progress at any point in time
    C) It shows various dependencies among the activities
    D) It shows the project start and finish dates

382. Mr. PM has been working on the enterprise learning management system project for 10 months with a fairly large team. Yesterday, the new system was made available to the whole organization with only one glitch viz. the mass email with incorrect login and password was sent out to all the employees. The project team worked on the issue diligently and within 4 hours sent out the correct email to everyone. Mr. PM met his manager on his way to the office this morning. The manager remarked, "I am very disappointed." What could be the reason?
    A) Manager's name was not mentioned in the email sent out to the whole organization thanking the team for hard work

B) Mr. PM did not ask the manager's permission if the problem should be fixed or not
C) Integrated Change Control Process was not followed to fix the issue
D) Risk register shows mass email risk with a planned response strategy but no risk owner

383. If you have to choose one of the following as NOT being a project, which one will it be?
    A) Creating a project management office in the IT department
    B) Shipping the 10 times larger than usual order received through the internet
    C) Building a 10 ft. x 15 ft. shed in your backyard
    D) Increasing parking spaces from 300 to 400 in a parking lot

384. Which of the following is an input to the Define Scope process?
    A) Requirements documentation
    B) Requirements traceability matrix
    C) Project scope statement
    D) Product analysis

385. A project had a list of identified risks. This list was in the risk register. Where can one find the overall project risks?
    A) Risk management plan
    B) Project management plan
    C) Project charter
    D) Risk register

386. Your management has asked you to review a troubled project and suggest the best course of action. The project is expected to be completed one week later than the baseline completion date. Though the project has a low risk, the Internal Rate of Return is expected to be 25% which is very promising. A closer review of the schedule reveals that most dependencies are of discretionary type. You asked management about resource availability to find out if more resources can be engaged to speed up the work but was told that no resources are available. What do you suggest?
    A) Move resources from non-important activities to major activities
    B) Fast track the schedule
    C) Change discretionary dependencies to lags
    D) Remove few non-critical activities to reduce the schedule

387. You being the seller's project manager are working on a project for a

buyer. This was a small project, with an unambiguous statement of work and well-defined deliverables. You have completed all the deliverables as specified by the statement of work and all these deliverables have been accepted by the buyer's representative. However, the buyer does not like the deliverables and is unhappy. How should the contract be treated in such a case?
   A) The contract should be treated as canceled
   B) The contract should be treated as pending
   C) The contract should be treated as complete
   D) The contract should be treated as if the work is still to be done

388. Validate Scope process is an essential scope management process. When is it performed?
   A) At the end of the project
   B) At the start of the project to validate the scope management processes
   C) Throughout the project, as needed
   D) At the end of Monitoring and Controlling processes

389. You are the project manager of a multi-phase industrial construction project. You started the Close Project or Phase process at the end of the first phase and are now using expert judgment to seek expertise from individuals with specialized knowledge in certain topics. Which of the following is the least likely specialized knowledge expert you will be considering?
   A) Regulations
   B) Legal
   C) Audit
   D) Scheduling

390. All of the following are examples of the cost of quality EXCEPT _____.
   A) Review and acceptance of requirement document by the key users
   B) Hiring a truck to move material closer to the site
   C) Performing additional tests before deployment
   D) Responding to a user request for defect repair

391. What is the BEST statement to describe sensitivity analysis?
   A) Estimates the impact on one variable by changing all other variables
   B) Estimates the impact of changing one variable when all other variables are kept constant

C) Estimates how risk tolerant the stakeholders are for the project
D) Estimates how risk tolerant the project team is compared to the rest of the stakeholders

392. In which process is the resource histogram created?
A) Develop Schedule
B) Plan Resource Management
C) Estimate Activity Resources
D) Acquire Resources

393. What is the type of organization where an individual working as a project coordinator does not have control over project resources? Instead, those resources are managed by the functional manager.
A) Project-oriented
B) Functional matrix
C) Functional
D) PMO

394. You are the project manager of a heavy construction project. The project needs a large excavator and you are to decide whether to buy or lease the excavator. The internal cost of procurement is 20,000 and the cost of the excavator is 350,000. The cost to lease will include 10,000 one-time mobilization fee and 10,000 per month lease. What will be the minimum months of use that will justify buying vs. leasing?
A) 34 months
B) 32 months
C) 38 months
D) 36 months

395. _____ is the cost management process that aggregates the estimated costs of individual work packages.
A) Determine Budget process
B) Plan Cost Management process
C) Control Costs process
D) Estimate Costs process

396. If a project is late and there is a need to compress the schedule to complete the project on time without reducing the scope, which technique can be used considering there are resources available?
A) Crashing the schedule
B) Analyzing the schedule
C) Forecasting the schedule
D) Fast-tracking the schedule

397. The PMO manager advised a new project manager who is initiating an agile project that he should use timeboxing to plan releases and iterations for his project. What is the biggest benefit of timeboxing?
    A) Delivers faster
    B) Minimizes scope creep
    C) Reduces cost
    D) Improves quality

398. Recognition and rewards are important techniques of the Manage Team process. With which statement about these techniques do you disagree?
    A) Rewards should be established by considering the cultural differences
    B) Rewards should satisfy a need of the stakeholder
    C) Display of the desired behavior can be recognized by a reward
    D) Reward decision should always be made formally

399. Which one of the following is the most common forecasting method used by project teams?
    A) Current rate of progress
    B) Original rate of progress
    C) Current rate of schedule and cost performance
    D) Manual bottom-up summation

400. Monitor risks process also includes updating the organizational process assets, _____, for the benefit of future projects.
    A) Policies and procedures
    B) Quality improvement initiatives
    C) Including the fallback plan, alternative strategies, and corrective actions
    D) Including the risk breakdown structure and risk management templates

Daud Nasir, PMP

4 - PMP MOCK TEST 3

200 Questions - Time Limit: 4 Hours

401. Which process group comes to mind when you hear this: "Develop project charter and identify stakeholders"?
    A) Initiating
    B) Executing
    C) Monitoring and controlling
    D) Planning

402. What is risk appetite?
    A) It is the degree of risk someone will be able to withstand
    B) It is the degree of uncertainty someone is willing to accept while anticipating a reward from it
    C) It is the measure of loss that can come from taking the risk
    D) It is the degree of the desire of someone to take on risk

403. Your team members are confused whether a project manager is a manager or a leader. You explain to them that a project manager needs to be a leader and a manager. Which of the following characteristics is a leadership characteristic that you will mention?
    A) Ask how and when
    B) Ask what and why
    C) Do things right
    D) Focus on the bottom line

404. A project manager has set up a regular weekly project meeting inviting all team members to attend since decisions are to be made. A good

discussion on a topic is followed by a decision by the project team. The project manager will accept the team's decision as long as it aligns with the project goals otherwise the decision will be modified. Which leadership style is being used by the project manager?
A) Transactional
B) Laissez-faire
C) Transformational
D) Charismatic

405. _____ is an output of the Validate Scope process.
A) Accepted deliverables
B) Verified deliverables
C) Accepted change request
D) Signed statement of work

406. You are managing a shipbuilding project when the sponsor invites you to an urgent meeting. He is worried about the quality of the work being performed. Even after you explain that all the testing has shown satisfactory results, he still believes that the end product will not be of quality. What will be your response?
A) Get help from senior management to remove the sponsor's doubts
B) Reperform some of the tests to confirm that the original tests were good
C) Form an audit team to perform a quality audit of the project
D) Explain to the sponsor that his worries are unfounded as all quality results have met the criteria

407. Scheduling software tools, work authorization systems, information distribution systems, configuration management systems, and interfaces to other online automated systems are all part of _____.
A) Deliverables
B) Organizational process assets
C) Project management information system
D) Organizational systems

408. A senior project manager is trying to explain the goals and objectives of portfolio management to junior project managers at her organization. Which one of the following would she mention as a goal of portfolio management?
A) Train, coach, and evaluate project managers
B) Provide centralized project control activities

C) Provide and manage project resources
D) Evaluate program and project proposal to derive maximum value out of investment

409. Which of the following is typically established first before moving on to the others?
    A) Scheduling tool
    B) Scheduling method
    C) Scheduling model
    D) Scheduling data

410. A programmer working on a global project repeatedly produced code with errors that required significant rework to fix. This is an issue of resource _____.
    A) Programming
    B) Allocation
    C) Competency
    D) Authority

411. A project manager working for a chemical equipment manufacturing company has been working on a long project. The project has finally reached completion and is in the Close Project or Phase process. The project manager has requested the customer to provide formal acceptance of the final deliverable, the new chemical mixing machine. All of the following statements are normally true in regards to the final acceptance of the new machine EXCEPT _____.
    A) The customer should conduct performance testing on the new machine
    B) The customer should confirm in writing that the new chemical mixing machine has been accepted
    C) The customer should use the machine for one year before confirming that all terms of the contract have been met
    D) The customer can use third-party testing to confirm if the machine meets the specifications

412. Stakeholder analysis involves all of the following steps EXCEPT _____.
    A) Understand stakeholders specialized knowledge
    B) Analyze communication requirements of stakeholders
    C) Identify legal and moral rights
    D) Establish expected contribution both tangible and intangible

413. A project has a budget of 700,000 and is expected to complete in two

years. The project is now 20 percent complete and is on track. What is the Budget at Completion (BAC)?
A) 700,000
B) 140,000
C) 70,000
D) Cannot be determined from the information given

414. A new scheduling guideline has been developed by the project management office at your company. The document provides information about resource optimization. Which one of the following it will not have mentioned?
A) It can change the schedule critical path
B) It reduces the impact of the low skill level of resources
C) It helps engage resources at or below their availability level
D) It removes resource over-allocation

415. You were managing a project where a seller under a contract was executing some work. Due to performance issues, you decided to terminate the contract before completion. This triggers _____.
A) Disputes
B) Negotiations
C) Product, service, or result transition
D) Final report

416. A junior project manager at your organization is confused about quality control (QC) vs. quality assurance (QA). How will you explain the difference between the two?
A) QA measures seller's performance while QC measures project performance
B) QC measures the quality of project deliverables and QA audits the quality plan
C) QC is controlling the quality and QA is accepting the deliverables after that
D) Audit department performs QA while project management office performs QC

417. Cost of nonconformance has all of the following characteristics EXCEPT _____.
A) Loss of customers
B) Liabilities
C) Safety measures
D) Rework

418. Which of the following is the Monitor and Control Project Work process concerned with?
    A) Rejecting change requests
    B) Approving change requests
    C) Monitoring of implementation of approved change requests
    D) Implementing approved change requests

419. What is not true about the project charter?
    A) Project charter is a contract between the sponsor and the project manager
    B) Project charter validates alignment of the project to the strategy and the ongoing work in the organization
    C) Project charter establishes a partnership between the performing and the requesting organization
    D) Project charter formally initiates a project

420. You are looking at the following list of activities (in sequence) for a small software functionality enhancement project.
    1) Gather requirements - 3 days
    2) Create Specs document - 2 days
    3) Design the changes - 3 days
    4) Code the changes - 5 days
    5) Unit Testing - 6 days
    6) Business Testing - 12 days
    7) Deployment - 1 day
    8) Post-deployment support - 10 days
    Calculate the minimum time it will take to deploy the project when all the activities are on a critical path and activity 6 is late by 6 days while activity 5 was completed one day earlier?
    A) 47 days
    B) 42 days
    C) 37 days
    D) 32 days

421. Thinking about project funding requirements, these can be _____.
    A) Cost-based or schedule-based
    B) Parametric or parabolic estimates
    C) Contingency and management reserve
    D) Incremental and/or lump sum

422. Which of the following is INCORRECT about conflicts?

A) Conflicts happen all the time
B) Conflicts should be attended to earlier than later
C) Conflicts should be resolved publicly to avoid any misunderstanding
D) Most conflicts can be resolved using a collaborative approach

423. Which of the following is driven by the stakeholders' risk appetite?
A) Risk responses
B) Risks identification
C) Cost of risks
D) Expected Monetary Value

424. If you are looking at the work performance data to determine the project's performance, what should you do NEXT?
A) Identify areas of improvement and create corrective actions
B) Compare the information with baselines and identify variances
C) Update the lessons learned document
D) Send the information to the project sponsor

425. As a project manager on a non-technology project, how will you ensure various project items remain consistent and operable?
A) Through the project management plan
B) Through the change control board
C) Through the control chart
D) Through configuration management

426. What is not true about milestones?
A) Milestones may be mandatory as per contract
B) Milestones cannot be estimated using the three-point estimation method
C) Milestones have zero duration
D) Milestones can be set up based on historical information

427. A project manager who was already managing a project was assigned a new project. Due to commitments on the other project, she wanted to create the work breakdown structure rather quickly. What will be your advice?
A) Only drill down 2-3 levels and create work package at a higher level
B) Get a head start by using a work breakdown structure from a similar previous project as a template
C) Work breakdown structure can be skipped in favor of a quick high-level activities list

D) Ask the sponsor to have the key users prepare the work breakdown structure

428. Which of the following BEST describes the difference between project management process groups and project life cycle phases?
A) Project management process groups are used in sequential while project phases are used in iterative projects
B) Project management process groups are independent of project phases
C) Project phases are repeated in project management process groups but may also continue from one project management process group to another
D) Project management process groups and project phases are the same things

429. A project manager has been asked to help in the pre-project work and determine the important factors that should be considered for the right project to be selected for implementation. What should the project manager do first?
A) Write the business case
B) Perform the needs assessment
C) Develop the project benefits management plan
D) Establish the project objective and the success measures

430. Your co-worker who is managing a project has acquired team members for his project. He wants to make sure that all team members along with their roles and responsibilities are captured in a document. You advised him to use _____ for this purpose.
A) Resource management plan
B) Resource calendar
C) Project team directory
D) Resource breakdown structure

431. All of the following statements are correct about vendor conferences EXCEPT _____.
A) The answer to a seller's question should be openly provided to all the sellers
B) First-time bidders should be given extra attention to encourage them to bid
C) Vendor conferences should have ample time so that all the sellers have a chance to ask questions
D) The objective is to have all sellers develop the same understanding of the bid

432. Which is an interpersonal skill a project manager uses in MOST of the processes?
    A) Active listening
    B) Leadership
    C) Decision making
    D) Facilitation

433. The project performance can be presented with two indicators that reflect the cost and schedule performance of the project. These are _____.
    A) Cost Planned Index (CPI) and Schedule Planned Index (SPI)
    B) Cost Variance (CV) and Earned Value (EV)
    C) Cost Planning Index (CPI) and Schedule Performing Index (SPI)
    D) Cost Performance Index (CPI) and Schedule Performance Index (SPI)

434. You are excited to start a new project for a highly reputed global company. Even before starting the project, the sponsor has asked for a quick turnaround and wants to move quickly through the initiating and planning process group and get to executing. Which of the following is the MOST effective approach?
    A) Create project charter and move into executing
    B) Create project charter, identify risks and stakeholders, and then move to executing
    C) Use expert judgment to move quickly through initiating and planning
    D) Make active use of progressive elaboration

435. You are a project manager working in a functional organization. One of your project team members is upset because he is overloaded with work request by others. He should be assigned work only by the _____.
    A) Project manager
    B) Functional manager
    C) Sponsor
    D) Project team members

436. You are managing a marketing project where your team is tracking daily unique visitors to the product webpage. Here are the numbers for the last 7 days. 320, 415, 276, 403, 350, 373, and 327. What are the upper and lower control limits if you plan to track it on a control chart? Standard deviation is 49.

A) 415 and 276
B) 404 and 300
C) 401 and 303
D) 499 and 205

437. As project manager of a system upgrade project, you have engaged your project team members, and are going through activities to improve team interaction. Which process group are you in?
A) Initiating
B) Planning
C) Monitoring and controlling
D) Executing

438. A project manager is performing an analysis to determine the best corrective action in terms of cost in case of project deviations. What is this type of analysis called?
A) Trend analysis
B) Cost-benefit analysis
C) Variance analysis
D) Root cause analysis

439. You are managing a construction project. Your team took a sample of wet concrete and sent it to the laboratory for testing the quality. Which project management process is your team performing?
A) Perform Quality Sampling
B) Control Quality
C) Perform Quality Inspection
D) Manage Quality

440. Selena is managing a project for an organization that requires that various quality results be reported in Six Sigma metrics. Instead of reporting a count of defects found, she has to report _____.
A) How many Sigmas were found
B) How many defects were not found
C) How many defects per million were found
D) Upper and lower specifications

441. Which of the following is NOT an input to the Plan Procurement Management process?
A) Project scope statement
B) Stakeholder register
C) Work performance data
D) Work breakdown structure

442. You are managing a new laptop deployment to the whole workforce of a multi-national company. The company has a presence in 45 countries with a global workforce of 65,000. The total number of laptops to be deployed is approximately 30,000. You have team members in each work location to perform the deployment. For each location, there is a specific process to set up the user account and several smaller issues need to be taken care of before the work is complete. What can you implement to ensure project quality globally?
   A) Checklists
   B) Work breakdown structure
   C) Quality management plan
   D) The WBS dictionary

443. The quality team performed analysis to verify if the gain from improving quality is equal to or lower than the incremental cost to achieve that quality. This is called _____.
   A) Just in time
   B) Benchmarking
   C) Mind mapping
   D) Optimal cost of quality

444. A project manager has been asked to hand over partially completed deliverables to the customer. This can happen in which of the following processes?
   A) Control Scope process
   B) Validate Scope process
   C) Cancel Project or Phase process
   D) Close Project or Phase process

445. You are working for a private firm and managing a technology project. The firm's culture distinctly puts employees into two categories: management and staff. Project managers fall somewhere in the middle. The management considers you as a staff member while the project team believes you are the management. So the team members are very reserved in your presence because they think you can impact their performance bonus. Which power does the project team think you have?
   A) Formal power
   B) Coercive power
   C) Pressure-based power
   D) Referent power

446. A contract had terms that defined that ten resources will be engaged on the project by the supplier to execute the statement of work and finish within 200 days. During execution, the buyer asked the seller to engage 2 more resources as the project was trending late. The seller added two more resources and asked the buyer for additional payment in the next invoice. Buyer believes that finishing work in 200 days requires that seller engage more resources without additional cost. Seller says that buyer has asked for more resources to be engaged so it is an additional cost. They tried to negotiate but it did not work out. What should they try next to decide?
    A) Negotiation
    B) Arbitration
    C) Mediation
    D) Litigation

447. You are managing a large end to end application development project. After completing the requirements gathering process, the project ended up with 3,000 requirements. Managing those requirements is a huge challenge, but you know of a tool that can help your project ensure that approved requirements are delivered at the end. What is this tool called?
    A) Requirements traceability matrix
    B) Project management plan
    C) Configuration management plan
    D) Requirements documentation

448. There can be event-based risks and non-event risks in a project. Which of the following are the two types of non-event risks that a project may be exposed to?
    A) Schedule risks and cost risks
    B) Variability risks and ambiguity risks
    C) Internal risks and external risks
    D) Explicit risks and implicit risks

449. A warning sign in regards to risk response is also called as _____.
    A) Risk trigger
    B) Probability
    C) Impact
    D) Threshold

450. What happens in the Manage Quality process?
    A) Audits the submissions by the vendor to ensure the deliverables

quality matches the planned quality
B) Provides the performance level to the project team to be able to audit the project quality measurements
C) Quality requirements of the project are audited and the results from quality control measurements are reviewed to verify that the quality standards imposed in the project are adequate and that relevant policies of the organization are followed.
D) Quality measurements are compared against deliverable specifications to ensure the deliverable meets the set criteria

451. During the team meeting to select a seller, after the submitted bids were opened and reviewed, project team members could not decide to whom the contract should be awarded. One member recommended a seller who is highly reputed in the industry, another member recommended a seller that has worked for the company several times in the past, and yet another member insisted that the seller who has the lowest bid should be awarded the contract. What should the project manager do?
   A) Verify the seller's reputation in the market
   B) Contact project managers who have worked with the seller in the past and ask their opinion
   C) Review the seller selection criteria
   D) Select the lowest bidder

452. You are managing a high rise building construction project. The project started six months ago and is now well under progress. The team consists of 40 internal resources and 3 sellers. All the team members record challenges and problems faced including recommendation and proposed actions to manage them in the form of videos and photos. Where exactly are these things being captured?
   A) Project performance report
   B) Lessons learned register
   C) Computer hard disk
   D) Work performance data

453. You have been assigned as a project manager for a large project. You have decided to split your project into phases. Which of the following may not be a benefit of establishing project phases?
   A) Better control of project work
   B) Opportunity to assess project performance
   C) Faster delivery of project deliverables
   D) Improved planning based on funding and go/no-go decisions

454. If the project is behind schedule, the earned value is _____.
    A) More than the Actual Cost (AC)
    B) More than the Planned Value (PV)
    C) Less than the Planned Value (PV)
    D) Less than the Actual Cost (AC)

455. What is the purpose of reviewing a defect repair?
    A) To ensure stakeholders are satisfied with the repair
    B) To verify the extent of the repair as per scope defined in the project charter
    C) To ensure the defect was repaired properly and as required
    D) To create a Pareto chart to see the major reason for the defect

456. Several project managers in your organization were discussing the need to update the project management plan during its development. They were unsure of the number of times the project management plan before it is baselined, can be updated without putting in a change request. What would you tell them?
    A) As many times as needed
    B) A change request is required for each update
    C) Only once without the change request
    D) No need to update as it is still being developed

457. Two team members were in disagreement over a design issue. One team member had been doing similar work over 15 years and was considered an expert in the field while the other team member had only one year of experience. The project manager was under pressure to complete a report on the project status that he needed to present to executives so he could not spare much time to resolve this issue. He made the decision based on what the expert resource was saying. What type of problem-solving was this?
    A) Problem-solving
    B) Compromising
    C) Forcing
    D) Withdrawal

458. Which of the following represents verifiable products, services or results?
    A) Work breakdown structure components
    B) Project scope statements
    C) Change requests
    D) Deliverables

459. Benchmarking technique results in one or all of the following EXCEPT _____.
    A) Identify best practices
    B) Generate ideas for improvement
    C) Provide a basis for measuring the performance
    D) Measure project performance against the plan

460. Which conflict resolution techniques are generally acknowledged and used in project management?
    A) Compromise, schmooze, flatter, and ignore
    B) Ignore, accept, reject, and modify
    C) Compromise, accommodate, collaborate, and force
    D) Withdraw, problem solve, ignore, and compromise

461. Business case, benefits management plan, and agreements, are all an input to which of the following process?
    A) Develop Project Charter
    B) Develop Project Management Plan
    C) Conduct Procurements
    D) Perform Integrated Change Control

462. A project manager asks for every detail from the team members. He meets team members in a daily meeting and gets the details of progress and issues, and provides direction of what steps should be taken to fix an issue. He also reviews every document that is created by the project. He even wants to know if someone wants to go for a coffee break. Which of the following is his management style?
    A) Interactional
    B) Servant Leader
    C) Transformational
    D) Transactional

463. Why is the benefits management plan an input to the Close Project or Phase process?
    A) To check if the expected outcome from the economic feasibility study occurred
    B) To determine if the project was formally authorized or not
    C) Benefits management plan is not an input to the Close Project or Phase process
    D) To measure whether gains from the project were achieved as planned

464. You have a seller working on a fixed price incentive fee contract. As

per the contract, the target price is 180,000 with a ceiling set at 240,000 and an incentive fee of 40,000 with an 80/20 split. The target was to finish the project in 12 months but it was completed in 18 months with a total cost of 260,000. What is the total price of the contract?

A) The total price paid to the seller was 240,000
B) The total price paid to the seller was 180,000
C) The total price paid to the seller was 260,000
D) The total price paid to the seller was 220,000

465. A public utility project to deploy a new garbage collection policy needed a flyer distributed to 100,000 households of the city. A team was developed who went door-to-door to distribute the flyer. In order to verify the flyer is delivered to all the households in the city, few random calls were placed to the residents to find out if they have received the flyer. The tool used to verify the quality is _____.

A) Expert judgment
B) Validate Scope
C) Statistical sampling
D) Benchmarking

466. A statement of work is usually prepared when a project needs to engage a seller to do part of the work. Which of the following is incorrect about the statement of work?

A) It includes desired results, deliverable specifications, and quantity to be delivered
B) It is a high-level brief document that helps in negotiations and modifications during contract administration
C) The seller should be able to determine if they can deliver the work from the statement of work
D) Just like the contract, SOW can be modified through contract change control system

467. A project manager left the company for some personal reasons right after he received approval of project charter. You were asked to take over the project. What will be your FIRST step?

A) Work on gathering detailed requirements
B) Check all stakeholders' alignment with the project charter
C) Redo risk identification
D) Start planning the project

468. A contract becomes legally binding when both parties have signed and accepted that contract. In which case the contract will not be legally

binding even though both parties signed it?
A) Seller does not perform the work as per contract
B) The buyer is unable to make payments to the seller for completed work
C) The contract has terms that are in violation of a law
D) It is unacceptable to the legal counsel of the buyer or seller

469. You are working as a project manager in an organization and having problems with securing resources for a project. Your manager has turned down each of your request explaining that the resources are already engaged in other work and they do not have time to engage with your project. You are working in _____ organization.
A) Functional
B) Weak matrix
C) Strong matrix
D) Balanced matrix

470. You are the project manager for a turbine installation project. During the development of the work breakdown structure, a team member starts talking about estimating durations of various activities. Your response was that _____.
A) If the team decides that they are ready for duration estimation then we should go ahead with it
B) Durations cannot be estimated until cost estimation has been completed
C) We should be estimating durations of activities now
D) Durations can be estimated only after the work breakdown structure is done and activities have been defined and sequenced

471. Which of the following is another name for the fishbone diagram?
A) Ishikawa diagram
B) Pareto chart
C) Flowchart
D) Histogram

472. A risk audit has various objectives. Which of the following is NOT one of them?
A) Evaluate the level of risk management effort in the project
B) Determine if valid risk response planning and follow up was done
C) Check occurred risks and their root causes
D) Check if any identified risk was missed when planning risk responses

473. Which of the following is an example of a user story?
   A) As an office assistant, I need to access the supplies cabinet, so I can check which supplies are running out.
   B) Users need notebooks to write stories. These stories can be short or long depending on user perception.
   C) Login capability to check the status of applications submitted by undergraduate students
   D) Management requires a monthly report on payments that were late

474. What approach should be taken by the project manager who finds out that the project she is managing requires more time to complete than what has been advised by the customer?
   A) Cut scope to remove activities from the schedule
   B) Inform the customers that their imposed deadline cannot be met
   C) Plan to have the resources work overtime to meet the deadline
   D) Check if the schedule can be compressed to bring the project in time

475. Terry is managing a project in a computer manufacturing company. Due to a shortage of raw material, one supplier could not complete the assembly of components on time. This was a risk already identified, analyzed, planned, and recorded in the risk register. As per the plan, Terry has decided to use similar parts supplied for another computer model about a year ago and left in the inventory due to canceled order. This has introduced new risk of a higher number of defective components due to long storage time. What should Terry call this type of risks?
   A) Unknown risks
   B) Secondary risks
   C) Known risks
   D) Responded risks

476. Your project has run into some trouble and you are analyzing exactly how much percentage variance you may have by the time project is done? Your project is 50% done and the value of the work completed till now is 200,000. Your Estimate at Completion is 500,000.
   A) 25% under the cost baseline
   B) 25% over the cost baseline
   C) 40% under the cost baseline
   D) 40% over the cost baseline

477. All of the following are correct statements about the contract change control system EXCEPT _____.
   A) Contract change control system is mainly used during the Control Procurements process
   B) Contract change control system is a part of the project's integrated change control system
   C) The buyer and seller both can submit a change request to the contract change control system
   D) The contract change control system should be defined separately from the terms of the contract

478. The project is officially approved to go ahead when _____.
   A) The project manager is assigned
   B) The stakeholders are identified
   C) The deliverables have been accepted
   D) The project charter is approved

479. Which of the following will you consider for the team management plan?
   A) Inspection
   B) Recognition and rewards
   C) Communication strategy
   D) Stakeholder engagement matrix

480. Which estimation technique results in the most accurate estimate for a new product development project?
   A) Top-down estimating
   B) Bottom-up estimating
   C) Analogous estimating
   D) Parametric estimating

481. A project team decides to use the six sigma technique to deliver 10,000 parts order to the manufacturer. How many defected parts is the project team willing to accept?
   A) Two hundred
   B) Three
   C) One
   D) Zero

482. A project manager of a high-rise condominium project is estimating resource requirements for the project. The project needs 1,000 standard light fixtures installed within 10 working days. Each day has 8 working hours and the plan is to engage two electricians for this

purpose. What is the minimum productivity required of each electrician?
A) 5 light fixtures / hour
B) 10 light fixtures / hour
C) 6.25 light fixtures / hour
D) 12.5 light fixtures / hour

483. Several senior managers at a large wholesale distribution company recently got trained in project management. They were very impressed with the structure and rigor of project management processes and decided that all orders received by the company will be considered projects. They even changed the titles of customer representatives to project managers and got them trained on project management fundamentals. Each order will be treated as a project request, a project manager is pre-assigned to projects based on the origin of the project, the status will be updated daily, issues will be recorded against the project and resolved, and scope validation will occur with customer's acceptance of the shipment. The orders can be anywhere from 10 through the internet to 300,000 through an electronic purchase order. In order to reduce the burden on the project manager, project charter and project management plan have been eliminated. What would be your comments?
    A) Any effort that is temporary with a start and an end date and results in a product is a project so the orders are treated correctly as projects
    B) Since there is a continuous flow of related projects, it can be considered as a program
    C) All the projects are operational activity and should not be treated as projects
    D) Orders that take more than 5 days to process should be treated as projects and the rest as operational activity

484. A project manager has been working on a new corporate intranet development project. The work has been going on quite smoothly. No budget or schedule overruns have occurred. The designers have created amazing web applications that meet the needs of the customer really well. In the last design review meeting, the lead designer suggested an application that will create real-time reports by combining employee personal data, payroll data, and data from the learning management system. The team really liked the idea because they felt the report will be a great time saver for any employee looking for the information. Surprisingly the requirements document does not mention any such report so it seems this is out of scope. What should

the project manager do?
- A) Consult the change control process and perform an impact assessment
- B) Include the application into requirements to deliver it with the rest of the intranet and thus exceed customer expectations
- C) Speak with the sponsor and inform about this great application that will be very productive
- D) Reject the application idea as it is out of scope. Focus on completing the project and do not entertain such ideas

485. You are a project manager managing a geographically distributed team. You have received several emails and voicemails from your team members with concerns about cost overruns, delays, and quality. What is the best way to track these concerns?
- A) An assumption log
- B) An issue log
- C) A risk register
- D) A change log

486. A project manager is facing a dilemma of how to meet the schedule deadline. The project is behind schedule but must be completed on the planned completion date. Which of the following cannot be a solution to this problem?
- A) Add more resource and crash the schedule
- B) Fast Track the schedule
- C) Remove an activity from the critical path
- D) Do resource leveling

487. A document contains the project objectives, criteria to determine if objectives are met, and evidence that objectives were actually met. What is this report called?
- A) Benefits management plan
- B) Business case
- C) Quality report
- D) Final report

488. An email is generally what type of communication?
- A) Formal written
- B) Informal written
- C) Formal electronic
- D) Informal nonverbal

489. There is a 70% chance that the material delivery will be late by two

days. It is also known that a two-day late delivery will result in a 10% schedule delay. What is the value of risk?
A) Risk = 0.7
B) Risk = 0.1
C) Risk = 0.07
D) Cannot be determined

490. As the project manager, you created and received approval of the project charter for your project. The charter has formally authorized you to start project work. It includes high-level requirements, assumptions, and constraints. How often are you planning to review the project charter?
A) Every time I meet the sponsor
B) Monthly
C) Quarterly
D) Never

491. You are managing an airport construction project but finding it difficult to meet the needs of all the stakeholders. You had classified the stakeholders and engaged them according to the stakeholder engagement plan but stakeholders' complaints are high in number. The issue log shows all the stakeholders' complaints and issues related to stakeholder engagement. Which another project document you would need to perform an analysis?
A) Project schedule
B) Project charter
C) Project communications
D) Change log

492. As the project manager of accounts payable system improvement project, you are in the Close Project or Phase process of your project. As part of this phase, you will review all of the following inputs EXCEPT _____.
A) Contracts
B) Risk report
C) Quality reports
D) Final report

493. You work for a government department as project manager for technology projects. The change control board for your project meets regularly once a month and processes any submitted change requests. This month you had multiple change requests from various stakeholders that will impact time and cost. Luckily six out of the

seven change requests submitted were approved. How will you proceed?
A) Update the business case and project charter
B) Use work authorization system to make sure the change requests get processed
C) Track approved changes against the cost and schedule baselines
D) Implement through Direct and Manage Project Work process

494. You are in the steering committee meeting presenting your project's latest performance report. You just presented that the CPI is 1.1 and the SPI is 0.87. Which of the following will be most helpful to make this presentation successful?
A) Provide an electronic copy of the presentation
B) Ask for feedback at the end of the presentation
C) Finish the presentation on time
D) Request for the specifically needed support

495. Which of the following is not a project document updated as part of implementing risk responses?
A) Issue log
B) Assumptions log
C) Risk register
D) Project team assignments

496. As the project manager of a payroll application upgrade project, you have to report the project status on a monthly basis to the steering committee. While presenting last month's status you informed the steering committee that the Schedule Performance Index is 1.06 and the Schedule Variance is 10,000. A steering committee member, who is attending this meeting the first time, is confused. She represents the finance department so her question is "What does this tell me as to how much we have saved or overspent till now?" What will you tell her based on the information given above?
A) We have underspent 10,000
B) We have overspent 10,000
C) We cannot determine that from this information
D) Earned Value Management is the best technique to see what the value of the work done is and it is presented using indices and variances

497. A project manager has many types of contracts to consider when deciding which will be more suitable for the type of work to be done. Which one of the following is NOT a type of contract?

A) Statement of work
B) Fixed-price
C) Cost plus fixed-fee
D) Time and material

498. You are managing a global software development project. There are several teams located in different countries. One of the teams is continuously late in producing its deliverables which is affecting another team's schedule. What will be your approach to fix this problem?
    A) Discuss the issue with the leader of the team that receives the late deliverables
    B) Discuss the issue with the leader of the team that produces the late deliverables
    C) Bring both team leaders in a meeting and discuss the issue
    D) No need to take action as the second team is still able to produce their deliverables on time somehow

499. Your company is bidding on a multi-million dollars contract to build parts for an innovative spaceship. Which one of the following is the riskiest contract for your company?
    A) Cost plus incentive
    B) Time and material
    C) Fixed price
    D) Cost plus fixed-fee

500. You are the project manager for a non-profit housing project. You had worked with most of the stakeholders before. One of the stakeholders had made quite a few changes on the last project. Which of the following is the BEST approach to manage this stakeholder?
    A) Set the expectations right at the start without identifying the stakeholder that too many changes will not be entertained as it is detrimental to the project progress
    B) Involve the stakeholder actively right from the start of the project
    C) Check if this stakeholder can be removed from the stakeholders list
    D) Discuss with the stakeholder, in an informal verbal way, the issue of too many changes

501. A multinational firm assigned Cathy as the project manager of the organizational transformation project. Cathy has identified few tools and techniques to connect people so that they can work together to create new knowledge and share tacit knowledge. She has identified

storytelling, communities of practice, conferences, and networking as the tools and techniques for this purpose. What are these tools and techniques called?
A) Collect Requirements process tools and techniques
B) Knowledge management tools and techniques
C) Information management tools and techniques
D) Lessons learned register

502. All of the following are established through a schedule management plan except _____.
A) Control thresholds
B) Level of precision
C) Level of accuracy
D) Reporting formats

503. You are the project manager of a business application enhancement project. During planning, you have identified that internal resources will not be available to perform some work so you have to contract out the work to a seller. You asked the internal resources to provide an estimate of the work. The estimate they provided was 150,000. You went through the procurement process by inviting bids, 30 prospective sellers obtained the statement of work and terms of the contract to review, 24 attended the bidders' conference, but only one submitted a bid for 300,000. All of the following may have been the reason EXCEPT _____.
A) Statement of Work was vague and not detailed enough to provide prospective sellers the opportunity to assess their capability to deliver the work
B) The terms of the contract were unfavorable for the seller
C) Prospective bidders have colluded in favor of the submitted bid
D) The internal team estimate must be incorrect

504. You were the project manager of project X, which was a finance application upgrade project that was completed successfully a year ago. Since then, you have moved on to a different role in the human resources department. Project Y, which is a follow up project to project X, is in its initiating processes. The project manager of project Y has identified you as a stakeholder of the project. How should she classify you?
A) High power, high interest
B) Low power, high interest
C) High power, low interest
D) Low power, low interest

505. Rolling wave planning is a technique where work in the near future is planned in detail while the work in the farther future is kept at a higher level of details. Rolling wave planning can be considered as all of the following techniques except _____.
   A) Decomposition
   B) Iterative
   C) Sequential
   D) Progressive elaboration

506. A project identified and analyzed a list of risks and planned responses to a few of them. One of the risks occurred and the project manager responded as per plan. The expected monetary value of the risk was 10,000 but the additional cost incurred, due to the occurrence of that risk, was 15,000. Still, the project manager believed that the outcome was better than expected. Why?
   A) Expected Monetary Value is not the cost of the impact
   B) The project was under budget and had extra funds available
   C) The project is still ahead of schedule and under budget
   D) The project manager does not understand the Expected Monetary Value concept

507. Which of the following is an input to Manage Stakeholder Engagement process?
   A) Change log
   B) Assumption log
   C) Change requests
   D) Work performance data

508. As a project manager, which one of the following will not be your concern when it comes to controlling resources?
   A) Dealing with resource shortages and surpluses
   B) Acquiring resources for the right cost
   C) Monitoring resource expenses
   D) Releasing resources for use at the right time

509. You have just come out of a project meeting where the project team members were analyzing schedule performance over the course of the project while validating the organization's schedule model. What is this type of analysis called?
   A) Model analysis
   B) Schedule analysis
   C) Regression analysis

D) Trend analysis

510. Which of the following is expected to be within the Initiating Process Group?
A) Develop Project Management Plan
B) Define Scope
C) Develop Project Charter
D) Collect Requirements

511. The project manager is reconciling the cost estimate with any funding limits imposed by the approved budget. What process is this?
A) Integrated Change Control
B) Estimate Costs
C) Determine Budget
D) Control Costs

512. All of the following are objectives of the Monitor Communications process EXCEPT _____.
A) Optimal information flow occurs
B) Information needs of project stakeholders are met
C) Trigger a review of the Communication Management Plan if needed due to an issue
D) Identification of new stakeholders

513. The _____ manager invited three project managers to a meeting to discuss projects' progress. She wants to ensure her role's commitments will be met but has the least concern with the department's overall strategic goals for the year.
A) Program
B) Portfolio
C) Functional
D) Project

514. You are the project manager of a financial services project. There is a tremendous pressure from the stakeholders to shorten the project schedule. You decided to use a schedule compression technique called crashing. You may do any of these activities EXCEPT _____.
A) Engage more resources
B) Reduce the scope of the project
C) Provide incentive to the vendor for early delivery of code
D) Get resources to work overtime

515. What is the duration of the critical path in this activity list?

Activity	Duration	Predecessor
A1	2	
A2	3	A1
A3	4	A1
B1	5	A2
B2	6	A3
B3	7	A3
C1	4	B2
C2	3	B3
D1	4	B1
D2	2	C1,C2
E1	3	D1
E2	4	E1,D2

A) Length of critical path is 22
B) Length of critical path is 21
C) Length of critical path is 20
D) Length of critical path is 24

516. If you receive a complaint from a stakeholder that she is not getting enough information, what will you do?
    A) Inform the stakeholder that you have been sending information as per communication management plan
    B) Ask the stakeholder to review all project documentation in the project repository
    C) Review stakeholder's information needs and then update the communication management plan if needed
    D) Review stakeholder's information needs and then send the communication management plan for review

517. Suzy has been asked by the sponsor to find out what is the To Complete Performance Index (TCPI) for her project. The project's Budget at Completion is 500,000 and the Actual Cost to date is 400,000. The project is 60% complete and the Estimate to Complete the remaining work is 200,000.
    A) TCPI = 0.80
    B) TCPI = 1.00

C) TCPI = 1.20
   D) Cannot be determined from the information given

518. A document that has a section on business need and implementation approach is called _____.
   A) Statement of work
   B) Business case
   C) Project charter
   D) Project management plan

519. You are the project manager of supply chain project. The project has a To Complete Performance Index (TCPI) of 1.1. What does this mean?
   A) The project has extra funds at hand
   B) Cost performance needs to be improved
   C) Schedule performance needs to be improved more than the cost performance
   D) Cost performance needs to be improved more than the schedule performance

520. Which project management process will you use if you want to find out how scope variance is impacting schedule or cost?
   A) Corrective action
   B) Control scope
   C) Integrated change control
   D) Preventive action

521. All of the following are examples of operational work EXCEPT _____.
   A) Upgrade of enterprise payroll application every two to three years
   B) Processing of invoices through accounts payable system every two to three days
   C) Daily newsletter email sent out with important notices
   D) Yearly employee performance reviews

522. What is false about project cost management?
   A) The currency exchange rate is only considered when using team members from other countries
   B) The culture of an organization influences cost management
   C) Productivity difference can result in varying costs for resources in the same roles
   D) The project management information system can provide various approaches to manage the project cost

523. For a new leading-edge product development project, the project manager decides to use _____ to estimate activity durations because there was very little information available about this project.
    A) Guesstimating
    B) Three-point estimating
    C) Analogous estimating
    D) Parametric estimating

524. A project manager was informed by the sponsor that the product from the project must be delivered one month earlier due to a sudden change in the market demand. Without changing the scope of the project, what technique can the project manager use to reduce the schedule by one month?
    A) Schedule compression
    B) Resource optimization
    C) Critical path method
    D) Monte Carlo simulation

525. During a quality audit, the audit team noticed that significant coding errors are occurring which are caught during the testing phase. The defected code is returned, for fix or rewrite, to the programmers. Three programmers have been replaced since the start of project for not being able to improve the code quality. On further drill down, the audit team found that most of the errors being reported are related to the nonconformance to the company's coding standard. They also found that a training course exists on company coding standards but the company policy says that training cannot be provided to temporary project resources and is only available to permanent employees of the company. What is the BEST thing to do?
    A) Prepare a quick presentation on the company's coding standards based on the frequent errors observed and train the temporary project programmers
    B) Ask that the training be waived for the programmers
    C) Use internal trained programmers for this project
    D) Recommend review of the company's training policy

526. As part of the Close Project or Phase process, project management plan, project calendars, and the change management documentation will be updated and stored. What are these documents part of?
    A) Project documents
    B) Historical information
    C) Lessons learned repository
    D) Project or phase closure documents

527. Out of the following, which input can help the project manager the MOST when creating a cost estimate for her project?
   A) Work breakdown structure
   B) Resource breakdown structure
   C) Parametric estimating
   D) Sponsor's commitment

528. Which of the following is the point where optimal quality is reached?
   A) The test results just about meet the specifications and the product is not of unnecessarily high quality
   B) Results from the quality audit are the same as results from quality control measurements
   C) Revenue from improvements equal the incremental costs to achieve the improvements
   D) Revenue from corrective actions equals the revenue from defect repair

529. As the project manager, you were talking to a team member and discussing how he should approach a certain task. From his body language, you were certain that he does not agree with your approach though he did not refuse. Which of the following BEST represents this situation?
   A) Transmission
   B) Negotiation
   C) Acknowledgment
   D) Distribution

530. _____ is NOT an input to the Direct and Manage Project Work process.
   A) Approved change requests
   B) Issue log
   C) Risk register
   D) Change log

531. Which of the following is NOT a tool and technique used in Manage Communications process?
   A) Communication technology
   B) Communication competence
   C) Communication activity
   D) Communication methods

532. A project manager at your organization was having trouble controlling

the project scope. You advised him to refer to _____ for guidance.
A) Requirements traceability matrix
B) Scope validation plan
C) Scope management plan
D) Scope control plan

533. What should be included in the scope management plan of an infrastructure project?
A) Process for preparing a project scope statement
B) Requirements and deliverables
C) Acceptance criteria for deliverables
D) Requirements prioritization process

534. A project manager is working on office space refresh project. While using earned value technique, he determines that the project will run over budget by 2,000 if current performance trend continues. The project manager has used _____ characteristics to identify the issue.
A) Knowledge
B) Earned value
C) Interpersonal
D) Problem solving

535. A project team working on a complex business application enhancement project stumbles on a serious issue. All project work comes to a halt since the team has no idea what the root cause is. You anticipate a delay due to this issue but unsure how much it will be. The team has asked for three days to explore the problem and identify the root cause and solution. How will you proceed?
A) Create a change request and submit for approval
B) Issue a "stop work until further notice" notification
C) Inform the sponsor and other potentially impacted stakeholders that a serious issue has come up and then provide a target resolution date
D) Add the issue to the lessons learned document

536. Which of the following is NOT a characteristic of the payment system when payments are being made?
A) The payment request is reviewed before payment is made
B) Payment is made according to the terms of the contract
C) Payment is linked to the seller's progress
D) Terms of payment are negotiated before the payment is released

537. Which document will you check to come up with an initial list of stakeholders during the Identify Stakeholders process?
   A) Project charter
   B) Stakeholder register
   C) Team roster
   D) Resource breakdown structure

538. If the customer asks for a major scope change in the middle of the project by speaking to the project manager (you) directly, what should be your response?
   A) Refuse and explain that changes are very expensive in the middle and should be done earlier to avoid the extra cost
   B) Ask the customer to send you details of the change in writing so that you can review the impact
   C) Inform customer that you have to ask sponsor if he is willing to consider the change
   D) Mention that any change to the scope means there will be an additional cost

539. A new project manager was unsure which technique she should use to come up with a cost estimate for her project. She reviewed the company's estimation guidelines and decided that parametric estimating is the best choice. Which of the following will she use?
   A) Lessons learned from a previous project
   B) Project cost summed up from each activity's estimate
   C) 300 per day for an expert resource
   D) Project cost distributed down to each activity

540. You are managing a global application deployment project. Part of the work is on a very specialized software for which it is really hard to find a resource. You were lucky that you got a contract resource engaged. The resource resigned in the middle of the project. What is the first thing you will do?
   A) Hire a new resource to fill the role
   B) Reject the resignation and demand that the resource come back to work and complete the project as per contract
   C) Submit a change request to fast-track the schedule
   D) Record issue on an issue log to evaluate the situation

541. Which of the following is included in a project charter?
   A) Project communication plan
   B) Cost estimate for each WBS work package

C) Resource requirement for each WBS work package
D) Purpose of the project

542. A project manager was informed by the team member that the internal failure cost is very high. Which of the following is an example of internal failure cost that the team member may be referring?
    A) Rework
    B) Quality control
    C) Liabilities
    D) Destructive testing

543. Which type of communication can the project status report be considered?
    A) Formal written communication
    B) Formal verbal communication
    C) Informal written communication
    D) Informal verbal communication

544. You are the project manager for a software development project. The code written by the programmers was tested by the testers. Some of the work was found to have significant logical errors that required a complete rewrite. The cost of redoing the work can also be called as _____.
    A) Cost of quality
    B) Cost of project
    C) Cost of non-conformance
    D) Cost of conformance

545. What is true about analogous estimating?
    A) It is very rarely used
    B) It has the same level of accuracy as the bottom-up estimating
    C) It is more accurate than the bottom-up estimating
    D) It is less accurate than the bottom-up estimating

546. You are the project manager for a dam construction project where major pieces of work have been contracted out to two sellers. You have observed that one of the sellers is not delivering the work as per contract. After reviewing the terms of that contract, you are quite clear that some of the contractual terms were not met by the seller. You decided to start some corrective action to make sure the seller performs as stipulated in the statement of work and the contract. All of the following can be an output of your effort EXCEPT _____.

A) Work performance data
B) Seller's performance evaluation
C) Updating the organizational process assets
D) A change request

547. Project manager circulates work performance reports to the project stakeholders. Which of the following is least likely to be part of a work performance report?
A) Defect histograms
B) Risk summaries
C) Reserve burndown chart
D) Stakeholder engagement matrix

548. At what stage, stakeholders have the MOST impact on the project?
A) During execution
B) At project start
C) At project end
D) Throughout the project life cycle

549. A change request is an output of the Validate Scope process. Which of the following is also an output of the same process?
A) Work performance data
B) Product analysis
C) Accepted deliverables
D) Inspection

550. A change submitted by a stakeholder was asking for the addition of scope that would add significant cost to the project. Which of the following is the MOST likely output of the Control Scope process in this case?
A) A change request to add extra cost to the budget
B) A change request to update performance baselines
C) Rejection letter to the stakeholder who suggested the change
D) Update organizational process assets

551. A project was ahead of schedule with certain hard to achieve deliverables completed earlier than the planned date. The team has been working really hard so the project manager decided to announce an award. Sponsor and other executive stakeholders were invited and two team members were awarded a gift and appreciation certificate. The award ceremony was followed by dinner attended by whole project team along with the executives. Starting next week, project progress started to slow down to the point that the next three

deliverables were late. What is the BEST step the project manager can take?
- A) Review the reward system for the project
- B) Improve the schedule performance of the project
- C) Hold a meeting with the project team to find out what is going on
- D) Use a problem-solving technique with the team members

552. Which of the following is NOT an update to the risk register as an output of the Monitor Risks process?
- A) Updates to Risk breakdown structure
- B) Updates to outdated risks
- C) New identified risks
- D) Updates to risk responses

553. You are in the processing of assessing various stakeholders' current engagement level. Which classification scheme can help you in this regard?
- A) Engaged, disengaged, neither engaged nor disengaged
- B) Unaware, resistant, neutral, supportive, leading
- C) Unanimity, majority, plurality, autocratic
- D) Proximity, manageability, connectivity, detectability, propinquity

554. Which of the following is INCORRECT about the project scope statement?
- A) It contains work packages
- B) It contains deliverables list
- C) It provides project exclusions
- D) It provides deliverables acceptance criteria

555. Which of the following CANNOT be derived from the work breakdown structure?
- A) Project objectives
- B) Work packages
- C) Cost estimates
- D) Resources required

556. Which of the following factors will not be part of the criteria to score potential physical resources to acquire for your project?
- A) Availability
- B) Cost
- C) Experience
- D) Ability

557. Which of the following is NOT a valid tool for risk identification?
   A) Assumptions analysis
   B) SWOT analysis
   C) Document analysis
   D) Trend analysis

558. One of the following relationships is rarely used when building the Precedence Diagrams. Which one is it?
   A) Start-to-Start
   B) Finish-to-Finish
   C) Finish-to-Start
   D) Start-to-Finish

559. Which of the following is NOT a tool and technique of the Control Schedule process?
   A) Pareto chart
   B) Leads and lags
   C) Fast-tracking
   D) Iteration burndown chart

560. When performing Earned value analysis, all of the following will be considered EXCEPT _____.
   A) Value of the completed work
   B) Planned cost of management reserve
   C) Authorized budget assigned to the scheduled work
   D) Actual cost of work performed

561. A project manager is preparing a document that mentions what information will be expected from the stakeholders, when it is expected, in which format, and to whom that information will be sent. The project manager is preparing _____.
   A) RACI chart
   B) Performance report
   C) Stakeholder register
   D) Communication management plan

562. Risk ranking is an output of _____.
   A) Expert judgment
   B) Qualitative Risk Analysis process
   C) Plan Risk Response process
   D) SWOT analysis

563. As the project manager you kept all the project documentation on your laptop's hard disk. You have planned for the worst risk, the hard disk crash so you took weekly backup on a portable drive that you carried in your laptop bag. One day on your way back from office, you stopped to buy a cup of coffee. When you returned to your car, you found the window was broken and the laptop bag was gone. Both laptop and the portable backup device were lost. You missed identifying theft as a risk. All of the following could have been a response planned for such a risk EXCEPT _____.
    A) Password secure the laptop and the portable backup device
    B) Hide the bag in the trunk of the car
    C) Keep another backup at the office
    D) Keep the bag with you all the time when not in a secure area

564. On a Power/Interest grid, the project sponsor should typically fall in which group?
    A) Keep satisfied
    B) Keep informed
    C) Monitor
    D) Manage closely

565. What can a project manager do to resolve a dispute with the seller? The dispute is over scope change where the seller believes that the scope is extra work and not part of the signed contract while the buyer believes it is already included in the contract.
    A) If the seller does not agree then the buyer can go to the court
    B) Alternative dispute resolution techniques can be used
    C) The contract can be terminated
    D) The contract can be changed to resolve the dispute

566. Which one of the following is the BIGGEST benefit of using a colocated team?
    A) Reduces the communication project manager has to do with the team
    B) Team communication is no longer required when team members are located in the same location
    C) Team communication and collaboration is more effective
    D) It costs much less because team members are located in the same location

567. _____ can be a constraint on the project communication.
    A) Schedule, cost, and scope
    B) Sponsor's reporting requirements

C) Global project with team members in different continents
D) Stakeholder identification

568. A project manager could not decide how to plan for project scope which has various stakeholders with different needs who are expected to have a large number of requirements. What can he do to ensure all such requirements are captured, analyzed, documented and managed successfully?
    A) Create a requirements traceability structure and prioritization process
    B) Document each stakeholder requirement and rank from most favorable to least favorable for the project
    C) Remove from the project all the stakeholders that have a negative approach to the project
    D) Ask the sponsor to identify which stakeholders should be satisfied

569. A project manager was advised by a senior project manager to show the planned quality performance on one axis and the actual performance on the second axis. What was he referring to?
    A) Control chart
    B) Histogram
    C) Scatter diagram
    D) Fishbone diagram

570. Which factor cannot influence the development of the project charter?
    A) Project life cycle
    B) Industry standards
    C) Infrastructure of the organization
    D) Regulatory requirements

571. All of the following are always characteristics of a project EXCEPT _____.
    A) Temporary
    B) Strategic
    C) Unique product, service, or result
    D) Drives change in an organization

572. You are the project manager of a software development project. You are estimating activity resources and need to decide on a developer resource. There are four resources available as given below. Which resource will you select if lower costs factor is much more important than delivering in a shorter time? Speed is given as lines of code

written per day and there are about 100,000 lines of code to be written. The error rate is lines of code that need to be rewritten. Cost is given in per hour rate.
   A) Anita is an in-house resource. Speed = 300, cost = 40, Error = 12%
   B) Barry is local resource. Speed = 400, cost = 50, Error = 10%
   C) Cathy is a virtual resource. Speed = 500, cost = 60, Error = 10%
   D) David is a virtual resource. Speed = 600, cost = 100, Error = 2%

573. Which of the following is an input to the Monitor Stakeholder Engagement process?
   A) Work performance analysis
   B) Work performance report
   C) Work performance information
   D) Work performance data

574. Which one of the following you will NOT consider when planning the communication needs of a project?
   A) Project team size
   B) Experience of the project manager
   C) Geographical locations of team members
   D) Data security

575. One of your team members came to you with a problem. He is having trouble understanding what is being discussed in the meetings. What will be your advice to him?
   A) Stop the person who is speaking and ask questions
   B) Take minutes of meeting to make the best use of time
   C) Face the speaker and maintain eye contact
   D) Focus on the speech rather than the speaker

576. A project manager has just started a new project and he is going through initial meetings with the sponsor and other key stakeholders. One Vice President (VP) who is a key stakeholder wants to know how much the project will cost and how long it will take. The project manager has just initiated the project and does not have details but still provides an estimate to the VP. Which technique did the project manager use?
   A) Analogous estimate
   B) Rough order of magnitude
   C) Parametric estimate
   D) Bottom-Up estimate

577. Which of the following is an input to the Identify Stakeholders process?
    A) Assumption log
    B) Risk register
    C) Change log
    D) Stakeholder mapping

578. What is a list of prequalified sellers?
    A) A list of sellers whose qualifications and experiences are found to be competent to perform the work
    B) A list of sellers whose qualifications and experiences are of the highest quality
    C) A list of sellers who have qualified people in their teams
    D) A list of sellers whose qualifications and experiences have been reviewed thoroughly

579. You are managing a software development project. Your design team has asked for an additional week to complete the design work which is on the critical path. What will you do?
    A) Fast track the schedule to cover up for the additional week
    B) Add one week to the project schedule
    C) Initiate a change request
    D) Reject the design team's request

580. A common way of representing the stakeholder engagement strategy is a _____.
    A) Stakeholder register
    B) Power/Interest grid
    C) Salience model
    D) Stakeholder engagement plan

581. A stakeholder on a project has asked for a change to the project that has an impact on the project budget. To implement the change, _____ has to be followed.
    A) Change's cost estimate
    B) Monitoring and controlling process group
    C) Change control board
    D) Cost performance baseline

582. An application enhancement project is being executed and has reached the end of design phase 10 days earlier than planned and 20% under the planned expense. The design has been reviewed internally by the project team. Next, the development phase is to start, followed by

multiple testing iterations. Design team and development team are not co-located. What is the FIRST thing the project manager will do?
   A) Validate the scope
   B) Control the quality
   C) Build the team
   D) Hire additional developers

583. Which of the following is NOT a characteristic of a decision tree?
   A) Shows the relative impact of choosing one decision over another
   B) Helps make the most appropriate decision
   C) Assists in identifying hidden risks
   D) Uses the concept of expected monetary value

584. How would you determine the risk exposure of a project risk?
   A) Multiply the probability of occurrence with impact
   B) Adding the probability of occurrence and impact
   C) Use the expert judgment
   D) Use the Delphi technique

585. You are managing a software development project. What is the main reason to create and contribute to lessons learned register?
   A) It is required by the project management plan
   B) To identify what worked and what did not work well
   C) To show the sponsor that the team has done a good job
   D) To help teams involved with future work packages and projects

586. Which of the following is LEAST valuable as part of the contract?
   A) Terms and conditions
   B) Work breakdown structure
   C) List of deliverables
   D) Incentives and penalties

587. You are managing a building construction project. During the recent check, you found out that your project is almost out of cement bags. The supply was planned in detail and this came as a shock. With the problem identified, you defined the problem by breaking it into smaller issues. What should be done next?
   A) Find the root cause of the problem
   B) Collect data
   C) Fix the problem
   D) Choose the best solution

588. The Control Schedule process in Schedule Management knowledge

area uses all of the following tools and techniques EXCEPT _____.

A) Iteration burndown chart
B) Expert judgment
C) Resource optimization
D) Leads and lags

589. One member of your project team is checking if all the steps to verify the key deliverable of your project were completed. Some of these steps include the acceptance criteria for the deliverable as defined in the scope baseline. What do you call the tool and technique that has been used here?
A) Quality control measurement
B) Quality metric
C) Checklist
D) Quality report

590. How will you calculate late start date and late finish date of an activity which has not started yet?
A) Calculate with the Critical Chain method
B) Calculate with Monte Carlo simulation
C) Calculate with a backward pass
D) Calculate with a forward pass

591. You are managing a project that is in the middle of developing a project charter. You will use one of the following as an input for developing project charter. Which one is it?
A) Work performance information
B) Organizational process assets
C) Project performance baseline
D) Project scope statement

592. The project management office at your organization is going through a project selection process. They are down to four projects which are to be compared using internal rate of return (IRR). Which project will you recommend?
A) Project with an opportunity cost of 200,000
B) Project with a benefit-cost ratio of 1.3
C) Project with a net present value of 150,000 and internal rate of return of 5%
D) Project with an internal rate of return of 10%

593. The success, of which of the following, is measured in terms of

aggregate investment performance and benefits realization?
A) Portfolios
B) Programs
C) Operations
D) Projects

594. If Actual Cost is more than the Earned Value, the project is _____.
A) Under budget
B) Over budget
C) Ahead of schedule
D) Behind schedule

595. During negotiation on the contract terms for a construction project, the project manager says, "I want to sign this contract with you because I really like you but my manager is quite upset that you are not listening to what he is asking and I am afraid if you do not accept our terms I won't be able to stop this contract going to another seller." The project manager is using a negotiation tactic, commonly known as?
A) Deadline
B) Delay
C) Good guy, bad guy
D) Divide and rule

596. You find it very valuable to attend the regular monthly project management training session. Most project managers at your office share your view and make effort to attend these sessions. It was mentioned in the last session that improvement in project management practice has been observed since the start of these training sessions a year ago. The manager of the project management office is quite pleased with these results because _____.
A) Stage gate reviews can be scheduled to enable projects to proceed to the next phases
B) More strategic projects can be initiated
C) Resources can be managed by project managers
D) Training, coaching and mentoring is one of the functions of the project management office

597. A project manager was having problems with issues popping up without any warning. The project team is regularly doing risk identification, analysis and response planning. What could have gone wrong?

A) The project team is doing lip service only
B) The project team is creating poor risk responses
C) The project team is less experienced
D) The project team needs training in issue management

598. Meetings are used as tools & techniques while managing the deliverables and the project work. Which of the following is not a type of meeting used in this process?
A) Iteration planning
B) Sprint
C) Retrospective
D) Scrum daily standup

599. In which process will you use a prequalified seller list?
A) Plan Procurement Management
B) Resource Procurements
C) Conduct Procurements
D) Contract Negotiation

600. What is the duration of activity F in the network diagram shown?

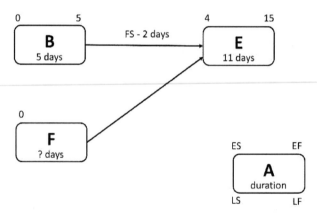

A) 2 days
B) 3 days
C) 4 days
D) 5 days

5 - ANSWERS & EXPLANATIONS TEST 1

1: C

Procurement audits are conducted during the Control Procurements process. The sellers are selected and the contract awarded in the Conduct Procurements process, so it is too early to perform an audit since there is nothing to audit. Procurement audits are not done in the Close Project or Phase process although the contract may be closed in this process. There is no process by the name audit procurements.

PMBOK reference: (12.3.2.5, pg. 498)

2: B

Next step is to implement the approved change. A change request is only closed, once the approved change has been completed and validated. Recommending corrective action is part of the integrated change control process. Question is asking what happens afterward. Preventive actions may get published, but such publication does not make the project move forward.

PMBOK reference: (4.3.1.3, pg. 93)

3: B

Removing few team members and bringing in new members will be more detrimental to the team morale which is already very low. Team development is not a core project management process, so it will be challenging to convince management to extend the schedule or budget for this activity; besides the focus should be on taking positive steps to improve morale. Bringing into management notice may not be a motivator for the team. The scenario does not mention any issue with WBS, so there is no need to recreate WBS. Recreating WBS will be a waste of time and may result in lowering team morale further. The best thing to do is to assess individual and team performance to understand the strengths and weaknesses. The assessment will help take the appropriate actions. Also, activating reward system can motivate team members to perform better.

PMBOK reference: (9.4.2.5, pg. 341 and 9.4.2.7, pg. 342)

4: C

Defining Activities, Plan Quality Management, and Estimate Costs processes have scope baseline as one of the inputs. Work breakdown structure (WBS) is a component of the scope baseline. Acquire Resources process only uses cost baseline as an input and does not need scope baseline.

PMBOK reference: (6.2, pg. 182; 7.2, pg. 240; 8.1, pg. 277; and 9.3, pg. 328)

5: B

Regression analysis is the technique to analyze interrelationships between various project variables to understand the contribution of these variables to the project success. Document analysis identifies lessons learned while trend analysis helps validate the models used in the project. Variance analysis helps improve organizational metrics.

PMBOK reference: (4.7.2.2, pg. 126)

6: A

Identify Stakeholders process may occur before or at the same time when the project charter is written. All the other three are correct statements.

PMBOK reference: (13.1, pg. 508)

7: D

The Identify Stakeholders and Plan Communications Management processes do not have 'update lessons learned register' as an output. Plan Quality Management process may have lessons learned register updated with the challenges faced while planning.

The main purpose of the Manage Quality process is to review the quality management plan, quality measurements, and compliance against a company's quality policies and procedures. Therefore, most information for lessons learned will come out of this process.

PMBOK reference: (8.2.3.5, pg. 297)

8: C

A constraint is a limiting factor that affects the execution of a project. A developer's absence of 5 days due to illness will impact schedule directly, so this is a schedule constraint. Unclear specifications resulted in low quality

work directly so this is a quality constraint. The per day cost of the tester being higher impacts the budget directly so this is a budget constraint. A programmer being less experienced than expected impacts productivity which is directly related to the resource and may have an indirect impact on schedule/budget/quality. Therefore, this is the best choice of being a resource constraint.
PMBOK reference: (4.3.3.6, pg. 97)

9: C

Propinquity is to compare the degree to which a risk is perceived to matter by one or more stakeholders. Dormancy is the time that may pass before a risk that has occurred is discovered. Connectivity is the extent to which a risk is related to other project risks. Controllability is the degree to which the risk owner can control the outcome of the result.
PMBOK reference: (11.3.2.3, pg. 424)

10: C

Schedule Performance Index (SPI) greater than 1.0 means the project is ahead of schedule. SPI of 1.0 means project is on schedule, and less than one means project is behind schedule.
SPI = Earned Value / Planned Value
PMBOK reference: (6.6.2.1, pg. 226)

11: B

Aggregate investment performance provides a measure of the success of portfolio management. Delivering on time, within budget, and with quality, establishes the success of project management, while the delivery of intended business benefits and the efficiency of delivering those benefits give a measure of program management's success. Operations management success is measured by continuing to run operation efficiently by optimal use of resources.
PMBOK reference: (Table 1-2, pg. 13 and 1.2.3.4, pg. 16)

12: B

A schedule can be compressed using crashing or fast tracking. Resource leveling is likely to extend the schedule rather than compress it. Schedule networking is the creation of a network diagram which happens at an earlier stage.
PMBOK reference: (6.5.2.6, pg. 215)

13: A

A root cause analysis should be done using a cause-and-effect diagram, also called a fishbone diagram, to find what the root cause of the customer's dissatisfaction is. Verifying quality measurements alone does not provide

the reasons of continued customer dissatisfaction. Identifying how many survey results are outside limits only tells the severity of dissatisfaction and not the reasons. Affinity diagrams help in organizing potential causes into categories.
PMBOK reference: (8.2.2.4, pg. 293)

14: D
The purpose of a template is to help the project save time and cost, and also reduce the chances of error. Therefore, a template should not be considered a project constraint.
PMBOK reference: (1.1, pg. 542)

15: D
The project management plan describes how the project will be executed, monitored, controlled, and closed. However, the project baselines measure performance by comparing the actual results with the baselines. Project baselines are a part of the project management plan. Both, project management plan and project baselines, cannot be changed without an approved change request.
PMBOK reference: (4.2.3.1, pg. 86-88)

16: B
The work will be complete once the customer has accepted the final deliverable. Acceptance of the deliverable by the customer happens in Validate Scope process. Monitor and Control Project Work process collects information from Validate Scope process for variance analysis. The Close Project or Phase process is to be started to formally close the project or phase at the end of the project. Control Communications mostly happens on a regular basis and is independent of acceptance of final deliverable or the process.
PMBOK reference: (4.7, pg. 121)

17: C
PESTLE stands for political, economic, social, technological, and environmental. It is an approach that gives a bird's eye view of the various dimensions of a project's risk exposure.
PMBOK reference: (11.2.2.5, pg. 416)

18: A
Executing process group is where the actual work is performed, and the maximum number of resources are engaged. Thus, this group has the highest level of effort spent. No matter the project type, whether equipment intensive or labor intensive, the effort level is highest in executing process group.

PMBOK reference: (1.9, pg. 555)

19: C
Establish a risk response strategy for all the risks after performing risk analysis. This strategy will address all the risks that require a response according to the plan. Developing a risk response strategy for the technology projects only is not the right approach since non-technology risk can materialize and become an issue.
PMBOK reference: (11.5.1.2, pg. 440)

20: D
Managing project resources and assigning project tasks is the responsibility of the project manager and is not taken care of by the project management office. All the other three functions are responsibilities of the project management office.
PMBOK reference: (2.4.4.3, pg. 49)

21: D
3 resources working for 6 hours/day = 18 hours of planned value of work per day. 18 x 8 days = 144 hours planned value of work until the end of 8th day. The 'twelve days' information is extra and not needed to find the solution.
PMBOK reference: (7.4.2.2, pg. 261)

22: C
In the Conduct Procurements process proposals are first invited from potential sellers and then evaluated. Though evaluation criteria are established in the Plan Procurement Management process, this is an incorrect choice since she is already in the Conduct Procurements process. Control Procurements process starts after the award of the contract. There is no process called Initiate Procurements.
PMBOK reference: (12.2, pg. 482)

23: D
Spikes are iterations timeboxed for doing research or running experiments. Continuous integration approach is to deliver frequently to a working product followed by testing cycles to confirm product is still performing as expected. In test-driven development tests are written before doing the coding. Kanban board is a visual display of work-in-process.
PMBOK reference: (The Agile Guide, 5.2.7, pg. 56)

24: D
The parametric estimation technique uses historical data and statistical analysis to come up with the project cost estimate. In the bottom-up

estimating technique, estimates at activity level are made and then summed up to the project level. Analogous estimating is a high-level estimating technique that takes historical information into account but does not use any statistical analysis. There is no such technique called risk-based estimating.

PMBOK reference: (7.2.2.3, pg. 244)

25: C

Analyzing activity durations to produce the project schedule is done in the Develop Schedule process, so this is not an objective of the Control Schedule process. All the other options are performed in the Control Schedule process.

PMBOK reference: (6.6, pg. 222)

26: B

You are referring to a prequalified sellers' list which is a short list of all the sellers capable of performing the work. Inviting the prequalified sellers only saves time going through the Conduct Procurement process. Negotiating a contract happens when a seller has been selected. The evaluation criteria are established before a list of sellers is created because sellers will be selected based on that criteria. Solicitation packages are sent out to the prospective sellers after the list becomes available.

PMBOK reference: (12.1.3.1, pg. 475)

27: D

Analyze stakeholders' interest and involvement in the project is done in the Identify Stakeholders process. All the other three can be the output of the Monitor Communications process.

PMBOK reference: (10.3.3.1 and 10.3.3.2, pg. 392-393)

28: C

It does not disallow scope changes but rather regulates changes to ensure scope creep does not happen. An ambiguous scope is not the only reason why scope creep occurs. The other three choices are correct about the Control Scope process.

PMBOK reference: (5.6, pg. 167)

29: A

For a new project, identification of stakeholders happens in the Initiating process group. Though stakeholders are identified throughout the project, the Identify Stakeholders process is a part of the initiating process group.

PMBOK reference: (Table 1-4, pg. 25 and 13.1, pg. 507)

30: B
Schedule Performance Index (SPI) = Earned Value (EV) / Planned Value (PV).
Now, here SPI = 0.8, PV = 150,000.
So 0.8 = EV / 150,000
Solving for EV, EV = 120,000
Schedule Variance = EV - PV = 120,000 - 150,000 = -30,000
PMBOK reference: (6.6.2.1, pg. 226)

31: D
Completing the project on time and within budget may not always satisfy project stakeholders. Stakeholders' satisfaction requires their needs being met through completed deliverables and their perception that they have received the best value from the project. Some projects create a transition state to achieve a future state so they have an impact on future projects in the organization. Though highly unlikely but a project may succeed without a project manager being formally assigned to the project. Projects are an excellent way to create value and benefits in organizations.
PMBOK reference: (1.2.1, pg. 6 & 1.2.2, pg. 10)

32: B
The six steps represent the problem-solving method. These steps are:
    1. Identify the problem
    2. Define the problem
    3. Investigate (collect data)
    4. Analyze and find the root cause of the problem
    5. Solve and find an appropriate solution, and
    6. Check the solution if it fixed the problem
PMBOK reference: (9.6.2.2, pg. 356)

33: D
Key stakeholders' responsibilities on the project may be addressed in the project charter. Stakeholders engagement level is addressed in the Plan Stakeholder Engagement process. Their influence and interest are determined in the Identify Stakeholders process.
PMBOK reference: (13.1.1.1, pg. 509)

34: D
Writing performance report of individual resources can be performed anytime during the project. These reports may also be written at the end of the project, but this activity is not directly related to the release of project resources. All the others are examples of releasing the project resources.
PMBOK reference: (4.7.1.8, pg. 126)

35: C

The formula to determine channels of communications is:

Number of channels = $n(n-1)/2$ where n is the number of stakeholders. So, originally there were 6 team members which means: $6(6-1)/2 = 15$ channels.

Now there are 11 team members, so $11(11-1)/2 = 55$ channels. So an additional $(55-11) = 40$ channels have been added.

PMBOK reference: (10.1.2.2, pg. 370)

36: A

The biggest benefit is that the project team can build beneficial relationships with the stakeholders by having a good understanding of their interests, influence, and involvement in the project. Though it is true that most stakeholders have very limited time to spend on the project, classifying them does not affect the time they have to devote to the project. Assigning responsibilities comes from defining roles and responsibilities, not by putting individual stakeholder into a different group. Classifying stakeholders in a group identifies how they are to be managed. Stakeholders do not need to know which group they belong to. In fact, releasing this information to stakeholders can sometimes backfire.

PMBOK reference: (13.1.2.4, pg. 512)

37: D

Monitor Stakeholder Engagement is the monitoring and controlling process in project stakeholder management knowledge area. All the other three are not the names of processes as defined in PMBOK guide.

PMBOK reference: (13.4, pg. 530)

38: C

It is unlikely that policy documents will be created from templates because each policy document is different and addresses different concerns. Also, policy documents are not created within projects but by the organization. The resource training procedure is developed by the human resources department. Both policy documents and resource training procedures will not be created within a project unless they are deliverables of a project. Requirement gathering is a process so no template can be used. Project scope statement can definitely be created from a template. This is the right answer.

PMBOK reference: (5.3.1.5, pg. 152)

39: C

There is no scope verification document mentioned in the PMBOK guide. The scope management plan has information on how to obtain the formal verification and acceptance of the project deliverables. Statement of work contains the work to be completed but does not provide information on how it will be verified. Communications management plan describes how and when communications will occur.

PMBOK reference: (5.1.3.1, pg. 137)

40: D

S-curve is a cumulative chart and not a probability distribution. All the others are types of probability distributions.

PMBOK reference: (11.4.2.4, pg. 432)

41: B

Make or buy decision is needed to plan the project approach, so it is a part of the planning process. Hence it cannot be an input to planning and initiating process groups. Monitoring and controlling has to do with comparing performance against the baseline. Once a make or buy decision is made, the project usually does not track whether the decision was right or wrong. Besides, the impact of a make or buy decision usually lasts beyond the project. Therefore this seems to be a weak choice. The make or buy decision is implemented in executing process group, so it is an implicit input to the executing process group. This is the best choice.

PMBOK reference: (12.1.3.2, pg. 476)

42: C

Project scope and product scope are not the same concepts, but sometimes product scope is considered as included within the project scope. Project scope, not product scope, is the work needed to deliver the product on time, within budget and within scope. Product scope is not a combination of project scopes of smaller components since each component in itself is a product.

PMBOK reference: (Key Concepts for Project Scope Management, pg. 131)

43: B

Project risk acceptance is one of the strategies that may be is the best in certain circumstances but definitely not in all cases. Risk identification whether positive or negative is just one step: identified risks also need to be analyzed, response planned and then implemented. To make risk management effective, risks should continue to be tracked after they have occurred, so that the response strategy can be modified to manage successfully the issues that arise later.

PMBOK reference: (11.7.2.3, pg. 457)

44: B

Looking for the expertise of individuals or specialized groups so that the response plan can be modified to make it more effective will be the most helpful. This is called expert judgment. Interpersonal and team skills may not help much since the plan is not being effective. A change request is not the first thing to be done since the project manager does not know yet how to improve the response. Risk audit will happen later to understand the effectiveness of the risk management process.

PMBOK reference: (11.6.2.1, pg. 451)

45: D

S stands for Supplier in SIPOC (Supplier, Input, Process, Output, Customer). It is a diagramming method that shows the value chain that helps understand many aspects of a process including bottlenecks, sources of errors, costs, delays, etc.

PMBOK reference: (8.1.2.5, pg. 283)

46: D

Understanding where the non-value added work is happening and what are the limitations being faced is done through process analysis. Quality assurance or the quality audit does not uncover non-value added work or limitations being faced, rather it verifies if the company policies and procedures are being followed. Scatter diagram compares two factors against each other and does not address the issues in question.

PMBOK reference: (8.2.2.2, pg. 292)

47: A

Since the penalty for each week of delay is 10,000, the crew must cost less than 10,000 for each week of work. The crew will work 5 days a week so 10,000/5 = 2,000 per day is the maximum the crew should cost.

Since the project will be only 3 weeks late and the penalty per week of delay is 10,000, the total penalty will be 30,000 which is less than the maximum penalty of 60,000. So there is no need to consider the maximum penalty amount. Similarly, since the penalty per week is the same, there is no need to consider the number of weeks of delay to find out the maximum crew cost per day.

PMBOK reference: (9.6.2.1, pg. 356)

48: D

Approve project charter is not a process. Collect Requirements is part of the planning process group. Initiation is what the initiating process group does. Develop Project Charter and Identify Stakeholders are the two processes of the Initiating process group.

PMBOK reference: (Table 1-4, pg. 25)

49: C

Validate Scope process does not ensure project completes on time and within budget. It also does not differentiate between change request work and other deliverables. Though it is concerned with meeting business requirements, it is definitely not involved with realizing business benefits. However, Validate Scope process is about formalizing acceptance of completed project deliverables.

PMBOK reference: (5.5, pg. 162)

50: C

FS = Finish-to-Start

Activity B has an early finish on 5th day but activity E does not start until 8th. So, 8 - 5 = 3.

The lag between activity B and activity E is 3 days.

PMBOK reference: (6.3.2.3, pg. 192)

51: A

Human resources are engaged in the Acquire Resources process. In Develop Team process, the engaged resources start working together as a team. In storming, the project team starts to address the project work as well as the approach to manage the project. There is no such process called as engage resources.

PMBOK reference: (9.3.3.2, pg. 334)

52: A

Negotiation is the quickest and cheapest method of conflict resolution followed by mediation which involves engaging a 3rd party to help come to an agreement. If this fails, then arbitration can be taken up where an arbitrator is appointed and agreed to by both the parties. The decision of the arbitrator is binding. It takes much more time but still gets settled outside the court. The most expensive and time taking technique is

litigation.
PMBOK reference: (12.3.2.2, pg. 497)

53: C
When estimating is done at the activity level and then summed up for the project, it is called bottom-up estimating. When estimating is done at a higher level and distributed down to the activities, it is called top-down estimating. Though expert judgment is used in parametric estimating, it alone cannot make a good estimate. This method will be more reliable when underlying data is highly accurate, parameters can be easily quantifiable, and the model is scaled to the project size.
PMBOK reference: (7.2.2.3, pg. 244 and 7.3.2.4, pg. 253)

54: A
The appropriate action is to solve the problem through a review of the quality plan, the filled checklists, and the problems identified by the design team. Define the problem, identify the root cause, generate solutions, select the best solution, and implement and verify the solution. This is essentially quality assurance which checks the adequacy of quality management processes. Reproducing the documents for 4 departments may fix those documents but does not guarantee that the rest will not have issues. Sharing the checklist with the design team and rejecting the design team's objection do not improve the quality of the documents.
PMBOK reference: (8.2.2.7, pg. 295)

55: B
Constraints are limitations or boundaries and not necessarily difficulties. Assumptions are assumed facts that may or may not be real but are considered to be real. Risks are potential difficulties that may or may not be faced by the project and may not necessarily hinder the team's ability to meet project goals. Issues are the difficulties that are being faced, and that can hinder the project team's ability to achieve project goals.
PMBOK reference: (9.5.1.2, pg. 347 and pg. 709)

56: A
Estimate At Completion (EAC) is the total expense at the end of the project. Hence, it is the sum of Actual Cost (AC) till now and the Estimate To Complete (ETC) the rest of the project work. EV and AC will provide Cost Variance (CV) and Cost Performance Index (CPI). CPI and AC will provide EV and hence CV. Same way CPI, AC, and EV provide CV only. All three wrong choices measure the past performance and do not provide any information regarding the future.
PMBOK reference: (7.4.2.2, pg. 264)

57: D
Verifying that project results comply with relevant quality standards is part of the Control Quality process and not a part of Manage Quality process. Therefore, this is the right choice. All the other three are objectives of the Manage Quality process.
PMBOK reference: (8.2, pg. 288)

58: A
Expert judgment is not an input; it is a tool and technique used to develop the project charter. The other three are input to the Develop Project Charter process.
PMBOK reference: (4.1, pg. 75)

59: B
In the Norming stage, the team members start to understand others' work styles and adjust their work habits for smooth interactions within the team. So in this stage, the team has a better understanding of the work to be performed and a good idea of how the project is to be managed. In the Storming stage, the team members do not trust each other yet. In the Performing stage, the team works like a well-organized unit. There is no stage that is called adjusting.
PMBOK reference: (9.4, pg. 338)

60: B
Alternatives analysis is where multiple approaches may be compared to select the best approach which is then recommended through a corrective action. Cost-benefit analysis is to find out the best corrective action in terms of cost while trend analysis is to forecast future performance. Variance analysis is to compare the planned vs actual progress to find if there is any deviation from the plan.
PMBOK reference: (4.5.2.2, pg. 111)

61: D
Closing processes should not be skipped for any kind of project. This process is an essential part of project management to confirm that the project has delivered what was planned in the benefits management plan. For abandoned and canceled projects, this process helps assess and record the reasons for not completing the project.
PMBOK reference: (4.7, pg. 123)

62: A
For a terminated project, the formal documentation will include the reasons of termination and the procedures for the transfer of both the complete and incomplete deliverables. The lessons learned register updates

happen throughout the project and is not necessarily a project end formal documentation. The documents for the organization to maintain and operate the product or service delivered are the operational and support documents and not the project end documents.

PMBOK reference: (4.7.3.4, pg. 127)

63: A

It is the Administrative Closure procedure in the Close Project or Phase process that addresses the actions and activities required to satisfy the exit criteria for the project or the phase. The Define Scope process establishes the deliverables acceptance criteria while the Validate Scope process, a monitoring and controlling process, is concerned with formal acceptance of deliverables by the sponsor based on the deliverable acceptance criteria. It does not talk about project or phase acceptance. Develop Project Charter process establishes the project or phase exit criteria but is usually at a high level.

PMBOK reference: (4.7, pg. 123)

64: A

The Control Costs process can only happen once a cost baseline has been established otherwise there is nothing against which costs can be compared and controlled. All the other three processes are required in order to establish a cost baseline.

PMBOK reference: (7.3.3.1, pg. 254)

65: A

A change request that fixes the problem by bringing the future performance in line with the project management plan is a corrective action. An action that reduces the probability of negative consequences of risks is a preventive action. A submitted change request can be a corrective action, a preventive action, a defect repair or an update to formally controlled documents. There is no change request defined as a supportive action.

PMBOK reference: (4.3.3.4, pg. 96)

66: D

Project performance baselines are developed in the planning process group while the project charter is developed in the initiating process group which happens before planning starts. The other three choices are used to develop the project charter.

PMBOK reference: (Figure 4-2, pg. 75)

67: C

Compliance of management policies is checked, the effectiveness of implemented risk responses is determined, and change to contingency reserve is analyzed, in the Control Risks process. Risk mitigation strategy is developed in the Plan Risk Response process.

PMBOK reference: (11.7, pg. 454)

68: A

Risks are not certain though these are believed to represent reality. Deadlines and constraints are certain and not just considered certain. Only assumptions are considered to be certain and real though they may be inconsistent, inaccurate, unstable, or incomplete. Hence assumptions is the correct choice.

PMBOK reference: (1.2.6.2, pg. 33 and 11.2.2.3, pg. 415)

69: C

Project planning may take too long when the focus is lost. This can happen if the project manager has weak management skills. There is less chance of developing an aggressive schedule when project team members are directly involved. The team will generally resist building an aggressive schedule. A realistic achievable plan can also be developed by the project manager with minimal involvement from project team members. However, this can be considered an outcome of involving the project team members. When the project team members are involved in project planning, they will know what they are to do, when, and how; this will save a significant amount of project manager's time and makes team members more committed to the project. This is a better and certain choice compared to the other ones.

PMBOK reference: (key concepts..., pg. 309)

70: D

If the approach being taken to develop an industry-leading product is totally new, the quality management plan should be created from scratch by involving subject matter experts and using the techniques like brainstorming. This should be continually updated with involvement of the stakeholders throughout the project. Delaying the plan is out of the question since there is nothing to verify that the work being done is of quality. Using an old plan cannot work effectively as the project has a totally new approach even if the old plan was from a successful product development project. Project team's preferred tests may not be the right tests so this option cannot be the best option.

PMBOK reference: (8.1.2.2, pg. 281)

71: B

The legal settlement is the agreement by both parties on a certain dispute. Close project or phase is too generalized as it deals with the whole project not necessarily with the completion of a contract. Control Procurements is the process where the seller is provided with formal written notice of completion of a legal agreement. There is no process called as Closed Procurements.

PMBOK reference: (12.3.3.1, pg. 499)

72: A

There is no information about the A, B, and C, start time; so it is possible that they start at the same time, staggered, or overlapped. Therefore, the option "Project B should start after project A and Project C after Project B" is incorrect. The work qualifies as project work since it has a definite start and an end, and it will result in a unique product. Therefore it cannot be considered as operational work. Since the deliverables of each phase and the overall project scope are well defined and clear, we can call these as three phases of the project.

PMBOK reference: (Table 1-2, pg. 13)

73: C

Check the quality control measurements taken during quality testing to verify if the deliverables (rivets) are of the correct size. Asking the seller for an explanation or submitting a change request both are incorrect steps without checking if there is actually a deviation from the required size or not. Rejecting the supply also requires a confirmation that there actually is a variation.

PMBOK reference: (8.3.3.1 and 8.3.3.2, pg. 305)

74: D

At any point during project initiating, planning, and executing, whether the project is 50% or more complete or not, once a new stakeholder has been identified, stakeholder register and stakeholder management strategy should be updated. All the other three options are incorrect.

PMBOK reference: (pg. 505 and 13.2, pg. 517)

75: C

These are constraints on the project. In other words, they set a boundary for the project. These cannot be called scope of work or deliverables but these set limitations of when and how work or deliverables are to be completed. These are not assumptions since these are not unknowns being taken as reality. Both assumptions and constraints are recorded on the assumption log.

PMBOK reference: (4.1.3.2, pg. 81)

76: D

I-shaped people are specialists in one domain only while T-shaped people are specialists in one domain and generalists in many others. More T-shaped people on the project means the team can be self-organized and the team members can swarm the tasks and work on various domains.

PMBOK reference: (The Agile Guide, 4.3.3, pg. 42)

77: A

Keeping lessons learned review confidential is detrimental to the project. The document should be distributed to all project stakeholders for their information and feedback. This way the document benefits the stakeholders by improving their understanding of the project and helps the current project with their input. It also incorporates their input to make this document a more effective one for future projects. Publishing lessons learned in the companywide newsletter will not be valuable as only project stakeholders are interested in the project information and they are the one that can contribute to the document. Individual performance review is not a lesson learned objective. Actually, it should never be used for that as team members will be reserved in making suggestions and bringing the issues to light.

PMBOK reference: (4.4.1.5, pg. 102 and 4.4.3.1, pg. 104)

78: B

You have transferred the risk to the insurance company. There is a fixed cost that is the cost of insurance, but this cost will likely be a fraction of the cost incurred due to the delay of work.

PMBOK reference: (11.5.2.7, pg. 445)

79: B

Control Quality process identifies the ways to eliminate causes of unsatisfactory performance because results are compared against the standards and defects are identified in this process. This provides the direction as to how the unsatisfactory performance can be corrected, whether rework is required, etc. There is no process called perform quality performance. Project Quality Management is the knowledge area and not a process. Plan Quality Management process develops the quality management plan in compliance with the organizational policies.

PMBOK reference: (8.3.3.3, pg. 305)

80: C

Implementing the approved changes is done in the Direct and Manage Project Work process. All the other three are done in the Perform Integrated Change Control process.

PMBOK reference: (4.6.2.2, pg. 119)

81: A

Work performance data and earned value measurements are only available once the executing processes start. Since the question is asking about planning processes, the three choices with these two items are incorrect. Hence, the correct choice is reporting formats and control thresholds. These two are among several other items established in the cost management plan based on how the costs are to be managed.

PMBOK reference: (7.1.3.1, pg. 238)

82: B

Tracking cost both ways requires effort and without the knowledge of how much effort is needed; you should not proceed with the change. You also cannot just track costs as requested by the customer, since you need to provide the data for your company's internal use which requires that costs be tracked by resources. A refusal without a valid reason will not be acceptable by the customer. So you should evaluate to find out the cost of complying with customer's demand. This will provide you the knowledge to make a further decision and/or communication. The change request from this exercise will then be reviewed by the change control board.

PMBOK reference: (4.6.2.5, pg. 120)

83: A

The Actual Cost (AC) for 6 months of work = 720,000 while the Planned Value (PV) for the same period is 600,000. There is no Earned Value (EV) information given. In order to find out the Schedule Variance (SV) and the Cost Variance (CV), EV is required. Hence, there is not enough information to determine how the project is doing.

PMBOK reference: (7.4.2.2, pg. 262)

84: A

Establish the cost baseline by including estimates is not an objective of the Control Costs process. The cost baseline is established in the Determine Budget process. All other three are objectives of the Control Costs process.

PMBOK reference: (7.4, pg. 259)

85: D

Ease of use of technology, the project environment, and urgency of the need for information, all can impact the type and frequency of use of communication technology and thus may strongly impact the project. For example, a co-located vs. remote team will impact the type of communication technology in use. The sender/receiver communication model describes the basic communication process irrespective of the technology used. Therefore, it will have no impact or the least impact, if any.

PMBOK reference: (10.1.2.3, pg. 370)

86: D
A deliverable is a unique and verifiable product that is produced by the project team and provided to the customer. The template or the plan can also be a deliverable if it is to be produced by the project team as a unique and verifiable output.
PMBOK reference: (4.7.1.2, pg. 125)

87: C
Project exit criteria are established first in the project charter. It may be elaborated further in the project management plan. Scope statement and business case do not address the exit criteria.
PMBOK reference: (4.1.3.1, pg. 81)

88: A
Rounding up to the nearest 100 means 9,701.34 will be rounded to 9,800. If it is round down to the nearest 100 then the answer is 9,700. If the rounding up is to the nearest thousand then it is 10,000 and round down results in 9,000.
PMBOK reference: (7.1.3.1, pg. 238)

89: C
Stakeholder engagement assessment matrix is not a tool and technique of the Manage Stakeholder Engagement process. All the other three options are tools and techniques of the Manage Stakeholder Engagement process.
PMBOK reference: (Figure 13-7, pg. 523)

90: C
Total work = 400,000 rivets
Total time = 500 days
Work productivity per day = 400,000 / 500 = 800 rivets per day
Work productivity of installer = 40 rivets per day
So, Number of installers = work productivity per day / work productivity of installer
Number of installers = 800 / 40 = 20 installers
PMBOK reference: (9.2.2.4, pg. 324)

91: A
Influence and potential impact of the stakeholders on the project success is analyzed and documented in Identify Stakeholders process. Manage Stakeholders Engagement process is where the stakeholder engagement plan is executed to engage stakeholders while Monitor Stakeholder Engagement process is about checking the effectiveness of the

stakeholder engagement plan and modifying the strategies as needed.

PMBOK reference: (13.1, pg. 507)

92: A

WBS does not contain the list of project activities but only contains work packages created through decomposition. WBS is not used to distribute work to project resources, though it decomposes work to work package level, after which activities can be created, estimated and resources assigned. Also, WBS leads the project team to create project deliverables. WBS is the work decomposed hierarchically to the work package level which can then be further decomposed into activities and assigned to teams and individuals.

PMBOK reference: (5.4, pg. 157)

93: A

The Monitor Risks process is concerned with managing risks and hence does not use earned value management technique. The Direct and Manage Project Work process only measures and provides work performance data and does not use earned value analysis. The Manage Communications process occurs after the earned value technique has been used to understand performance variances and a project performance report has to be communicated to the stakeholders. The Control Schedule process is the right choice since it uses the earned value management technique to understand the performance variances.

PMBOK reference: (6.6.1.1, pg. 224)

94: D

Issue log is not an input to the Control Quality process but rather it is one of the outputs of the process. All the other three are input to the process.

PMBOK reference: (8.3.3.6, pg. 306)

95: A

The project manager will use influencing skill to encourage the nominated risk owners to take the necessary actions and implement risk responses. The nominated risk owner is an individual who has been identified as the owner of a risk. This person is responsible to come up with a risk response plan which is documented in the risk register along with the name of the nominated risk owner. Therefore, using active listening and emotional intelligence is not directly related to encouraging the assigned individuals to take action. Focus groups is a data gathering technique and not an interpersonal & team skill.

PMBOK reference: (11.6.2.2, pg. 451)

96: B

It is to develop a good working relationship with the seller by clarifying the structure of the contract, roles and responsibilities, and other terms. Pressurize the seller to do more work for the same price or push to reduce the price can backfire later even though the seller may agree at the time. So these are not good practices. Terms and conditions were already reviewed and were part of the sellers' proposal. Changing terms at this time will be to bring clarity and make it executable for both the buyer and seller.

PMBOK reference: (12.2.2.5, pg. 488)

97: A

If a completed deliverable is rejected by the sponsor/customer, a change request may be required to fix the defects so that it can be resubmitted for acceptance. Validation of change request completion is part of the integrated change control process. Change requests do not result from acceptance of deliverables but from the rejection of deliverables.

PMBOK reference: (5.5.3.3, pg. 166)

98: A

Explicitly means that constraints and assumptions are clearly defined and implicitly means not directly mentioned but understood well. So defining activities would be considered implicitly in order to ensure the project objectives are met. The deliverables and the WBS are also considered explicitly in this process. Critical path analysis is done at a later stage.

PMBOK reference: (6.2.1.1, pg. 184)

99: D

This is an example of alternatives analysis to understand duration variables to get the work done. There is no need to take any action as the resource outage happened when the resource was not needed but is expected to be back to work when the resource has to start project work. Calling resource to let him know that he needs to return on time is not a prudent choice as it shows apathy. No need for a replacement resource as no work is being affected. Also, there is no need to add contingency to the schedule.

PMBOK reference: (6.4.2.6, pg. 202 and)

100: A

Answering questions of prospective sellers happen during the Conduct Procurements process. During the Control Procurements process, the contract has already been awarded so there are no more prospective sellers. All other three options are part of the Control Procurements process.

PMBOK reference: (12.3, pg. 494)

101: D

Sellers who have failed to deliver in the past may not be responsible for the failure. Hence simply disqualifying a seller based on that may result in losing a well-qualified seller. Fixed price contracts are less risky when the requirements are well-defined and articulated; otherwise shifting the risk to the seller does not mean the project will be successful. Procurement planning starts along with general project management planning. Going through make-or-buy decision is a good practice because it helps analyze what risks are involved in doing the work in-house versus asking the seller to deliver the work. So this is the correct choice.

PMBOK reference: (12.1, pg. 466)

102: D

Instant messaging is not needed for co-located team members. Distributing contact information to the whole team is not too helpful when the team is co-located. Sending the technical team lead for training can be done only if this is a major weakness of that individual but it is irrelevant to the team being co-located or not. Having all team members participate in an offsite event is an excellent way to develop the trust and bring the team members together.

PMBOK reference: (9.4.2.4, pg. 341)

103: B

Government regulations require public invitation to sellers for certain types of contracts. This seems to be the best reason why project manager advertised. The question is asking why to advertise when the project manager has six known reputed sellers. So whether it is the newspaper or internet, the cost of advertising is not the issue. Using advertising to delay the award of the contract is an unethical choice. Best seller would be someone who meets the criteria and from the question, it seems all six meet the criteria.

PMBOK reference: (12.2.2.2, pg. 487)

104: A

The change does not really add value, so you should refuse to upsell something knowing that it is of no value. Honesty requires that no misleading statement is made, no half-truth is stated, and no information is withheld. No need to evaluate budget and schedule impact as you do not recommend this change. Also, this is not scope creep. The scenario actually mentions contacting the customer to extend scope, budget and time which means it will be processed as a change request if agreed to.

PMBOK reference: (PMI's Code of Ethics and Professional Conduct, Section 5.3.1)

105: C

Activity	Planned Value (PV)	Actual Cost (AC)	Earned Value (EV)	CPI	SPI
A	1,200	1,000	1,100	1.1	0.9
B	600	500	600	1.2	1.0
C	300	300	300	1.0	1.0
D	1,800	2,000	1,800	0.9	1.0

As shown in the table, activity B and C, both are on time and within budget but activity B is doing better on the budget compared to activity C. So Activity B is the right answer.
PMBOK reference: (7.4.2.2, pg. 263)

106: A
Expected monetary value (EMV), for each option that was evaluated, is the output of decision tree analysis. This information can be used to decide the best course of action. Expected monetary value is not the cost of managing the risk.
PMBOK reference: (11.4.2.5, pg. 435)

107: A
Strategic planning does not provide a list of individual projects. It lists the overall goals of the organization along with the high-level approach to achieve these goals. It may furnish the list of milestones and activities of the project. Portfolio planning is more about the approach portfolio management is taking and what is the necessary communication that needs to take place. Program planning, on the other hand, tracks the interdependencies and progress of program components that includes all related projects. Therefore, this is the right choice.
PMBOK reference: (Table 1-2, pg. 13)

108: A
Noise is something that either distracts the receiver of the information or creates obscurity in the message when it is being received. In other words, it interferes with the understanding of the message by the receiver. Noise does not change the message but it impacts the understanding of the message. Noise can be persistent or occasional, it can affect both ways. The noise in the question is the one discussed in communication models and not just the physical noise.
PMBOK reference: (10.1.2.4, pg. 373)

109: D

Alternative resources must meet the mandatory criteria if any. When the desired resources are not available, lower or different competencies may be acceptable, the training plan may need to be modified to accommodate them, and the cost may be different.

PMBOK reference: (9.3, pg. 330)

110: B

Manage Stakeholder Engagement does not involve tracking the team member's performance. Neither Monitoring and Controlling nor Develop Team processes track performance or provide feedback to the team member. Manage Team is the executing process where team member performance is tracked and feedback is provided as well as issues are resolved.

PMBOK reference: (9.5, pg. 345)

111: D

Pre-acquisition, Multi-criteria decision analysis, and negotiation are the tools and techniques of the Acquire Resources process. Networking is not one of the tools or techniques although it may indirectly have an impact when using the Acquire Resources process tools and techniques.

PMBOK reference: (9.3.2, pg. 332)

112: D

A project team should not focus on delivering more than what the stakeholders are expecting because of three main reasons. One, the value of extra functionality or additional delivery is very little in the eyes of the stakeholders because they believe they do not need it. Second, trying to deliver extra can backfire by putting the in-scope work at risk of being late, over budget, or prone to defects, and three, more focus on exceeding expectations means the other three choices mentioned may not get full attention which can result in increased risk.

PMBOK reference: (13.3, pg. 524)

113: D

Negotiation, observation/conversation, political awareness, and a few other techniques are interpersonal skills used for managing stakeholder engagement. Decision making is a technique used for planning stakeholder engagement but not for managing stakeholder engagement.

PMBOK reference: (13.3.2.3, pg. 527)

114: A

The method you used for the estimate along with other information forms the basis of estimates. The estimation method provides a clear understanding of how the resource estimate was established. Scope baseline is an input to the Estimate Activity Resources process and helps in identifying resource requirements. Resource breakdown structure is the hierarchical representation of resources. Your estimate is independent of the software used so this information does not improve understanding of the estimate.

PMBOK reference: (9.2.3.2, pg. 326)

115: A

Scope addition means a change request has to be processed and approved; therefore such communication should be formally written. Instant messaging is an informal written communication so cannot be considered for the purpose of a change request. Formal or informal verbal communication and informal written communication are inappropriate in this situation.

PMBOK reference: (Key concepts for project communications management, pg. 360 and 10.3.3.2, pg. 393)

116: A

Preventive action is an intentional activity that ensures the future performance of the project work is aligned with the project management plan. In other words, it reduces the chances of negative outcomes of the actions. An activity that can help improve the performance back to the desired state is a corrective action. The other two options are illogical statements.

PMBOK reference: (4.3.3.4, pg. 96)

117: D

Lessons learned during the project are transferred to the lessons learned repository as part of the project closure in Close Project or Phase process. Lessons learned register is created in the Manage Project Knowledge process and updated in Direct and Manage Project Work and Monitor and Control Project Work process.

PMBOK reference: (4.7.3.4, pg. 128)

118: A

The roles and responsibilities should be clearly defined and documented in the change management plan. This helps in going through the process smoothly without any lost time. CCB is not part of the project manager's role and responsibilities so should not be included there. There is no need to have detailed contact information of all CCB members. Usually, CCB meetings and reviews are initiated by an assigned member who receives the change request for review and approval. Having the CCB on the intranet is only one way of making it accessible. Depending on the organization's

information system, CCB meetings could be held online/virtual or face-to-face.
PMBOK reference: (4.6.2.5, pg. 120)

119: A
The creation of the statement of work, which includes identifying deliverables that can be achieved through sellers, happens in the Plan Procurement Management process so the project manager must be in Plan Procurement Management process. The Control Procurements process follows the Conduct Procurements process which follows the Plan Procurement Management process.
PMBOK reference: (12.1.2.3, pg. 473)

120: A
Autocratic decision making is a technique where one individual takes responsibility for making decisions for the group. Therefore there is no voting involved in this technique. All the other techniques are voting techniques.
PMBOK reference: (5.2.2.4, pg. 144)

121: D
An activity with zero float is a critical activity.
Float = late finish - early finish.
So activity X has a float of 4, activity T has a float of 6, activity F has a float of 3 and activity M has zero float. Therefore, activity M is a critical activity.
PMBOK reference: (6.5.2.2, pg. 210)

122: A
The resource availability information goes into a resource calendar and not in the activity attributes. Therefore updating the resource calendar is the correct choice. Schedule baseline will need to be modified only if the four weeks of absence will affect the project and a change request in this regard has been approved. Same is the case with the critical path; no change unless the baselines are affected. The question does not provide any other information regarding the impact of the resource vacation on the baselines. So asking the resource not to take the vacation is a weak choice as there could be many factors that may affect the baselines.
PMBOK reference: (9.3.3.3, pg. 334)

123: C
Develop Schedule process will be least impacted by the scope and cost of the project. This is because their impact has already been taken care of by the estimating process. Constraints have to be considered explicitly so that everyone is clear of the limitations. Lead time and lag time will have an

impact on schedule development but they can only result in zero or positive float. Forced milestones and external deadlines will add constraints into the schedule and can create zero, positive, or negative float. So this is the best choice.

PMBOK reference: (6.5.2.2, pg. 209)

124: A

Risks are what may happen not what will happen. If you are certain something will happen then it is not a risk but rather an issue. It may not have happened in the previous projects but can happen in this project. It is obvious that the Identify Risks process identifies risks to the project. But this is a weak answer.

PMBOK reference: (11.2, pg. 409)

125: C

Management by walking around (MBWA) is not directly about quality but mainly about motivating employees. Hence the project quality management area does not include MBWA concepts. Total Quality Management (TQM), Lean Six Sigma, and Plan-Do-Check-Act (PDCA) by Shewhart, all relate to quality.

PMBOK reference: (Trends..., pg. 275)

126: B

An assumption is something that is believed to be true without any proof that it is true. Among the four options, there are three assumptions viz. the entire team is fluent in the English language, all resources are technically competent, and costs in all countries are within budget. Only the entire team's fluency in English is an assumption related to communications planning. The others are related to resources and cost planning. Team members acquired in various geographical locations is not an assumption but a fact.

PMBOK reference: (Tailoring considerations, pg. 365)

127: D

Each project is unique and so are the stakeholder's expectations and needs. So the plan should be used as a template and modified to fit the current project. Project quality management plan is the responsibility of the project manager and not the customer. Creating a new plan from scratch will result in a lot of unnecessary effort which can be saved by using the old plan as a template.

PMBOK reference: (8.1.1.5 and 8.1.2.2, pg. 281)

128: C

Once the bid solicitation process is completed, the contract is awarded to the selected contractor. 'Advertisement' is a tool used in the bid solicitation process. Creation of qualified sellers' list happens before bid solicitation starts. Prospective sellers' proposals are received during the bid solicitation process.

PMBOK reference: (12.2.1.4, pg. 486)

129: C

Team building, communications, and conflict resolution all three are challenging when team members are not colocated. Reporting would be the least challenging among the four choices because it follows a set process and involves comparatively less soft skills than the other three choices.

PMBOK reference: (9.3.2.4, pg. 333)

130: C

Installing an electric outlet is part of the scope so adding another outlet is adding additional work to the scope of the project. Since no information has been given whether integrated change control process is being followed or not, this request will account to adding unauthorized scope and hence will result in scope creep. There is no mention of cost or schedule so both cost overrun and schedule delay are incorrect choices. Micro-management is a relative term and since there is no mention of what and how the project was to be managed, it cannot be considered micro-managed when a scope addition is requested.

PMBOK reference: (5.6, pg. 168)

131: D

The affinity diagram is a data representation technique. All the other options are product analysis techniques.

PMBOK reference: (5.3.2.5, pg. 153)

132: C

For the Collect Requirements process, data representation techniques include mind mapping and affinity diagrams methods since both involve visual presentation. Data gathering includes brainstorming, interviews, focus groups, and a few others. Data analysis involves document analysis, while interpersonal and team skills include nominal group technique, observation, facilitation, and others.

PMBOK reference: (5.2, pg. 138)

133: C

It is a detailed description of the procurement items so that the sellers can come up with a good estimate for time and cost and check if they are capable of providing the product or service. Terms and conditions (T&C) of the procurement are separate from the statement of work (SOW). T&C

provide how the work defined in the SOW is to be performed. Project charter defines work at a very high summary level. The project statement of work usually refers to the scope statement and may or may not be the same as the procurement statement of work.

PMBOK reference: (12.1.3.4, pg. 477)

134: B

Risk mitigation planning comes after risks have been analyzed. The risk register is an input and an output for recording risks, and it is not used for analyzing the risks. Customer's experience is of value but cannot be the tool and technique that can be used in isolation. Expert judgment includes customer's experience and the project team's experience, so this is the best choice.

PMBOK reference: (11.3.2.2, pg. 422)

135: D

Project quality report identifies where the project plan does not follow company policies and procedures. The executive report is a very general term but may refer to project status report prepared for the executive audience. The project performance report provides the status of the project's progress. Project problems report may only show measurements compared against the project standards.

PMBOK reference: (8.2.2.5, pg. 294 and 8.2.3.1, pg. 296)

136: C

A control chart is the best tool for this purpose as it shows the measurements and deviation from acceptable limits. Fishbone diagram and Pareto Chart are used to identify the root cause of an issue and major issues respectively. Scatter diagram shows the relationship between two factors and does not show up against a standard.

PMBOK reference: (8.3.2.5, pg. 304)

137: B

In a large project, project management team plans most of the project and the kick-off meeting is done at the start of executing. In a small project, the whole project team is involved in project planning and so kick-off meeting is held at the start of planning processes. It is not a good idea that only the project manager plans the project. Involving the project team in the planning processes improves the quality of the plan.

PMBOK reference: (4.2.2.4, pg. 86)

138: B

Cost Variance (CV) = Earned Value (EV) - Actual Cost (AC)
Since both EV and AC are known, CV can be calculated as follows:

CV = 24,000 - 19,500 = +4,500
PMBOK reference: (7.4.2.2, pg. 262)

139: D
Finish-to-Start is the most common activity to activity relationship used. In fact, some schedules, if not needed to be fast tracked, are built entirely with this relationship.
PMBOK reference: (6.3.2.1, pg. 190)

140: A
The three-point estimation is an estimation technique that is not directly used for forecasting project budget at completion. The other three techniques of earned value management are used for this purpose.
PMBOK reference: (7.4.2.2, pg. 265)

141: C
Spelling errors: Both activities mentioned are quality control activities.

Nuts counting: Counting nuts being produced is work performance data, and counting the defects is quality control activity.

Book title printing: Both represent the same activity which is a quality control activity.

Wheel diameter: Measuring the diameter of the wheel to see if it is within limits is quality control activity but making sure that the limits set are correct is a manage quality activity. This is the correct choice.
PMBOK reference: (8.2.1.2, pg. 291)

142: B
The technique that represents data by visually organizing information about stakeholders and their relationships with each other and the organization is called mind mapping. Salience model classifies stakeholders based on power, urgency, and legitimacy. Stakeholder cube used three different factors to classify stakeholders like power, interest, influence, and impact. Stakeholder engagement assessment matrix shows the current and desired level of engagement of stakeholders.
PMBOK reference: (13.2.2.5, pg. 521)

143: C
Since additional resources are available that can be engaged by the project, you should crash the schedule. Fast tracking would be running activities in parallel. This increases risk compared to crashing the schedule. Resource leveling usually results in extending the schedule. Estimating activity resources is irrelevant in this case.
PMBOK reference: (6.5.2.6, pg. 215)

144: D
Both of these are examples of project records. With regards to communications, project records include all documents that describe and explain the project and any method of physical or electronic organization of such documents/information. Both items can also be the project deliverables if these are defined as such in the scope statement. The memos are usually for the purpose of internal communication but meeting minutes can be created for internal and external meetings. Information management systems are the facilities, processes, and procedures used to collect, store, and distribute information.
PMBOK reference: (10.2.3.4, pg. 388)

145: A
Project team members' performance will be best when they understand their roles and responsibilities, and their individual authority level matches the responsibilities. A project manager's experience, technical expertise of the team and co-location may not be much effective without it.
PMBOK reference: (9.1.3.1, pg. 318)

146: C
This is an example of expert power where a project manager asks for your advice because he believes that you have the knowledge and experience to guide him well. There is no indication of formal, relational, or ingratiating power display in this scenario.
PMBOK reference: (3.4.4.3, pg. 63)

147: C
The documentation of the acceptance of deliverables also occurs in the Validate Scope process. This formal documentation is sent to the Close Project or Phase which occurs after completion of deliverable acceptance. Control Procurements is for deliverables completed by the seller under a contract only. So this cannot be the complete answer. Manage quality process is unrelated to deliverable acceptance.
PMBOK reference: (5.5.3.1, pg. 166)

148: A
The question asks about increasing the acceptance of deliverables, not speeding up the acceptance of deliverables. Therefore, offering a discount on fees for quick deliverable acceptance is a wrong choice.
The deliverables are accepted when they appear to meet the requirements. The clearer it shows that they meet the acceptance criteria, the higher the chances that the deliverables will be accepted. So sending a written request to accept deliverables does not impact the appearance of meeting acceptance criteria.

Stakeholders cannot define deliverables without intervention and help by the project team since the project team is the one that has to agree to and complete the deliverables. So this is a weak choice.

Involving stakeholders during initiating increases the understanding of both the project deliverables and their acceptance criteria; this includes all stakeholders and the project team. This has a direct impact on the acceptance of deliverables because stakeholders have a clearer understanding of what is being delivered and how it meets the criteria.

PMBOK reference: (Key concepts for project scope management, pg. 131)

149: C

Work performance reports' is the input to the Manage Team process. It is created from work performance information which is generated from work information data. There is no such thing as work performance standards in this context.

PMBOK reference: (Figure 9-12, pg. 345)

150: D

No matter what the project is, the project or project phase is authorized to proceed in the Develop Project Charter process. Though the Develop Project Charter process is part of the initiating process group, it is a better choice since it is more specific than the initiating process group. The other two choices are incorrect.

PMBOK reference: (4.1, pg. 75)

151: C

The reason there can be a wide difference between bids is that each prospective seller has a different understanding of the statement of work and terms and conditions. Both of these documents should be evaluated if these are clear enough and provide the same understanding of the work to all prospective sellers. Awarding the contract to the lowest bidder may be asking for trouble later as the lowest bidder may not have a good understanding of the work. Canceling a bid and re-advertising is a lengthy and expensive process. Without knowing what caused current variations, you may end up with the same situation again. Who is the best supplier? The one who has the best understanding of the work and has the capability to deliver it. The price difference is big and it will be almost impossible to determine who the best bidder is.

PMBOK reference: (12.2.2.4, pg. 487)

152: B

It will be quicker to ask for help from others and easier to get the needed information than trying to figure out which terms to search to get that information. The challenge is finding the right keywords; once the correct keywords are known then the search will be quick and simple. The situation does not say anything about the team member's web search skills so that is an incorrect answer. Lessons learned register will not help in this case.

PMBOK reference: (4.4.2.3, pg. 103)

153: B

Providing the name and contact information on the white paper gives an opportunity for the reader to contact the project manager and ask for advice. This is an example of interaction. A web-based learning course may or may not have any interaction element with it. Circulating monthly journal among team members and archiving lessons learned in the repository do not have any interaction element to it though both are part of information management.

PMBOK reference: (4.4.2.3, pg. 103)

154: C

The bidders' conference is held in the Conduct Procurements process which includes inviting sellers to bid for the work and awarding the contract. Plan Procurement Management happens before bids are invited and Control Procurements happens after the bid has been awarded. There is no process called as Close Procurements.

PMBOK reference: (12.2.2.3, pg. 487)

155: B

The organization must have a high cost of quality. Remember that the cost of quality includes both the cost of conformance and the cost of non-conformance. So significant effort and money are being spent to achieve a high quality. This can happen when the investment in quality is more than the optimal cost of quality.

Low cost of quality will result in low quality so this is an incorrect choice. Project schedule's robustness does not generally impact the quality. Using a standard quality management plan alone cannot guarantee quality. It is what is in the plan that counts more than whether a standard plan is used or not.

PMBOK reference: (8.1.2.3, pg. 281)

156: C

Review and update the stakeholder engagement assessment matrix and then track changes in the level of engagement. She already knows that it is a stakeholder engagement problem. So fix that first, and then if there still are problems, an audit can be used as a tool to uncover those. Informing stakeholders of what has been missing without a plan as to how this will be fixed is a bad idea and will just reduce stakeholder satisfaction and confidence in the project manager. First, issue log is updated by the project team, not all stakeholders. So sending an email to stakeholders does not make much sense in this regard. Besides this step will not produce any results to fix the issue at hand.

PMBOK reference: (13.4.2.3, pg. 534)

157: C

Absolutely. Completed deliverables should be validated at the end of each phase before the project moves to the next phase. You do not need the sponsor's approval since this is an essential part of deliverable completion. Even though the customer may or may not have been reviewing deliverables as these were being completed, these still need to be formally accepted by the sponsor/customer. Deliverables due in a phase are accepted by the customer and mostly handed over at the end of that phase. In this case, if the customer is asking for that, then there is no reason to delay until the end of the project. Earlier validation of deliverables will result in lower cost of changes if identified.

PMBOK reference: (5.5, pg. 163)

158: B

Leading the project team to achieve project objectives is always the responsibility of the project manager. Prioritizing projects based on business need is usually done by the portfolio management team. Writing performance reports for project resources is mostly done by functional managers. Meeting the project's profit margin is only valid when working for an external customer.

PMBOK reference: (3.2, pg. 52)

159: A

The processes, policies, and procedures of the organization are the organizational process assets. The question is asking about the process and not the approval requirement; so government requirement, which is an enterprise environmental factor, is a wrong choice. A program is a group of related projects managed in a coordinated way to obtain benefits.

PMBOK reference: (2.3, pg. 39)

160: D

Impact/Influence grid is a data representation technique used for classifying the stakeholders after they have been identified. This happens in the Identify Stakeholders process.

PMBOK reference: (13.1.2.4, pg. 512)

161: C

Implement strategy in a way to maximize value is a strategic and business management skill and not a technical project management skill. All other choices are technical project management skills.

PMBOK reference: (3.4.2 and 3.4.3, pg. 58)

162: A

Risk register updates and corrective action in the form of a change request, are the output of the process. Contingent response strategies, if being referred to contingency planning, is an output of the Plan Risk Response process. Audits is the tool and technique used in Monitor Risks process.

PMBOK reference: (11.7, pg. 453)

163: A

The five stages of team development in the Tuckman ladder, in order, are: Forming, Storming, Norming, Performing, and Adjourning. The other three choices are incorrect as storming happens before norming and there is no such stage called adjusting.

PMBOK reference: (9.4, pg. 338)

164: D

Since the problem has already occurred this has become an issue and is no longer a risk so it should be treated as an issue. This is true but a weak answer. The best way to handle is to evaluate the impact of this issue on performance baselines and proceed further from there. Of course, the expectation is that appropriate communication has occurred so that the next shipment does not end up on the wrong side. It is of no value to have this added to the risk register, analyzed and response planned since it has already occurred. The contingency reserve is not for unplanned risk; it is set up and used for planned risks.

PMBOK reference: (11.6.3.1, pg. 451)

165: D

Engaging a seller through a contract is a time consuming and expensive process so canceling the contract for a missed deliverable is not prudent without giving notification and a chance to the seller to correct the issue. Similarly, issuing a warning before any communication on missed deliverable seems too aggressive and can damage the relationship. The creation of the interview schedule is the responsibility of the seller and as such should be created by the seller to avoid unnecessary complications. The best choice is to ask the seller to stop the work and submit the schedule for approval. Once the schedule is approved, the work can be restarted based on the schedule. This is usually done as part of the inspection.

PMBOK reference: (12.3.2.4, pg. 498)

166: A

The project management office is an organization, so this cannot be the correct answer. The integrated change control system is to manage the change requests, not the schedules, so this is incorrect. Organizational process assets include processes, procedures and knowledge base, so this is also not the right choice. Enterprise environmental factors include the organization's information technology software. Since desktop scheduling software falls under information technology software, this is the best answer.

PMBOK reference: (2.2.1, pg. 38)

167: B

Monitor Risks process is where risks are monitored whether residual or not. This process also ensures that any new risk identified is recorded on the risk register and analyzed. Identify Risks and Plan Risk Management processes do not include monitoring residual risks. So these two options are incorrect. There is no process called as residual risk management.

PMBOK reference: (11.7, pg. 454)

168: C

It is the project team's responsibility to ensure that products or services, acquired from the seller under a contract, meet the needs of the project and also comply with business policies of the buyer. Procurement department ensures that the contract is sound, valid, and executable. The project sponsor is minimally involved with procurements. The seller is only responsible for delivering the products or services under the contract and cannot be held responsible for whether these meet the needs of the project.

PMBOK reference: (Key concepts..., pg. 461)

169: C

In the cause-and-effect diagram, problems or potential problems are linked to the factors. The effects are linked to the causes. So this is the best choice. In process analysis, non-value added work is identified. Through the Pareto chart, highest occurring problems are identified. Quality assurance checks compliance against the company's quality policies.

PMBOK reference: (8.2.2.4, pg. 293)

170: A

Development approach helps in the selection of the scheduling approach, scheduling model, estimation methods, and scheduling tools. The scheduling management plan, which is the output of the process, addresses

all the other three choices.
PMBOK reference: (6.1.1.2, pg. 180)

171: B
Aggressive scheduling means the project manager is crashing and fast tracking the schedule which will likely increase the risk. Tight budget means the cost overrun risk has also increased. So it will be correct to say he is seeking risks or taking on more risks.
PMBOK reference: (6.5.2.6, pg. 215 and 11.1.3.1, pg. 406)

172: D
The control chart and statistical sampling are quality control tools and techniques. Benchmarking is a quality planning technique. Problem solving is the best choice which can help determine the best solutions to solve the identified problems.
PMBOK reference: (8.2.2.7, pg. 295)

173: A
Inflating task estimates is a bad practice as it hides the actual estimate and thus weakens the control. Threatening that you will not manage the project will likely result in your removal from the project and maybe even from the organization. The purpose of the contingency reserve is to provide funds for known risks. A high reserve will raise eyebrows and unnecessary questions and will require justification. With a 25% of budget added to contingency, it will be extremely difficult to justify. The actual cost estimate should be presented with a brief that provides an explanation of what will be the impact on the project if the budget is cut.
PMBOK reference: (7.3.3.1, pg. 254)

174: A
The biggest benefit of colocation that is lost is the concept and feeling of a team. Instant messaging and daily conference calls may help with reporting but will have minimal impact on that lost benefit of colocation. Coming in once a week can definitely help with team building but may be difficult to manage as all team members have to come to the office on the same day. This may also involve expense on a continuing basis which could be a constraint. The most productive step will be to bring the team members together and develop a collaborative environment. Bringing them together for an offsite event will help them socialize with each other and develop a relationship. This is, therefore, the best choice.
PMBOK reference: (9.4.2.4, pg. 341)

175: B
A business case, project requirements document, and project scope

statement do not include a summary milestone schedule. Only project charter documents the summary milestone schedule so this is the correct choice.

PMBOK reference: (4.1.3.1, pg. 81)

176: C

To build a new system is definitely project work so it cannot be considered operational work. Several projects can be directed at different aspects of the information system, where some deliverables may be well defined and others require an agile approach. Hence, a hybrid approach may work well. Since the overall building of the system has a very specific outcome already defined, this is a large project with various sub-projects and should not be considered as a program.

PMBOK reference: (The Agile Guide 3.1.10, pg. 29)

177: B

Changes that are requested but the buyer and seller cannot agree on the change being within or out of scope and/or they disagree about the value of the change are called contested changes or claims. These are not enterprise environmental factors. A change can be a preventive or a corrective action or even a defect repair, but the question is asking about changes not agreed to by both buyer and seller.

PMBOK reference: (12.3.2.2, pg. 497)

178: C

The company should select the new product development project because it has the highest internal rate of return of 25 percent. Higher the internal rate of return, the better it is.

PMBOK reference: (1.2.6.4, pg. 34)

179: B

Activities cannot be summed up in milestones since milestones have zero duration and zero cost associated with them. WBS work packages cannot be called milestones; instead, these are chunks of work to produce the deliverables. Milestones may be required in a schedule if requested as part of the contract otherwise a valid schedule can be developed without milestones. Milestones can be a requirement of the sponsor to track project's progress in definite terms.

PMBOK reference: (6.2.3.3, pg. 186)

180: C

The increase in the number of stakeholders is not a strong enough reason to change the communication technology in use. Having new team members located in a different country when the whole team was colocated will likely require the use of different technology for communications. A new regulation regarding data privacy may necessitate a change in the type of technology being used for communication to secure the data. A new document management system deployed by the organization will also likely require everyone to use this new system for the distribution, storage, retrieval, and management of documents.

PMBOK reference: (10.2.2.1, pg. 383)

181: A

A project manager has low authority in a weak matrix organization but carries little to none authority in an organic, functional, and multi-divisional organization.

PMBOK reference: (Table 2-1, pg. 47)

182: A

The project manager manages the project and thus cannot be the one who authorizes it. The project management office, sponsor, program manager, and portfolio manager can initiate and authorize the project depending on the process established for this purpose in an organization.

PMBOK reference: (4.1, pg. 77)

183: B

She is comparing how much contingency reserve is left and what is the amount of the remaining risks on the project. Just finding out how much has been spent and how much reserve is remaining does not provide any value. Comparison of spend on managing risks versus other spends or contingency reserve spend versus management reserve spend is not part of reserve analysis and does not provide any real insight to help in risk management.

PMBOK reference: (11.7.2.1, pg. 456)

184: C

Proposal evaluation criteria are established in the Plan Procurement Management process. Contract negotiation happens in the Conduct Procurements process. Litigation is not the main tool used in the Control Procurements process as it happens in very few cases. The main tool and technique is inspection which is the structured review of the work done by the seller so this is the main tool and technique used in this process.

PMBOK reference: (12.3.2.4, pg. 498)

185: B

Activity	Duration	Predecessor	Cost of Activity	Cost of Crashing (per day)	Max Days it can be Crashed
A	7		2,000	200	0
B	9	A	3,000	200	2
C	8	B	2,000	300	2
D	9	C	4,000	300	3
E	5	C	3,000	500	3
F	4	D,E	1,000	100	0

Critical Path is 37 days. So crashing the schedule by seven days can be achieved by crashing activities B, C, D (2+2+3) for a cost of (2 x 200 + 2 x 300 + 3 x 300) = 1,900.

PMBOK reference: (6.5.2.6, pg. 215)

186: B

Refactoring is to improve the design of the product by enhancing its maintainability and other characteristics. This design improvement will reduce the technical debt which is the cost of non-conformance. The iterations are timeboxed while the user stories are already being created. So both of these will have no impact on reducing technical debt. A burn-down chart shows the amount of work left against the remaining time.

PMBOK reference: (The Agile Guide, Table 5-1, pg. 58)

187: B

This is work performance data that can be analyzed using various techniques. Quality audits are usually performed by a 3rd party but in any case, a formal report is produced after the audit. Time and cost estimations happen during the planning process and do not include measurements from quality tests or how much work has been completed.

PMBOK reference: (4.3.3.2, pg. 95)

188: B

The best use of Estimate At Completion (EAC) and Estimate To Complete (ETC) is for forecasting. These can be derived from schedule performance data and/or cost performance data. These do have some value in the lessons learned but their most beneficial use is as a forecast.

PMBOK reference: (7.4.2.2, pg. 264)

189: A
Upcoming regulation changes may complicate approval of the flying car design is an example of ambiguity risks. All the other options are examples of variability risks which are related to variations in various factors related to project.
PMBOK reference: (Non-event risks, pg. 398)

190: C
Crashing non-critical tasks will not help in schedule compression so the focus should be to crash the critical tasks only. Crashing the tasks that have the highest costs has no impact on schedule compression especially if the tasks are not on the critical path. Besides cost is not an issue so this cannot be the best choice.
PMBOK reference: (6.5.2.6, pg. 215)

191: C
Three point estimation is a technique used for time estimation and not for schedule control. All other three are tools and techniques of the Control Schedule process.
PMBOK reference: (Figure 6-22, pg. 222)

192: B
Work performance report is not an input but rather an output of the Monitor and Control Project Work process. All the other three are input project documents to the process.
PMBOK reference: (4.5.1.2, pg. 108)

193: A
Standard Deviation (SD) = (Pessimistic - Optimistic) /6
SD = (24 - 12) / 6 = 2
PMBOK reference: (6.4.2.4, pg. 201)

194: D
Bidders' conference happens in the Conduct Procurements process. Statement of work is created and contract terms are defined in the Plan Procurement Management process. Managing the contractual relationship between the buyer and seller is what happens in the Control Procurements process.
PMBOK reference: (12.3, pg. 491)

195: B
The first thing you should do is evaluate the impact of resource capability on project cost and schedule. After that, you can either request for more resources or submit a change request since you now know what

needs to be done to achieve project goals. You can also speak with the buyer to alleviate his concerns because you now know what the impact is and how you will manage it. The question does not say if the cost of engaged resources is less than planned so the choice of asking to submit a change request cannot be the first thing to be done.

PMBOK reference: (9.5.3.1, pg. 350)

196: D

Manage Communications is part of the executing process group. There is no process called Monitor and Control Communications or Control Communications. Only Monitor Communications is part of the monitoring and controlling process group.

PMBOK reference: (10.3, pg. 388 and Table 1-4, pg. 25)

197: C

You are upset because the scope control process was not followed. Though the decision may seem good it may have repercussions later on because neither complete review and analysis was performed nor its impact on all other project deliverables was considered. Reduced profit and exclusion from decision making are wrong reasons to be upset. Deliverables can be changed once baselined but only through following the integrated change control process.

PMBOK reference: (5.6, pg. 168)

198: B

The schedule management plan will provide the guideline and criteria to create and manage the project schedule. Schedule baseline is the end result of creating schedule. The resource management plan is about managing resources, not schedule. There is no such plan as an activity management plan.

PMBOK reference: (6.1.3.1, pg. 182)

199: D

"If I do not get the document from you within two days, I will speak with your manager." The project manager is using coercive power to get the work done. Complaint to the manager may bring the issue of resource's performance.

"I want you to complete this report by end of tomorrow." This statement is made where there is a formal power in play.

"Should I meet in person or just send her an email. Which is the right approach?" Here the project manager is relying on the expert judgment of the resource.

"Come on. You know you owe me. Get me the report tomorrow." This is an example of use of guilt-based power by the project manager.

PMBOK reference: (3.4.4.3, pg. 63)

200: D

The project resources that are being charged to the project should be fully included in the budget. Some resources working on the project may not get charged against the project. It is possible that the expense may be coming out of an operational budget while the resource is partially working on the project. Same is the case of equipment; the equipment used on the project may be expensed from an operational budget. Payments made to the vendor for the contract work done for the project, and included in the statement of work to be paid from project budget, will be part of the budget. But the statement "All payments made to the vendor" is vague and can include any expense. For example, annual license fee paid to the vendor may come out of operational budget rather than the project budget.

PMBOK reference: (7.2, pg. 241)

Daud Nasir, PMP

6 - ANSWERS & EXPLANATIONS TEST 2

201: A

Preferential logic/discretionary dependencies can create arbitrary float values and if not fully documented will make it difficult to modify the schedule. All the other options are made up terms.

PMBOK reference: (6.3.2.2, pg. 191)

202: C

When a deliverable has not been accepted, document the reasons and submit a defect repair change request. As per the contract, the project team has to complete the deliverable that satisfies the acceptance criteria. Finger pointing at who is responsible for failed deliverable will just result in wastage of time. There is no need to review the relevant term if the project manager already agrees with buyer's interpretation.

PMBOK reference: (5.5.3.3, pg. 166)

203: B

The project management plan is neither an input nor an output of the Develop Project Charter process. A project charter is an output of the process which then becomes input to the Develop Project Management Plan process where the project management plan is created. Agreements and business case are input to the Develop Project Charter process.

PMBOK reference: (Figure 4-2, pg. 75)

204: D

Team development needs to happen in any environment or organizational structure. Even a team working together in operational role needs to be developed because new challenges and issues arise all the time, which require that some effort is spent on further developing or re-developing the team. When the whole team reports to one functional manager, it becomes much easier and simpler to manage the team development as the functional manager is well aware of the needs and strengths of each team member. Comparatively, in a project-oriented organization, though the whole team reports to one project manager, the team itself is together only for the project and sometimes a few projects. This makes team development more challenging due to the temporary nature of the roles.

PMBOK reference: (Table 2-1, pg. 47 and 9.4, pg. 337)

205: A

Risk response is not a type of risk attitude shown by the organizations. It is the result of showing an attitude represented by the other three choices.

PMBOK reference: (11.1.3.1, pg. 407)

206: B

Fixed price contract is most commonly used when the product specifications are well defined and detailed. Time and material contract is commonly used when outside help is needed with an internal project. Time lapsed would be a time and material contract if defined as a contract. In cost reimbursable contracts, the scope is expected to go through significant change during the project life cycle.

PMBOK reference: (12.1.1.6, pg. 471)

207: C

The purpose of a quality audit is to identify what needs to improve and how improvements can be made. It does not pinpoint individual performance or provide material for performance evaluation. Therefore, the best option is to explain to the team that it will benefit the project and the team, by identifying which policies and procedures are ineffective and inefficient.

PMBOK reference: (8.2.2.5, pg. 294)

208: A

As the project progresses from initiating to planning to executing to closing, the stakeholders' influence keeps reducing. This is because the cost of making a change keeps on increasing as the project progresses. The stage where most of the budget is spent and maximum resources are engaged is the executing stage. The level of influence stakeholders can exert in the executing stage as compared to initiating and planning stage has reduced.

PMBOK reference: (1.5, pg. 549)

209: A

Scope management plan details how the work breakdown structure will be created while the requirements management plan describes which traceability structure will be used. The scope management plan also defines how the deliverables will be accepted and how the scope baseline will be approved. The requirements management plan discusses how the user requirements will be collected and which traceability structure will be used.

PMBOK reference: (5.1.3, pg. 137)

210: A

Assessment of the team's performance on the project can help identify which training may be needed to improve the team's effectiveness and performance. An Individual team member's performance contributes to the overall performance of the project in general but stating that collective performance of all individuals is the project performance is misleading as there are many other factors that play a role in establishing a project's performance. 3rd party project appraisals or audit are focused on project performance, not individual's performance.

PMBOK reference: (9.4.3.1, pg. 343)

211: B

Team building activities should not be work-related. In most cases, it will develop a feeling that the team members are being tricked to do more work in the name of team building and this can be damaging to the team building itself. The purpose of team building is to improve social relations and collaboration among team members and can be taken up formally as an agenda item or informally as an offsite event.

PMBOK reference: (9.4.2.4, pg. 341)

212: D

Using resource management software to monitor resource utilization helps ensure right resources are working on the right activities at the right time and place. Ensure the right resources are identified for the right activities happens in the Estimate Activity Resources process. Ensure resources are acquired for the right cost at the right time is done in the Acquire Resources process. Resource problem tracking is done using a problem solving technique.

PMBOK reference: (9.6.2.4, pg. 357)

213: A

The first thing to do is to record the issue on the issue log and then track it to resolution. Each issue should be recorded on the issue log and then tracked and managed to determine what actions should be taken to resolve it. You need to understand the impact before deciding that you have to hire an external resource. First come first serve is not the principle used when making business decisions. After you have understood the impact, you should inform the management of how your project is getting impacted and then you may request for the resource's reassignment to your project. Compressing schedule will not result in anything except increasing risks for the project and may not be viable at all for this project.

PMBOK reference: (4.3.3.4, pg. 96)

214: D

The given Actual Cost (AC) = 300,000 is not needed to determine the Earned Value (EV).

Budget At Completion (BAC) = 400,000. Since project is 75% complete, 75% of 400,000 = 300,000.

So the Earned Value (EV) = 300,000

PMBOK reference: (7.4.2.2, pg. 261)

215: D

Creating the project scope statement, developing the stakeholder assessment matrix, and gathering detailed requirements, all are planning activities. The project has to be initiated which happens with developing of the project charter and getting it approved.

PMBOK reference: (4.1, pg. 75)

216: B

The on-demand scheduling approach is based on the Theory of Constraints to limit the team's work in progress. Supply and demand principle is not directly applicable to this situation. Precedence Diagramming Method is a networking diagramming technique. Monte Carlo simulation is used for schedule analysis.

PMBOK reference: (On-demand scheduling, pg. 177)

217: C

You will explain that there is a cost of quality; it can be the cost of conformance or cost of nonconformance. That is, either preventive measures are taken to produce a quality product or corrective measures are taken to fix defects in quality.

PMBOK reference: (8.1.2.3, pg. 282)

218: C

Quality is not meeting scope but the needs, even if these are not implied. For example, a seller building a house that is not habitable is not meeting quality. Even if the contract does not say the house has to be habitable, the need of it to be habitable is implied and cannot be ignored.

PMBOK reference: (Key concepts..., pg. 273-5 and 8.1.1.2, pg. 279)

219: D

The programmer, the vendor, and the workplace manager are all stakeholders because they influence the project and can be affected by the project. The seller responsible for fixing broken chairs does not influence the project and is not impacted by the project, so that seller will not be a stakeholder.

PMBOK reference: (Figure 1-4, pg. 551)

220: D

A purchase order or invitation to bid is issued during the Conduct Procurement process. The process is completed when the contract is awarded. In this case, the process will be complete once the purchase order is issued, and the seller has accepted. The purchase order is planned in the Plan Procurement Management process. Control Procurements process happens after the contract is awarded. There is no process called Deliver Procurements.

PMBOK reference: (12.2.3.2, pg. 489 and 12, pg. 459)

221: C

Parametric estimating takes historical data into account and performs statistical analysis so it is much more accurate than an opinion based on expert judgment. You should use 750,000 estimate.

PMBOK reference: (7.2.2.3, pg. 243)

222: D

Using data from previous similar projects to come up with the cost estimate of a new project is done in the analogous estimating technique. Ball Park estimate is a high-level estimate that mostly takes expert judgment into account. Bottom-up estimating is to estimate at the activity level and then sum it up to the project level. Parametric estimating takes historical data and statistical analysis to come up with an estimate.

PMBOK reference: (7.1.1.4, pg. 237 and 7.2.2.2, pg. 244)

223: A

Project scope management is not about completing the project on time and within budget, even though these will be affected by how the scope is managed. The key purpose of project scope management is to make sure that the project includes all the required work and only the required work. Project scope management is a component of overall project management. There is more to project scope management than gathering requirements, defining scope, and creating deliverables.

PMBOK reference: (Project scope management, pg. 129)

224: D

It does not make sense to restart the whole project. The work that has already completed would be a waste in this case, i.e. loss of time and money. All others are valid options.

PMBOK reference: (12.3, pg. 494 and 12.3.3.4, pg. 499)

225: A

A corrective action is a type of change request. When implementing risk responses a change request may be created to update the cost and/or schedule baselines. A corrective action will be taken if a risk occurs while a preventive action, in most cases, will happen before the risk occurs so that either its chance of occurrence or impact can be reduced. All the other three options do not address the question.

PMBOK reference: (11.6.3.1, pg. 451)

226: C

The project has an approved budget in US dollars but the cost of deployment in each country will be different and will be estimated independently. So not only that each country's deployment cost is constrained by the approved budget in US dollars but also the fluctuating currency exchange rate will put a budget constraint on the project. There is no mention of a fast track schedule and scope creep. Cost estimation will be independently done for each country but the currency exchange rate will fluctuate this estimation when summed up at the project level. So it is the budget constraint that this scenario is concerned with.

PMBOK reference: (7.1.3.1, pg. 239 and 7.3.1.5, pg. 251)

227: A

Smoothing technique focuses on areas of agreement but requires conceding something to come to an agreement. This can result in a lose-lose situation in the long run. Directing/Forcing is a good technique if one is in a position of power and chances of a dissent are rare. This can also result in a lose-lose situation. Reconciling/Compromising is another good technique that works really well in situations where both parties have somewhat equal or powerful impact but this happens with a sacrifice which may not be the best option for the project. Confronting a problem using a collaborative/problem-solving approach is the best technique because the focus is on understanding and removing the root cause of the problem. Even if the root cause is not fully removed, the knowledge of its impact is very helpful in managing it.

PMBOK reference: (9.5.2.1, pg. 349)

228: D

Gantt chart is used in the Develop Schedule process. It represents the work planned over a period of time. All the other are tools and techniques used in the Control Quality process.

PMBOK reference: (8.3.2, pg. 302)

229: A

The store department's objection was that the work packages were too high level, so using analogous and then the parametric technique for estimation does not address their objection. Work packaging by type of resources rather than by the departments will be a difficult approach as work usually cannot be isolated by resources throughout the project as it moves between various resources. In this scenario, several departments are involved and it is reasonable to assume that work between departments overlaps. So this is not a good approach. By doing a rolling wave planning, work packages do not need to be defined in detail now but later as the work gets closer and requirements and scope gets clearer. This would be a good technique to alleviate the store department's concern and help in good estimation at the right time.

PMBOK reference: (5.4.2.2, pg. 160)

230: A

Advertising is used as a tool in Conduct Procurements process where responses are solicited from sellers who are interested in bidding for the contract. The procurement management plan and procurement documents are prepared in the Plan Procurement Management process. The Control Procurements process happens after the contract has been signed. There is no process called as manage procurements.

PMBOK reference: (12.2.2.2, pg. 487)

231: D

A notice with such conviction only comes out when there is the formal power. Since there is no mention or hint of disciplinary action, it cannot be called the coercive power. The power that the senior project manager was asked to display was expert power because of his/her experience. The question is not what senior project manager displayed but rather which power he referred to, i.e. formal power.

PMBOK reference: (3.4.4.3, pg. 63)

232: D

Formal acceptance by the customer is obtained in the Validate Scope process. No change request is needed once the final product has been transitioned to the customer. The question does not say if it is a contract or not, so procurement closure cannot be the best choice. One of the activities performed during the Close Project or Phase process is the update of lessons learned register. This is the best choice among the four.

PMBOK reference: (4.7.3.1, pg. 127)

233: B

What is it that the experts provide and non-experts do not? Expert Judgment. Expert opinion can be obtained from people with specialized knowledge of environmental regulations and legislation as well as the audit process. This scenario is directed toward clearing the audit, it means the project is wrapping up and your concern is to close the project really well so that no issues come up when audited. Scope validation is not in question. Enterprise environmental factors and organizational process assets are not tools but input/output to a process.

PMBOK reference: (4.7.2.1, pg. 126)

234: B

All of these factors will result in initiating a project. They may also lead to hiring a project manager, but the purpose of hiring the project manager will be to initiate the project. Engaging a stakeholder may happen for any other reason in addition to the above reasons. In this case, it will only happen when a project has been initiated.

PMBOK reference: (Table 1-1, pg. 9)

235: D

Source selection happens in the Conduct Procurements process. Once the seller is selected and the contract is awarded, this process is complete. There is no process called as Request Seller Responses.

PMBOK reference: (12.2.3.1, pg. 488)

236: B

The project team is responsible for the quality of the deliverables for all types of projects. The Seller, sponsor, and quality assurance team can play a secondary role but they are not directly involved in the project and hence cannot be held responsible.

PMBOK reference: (Management responsibility, pg. 275)

237: D

Assumption log and risk register are updated during the Identify Stakeholders process and thus these are the outputs of that process. RACI chart defines the roles and responsibilities of the project team but does not impact how stakeholder should be engaged. Issue log is an output of the process because it may be updated to reflect a change to a recorded issue related to the stakeholder engagement.

PMBOK reference: (13.3.3.3, pg. 529)

238: A

People who will be directly affected by the project are called stakeholders. They are identified and recorded on stakeholder register during Identify Stakeholders process of the Initiating process group. Although the identification of stakeholders and update of the list happens throughout the project life cycle, it is the Initiating process group where the list is created.

PMBOK reference: (13.1, pg. 507)

239: B

Among the four choices, only network diagram shows the longest time between the planned start and finish dates. It shows various routes from start to finish date and the longest one can be determined from among all the routes shown. This is also called a critical path which can be determined by analyzing a network diagram using critical path method.

PMBOK reference: (6.5.2.2, pg. 210)

240: C

Since he is highly interested he should be kept informed on project progress and because he is an expert in domain knowledge, he should be solicited for opinion and feedback on estimation, planning, risks, and issues. Due to low influence, this stakeholder does not need to be managed closely. Sending only the regular project reports will satisfy his high interest but will not benefit the project.

PMBOK reference: (13.1.2.4, pg. 512)

241: A

Review of individual member's performance, including the project manager, is not put on a dashboard so this report does not show the performance of project manager vs. other team members or any resource. The question does not mention any rating so it cannot be the choice about seller's performance. Though seller rating is linked to the performance of work, it is not what this report refers to. The report shows the schedule, budget, and scope including % complete and status of actual performance vs. planned. This is a common project status report that gives a good understanding of where the project stands in terms of performance.

PMBOK reference: (4.5.3.1, pg. 112)

242: A

The Validate Scope process is asking the sponsor/customer to formally accept the completed deliverables. Therefore, acceptance of deliverables must be the main objective of this process. The only feedback that we receive from a customer is regarding acceptance or rejection of deliverable and the reason for it. So this is not the correct answer. Though the Project or Phase Close process cannot start until the Validate Scope process has completed, starting a later phase cannot be the main objective of the current phase. Validate scope process is related to the project scope management and is not directly related to completing the project within time and budget.

PMBOK reference: (5.5, pg. 163)

243: D

A discussion about performance in the presence of a human resource representative is an oral discussion in a formal setting. It will be written if the decision or agreement made in the meeting is recorded and distributed. It could have been considered informal if the HR representative was not present and the discussion was more around exploring problems with the team member.

PMBOK reference: (10.3.2.4, pg. 392)

244: A

The best option is to hire the team leader's son if he meets all other criteria. If the son meets all criteria but the experienced resource is hired against the country's norms, the project is being set up for problems. The productivity expected from hiring an experienced resource may be totally gone. Replacing team leader does not change the normal practice. Maybe the new team leader also has a son or daughter or some other relative interested in the job. Though team leader is responsible for getting the work done, the project manager needs to do the due diligence and make sure whoever is hired has the capability to get the job done since ultimately the project manager is responsible for delivering the project. According to PMI's code of ethics and professional conduct, we are to make decisions based on the best interests of society. Therefore we are to inform ourselves about the norms and customs of others and avoid engaging in behaviors they might consider disrespectful.

PMBOK reference: (9.3.2.1, pg. 332 and PMI's code of ethics and professional conduct, 2.2.1 and 3.2.1)

245: D

If there is an issue with a team member's performance, it will be discussed in private with the relevant manager or leader but definitely not in a status review meeting with executive stakeholders. All the other options are information that may be presented to these stakeholders.

PMBOK reference: (10.2.1.3, pg. 382)

246: C

Risk identification happens throughout the project but a good practice is to set up regular reviews periodically to review current risks and identify and analyze new risks. For example, for a yearlong project, a monthly review can be a good practice or even a semi-monthly if it is expected that risks will change.

PMBOK reference: (11.2, pg. 411)

247: B

Probability is associated with risks as the chance of risk occurrence. An issue has already occurred, so it does not have a probability associated with it. Issues are classified into different types, prioritized with a level of urgency, and are tracked using statuses.

PMBOK reference: (4.3.3.3, pg. 96)

248: B

Benchmarking can help compare the results of stakeholder analysis with the data from highly successful projects within the organizations or other reputed organizations. Checklists is a data gathering technique but may have very limited use when planning to engage stakeholders. Cultural awareness and political awareness are interpersonal and team skills and not data gathering techniques.

PMBOK reference: (13.2.2.2, pg. 520)

249: D

The resource cost for additional resources has to come from somewhere. Management reserve is kept specifically for the purpose of unknown risks and unexpected expenses. The scenario does not mention anything about risks occurring so it means this was unexpected. Hence funds should be requested from the management reserve. Purpose of adding more resources is to stay on schedule so there is no reason to modify schedule baseline. No risk has been mentioned so no risk can be closed. There is no change to the scope so no need to review the scope.

PMBOK reference: (7.4.2.2, pg. 265)

250: C

Independent cost estimate provides an estimate of costs that can be used to compare prospective sellers' bids. Since it is independent it is expected to be free from bias. Bottom-up estimating is unlikely to be used for an independent cost estimate as it is an expensive and time taking process. Bidders' conference helps ensure prospective sellers have the same understanding of the procurement. Procurement audit is done after a contract has been awarded.

PMBOK reference: (12.1.3.7, pg. 479)

251: B

The probability of occurrence of a risk or its impact if that risk occurs goes up and down during project execution as the project's internal and external conditions change. Risks that are close to being one requiring a response can be put on a watch list and monitored so that if their probability of occurrence or impact increases, a response can be planned.

PMBOK reference: (11.3.2.3, pg. 423)

252: B

If the project's cost is affected, then the project's cost baseline needs to be updated after the change is approved. Earned value is the work completed so it does not get affected by an approved change to the project's cost baseline. The integrated change control system does not need an update. Project charter seldom gets updated but if it does then it is because the project objectives have significantly changed.

PMBOK reference: (7.4.3.3, pg. 269)

253: D

Mind mapping is not a tool used for the individuals and team assessment. All the other three can be used for this purpose.

PMBOK reference: (9.4.2.7, pg. 342)

254: B

Variance analysis is performed in the Control Scope process to determine if there is a variance between the baseline specifications and the actual results and then decide if a change request is needed. Define Scope process is where the scope statement is written and the specifications were established. Control Quality process deals with the quality of the project and product and not the specifications. Perform integrated change control process happens when there is a change request to be processed.

PMBOK reference: (5.6.2.1, pg. 170)

255: A

An approved change request impacting the project performance baselines requires that the baselines must be updated. Adding more resources to the project on a fixed-price contract, rework by the supplier to fix a defect, and buying a new machine by the contractor may or may not require a change request. Since the situation does not provide any other information, none of these options will result in an update of the project performance baselines.

PMBOK reference: (4.3.1.3, pg. 93)

256: D

Negotiation is the preferred approach because it saves time and money and brings minimum disruption to the project. Court and arbitration take significantly longer time. Mediation takes more time than negotiation; a third party has to be involved and of course, needs to be compensated in most cases. So it has both time and cost impact greater than negotiation.

PMBOK reference: (12.3.2.2, pg. 497)

257: D

Recommendations from the quality audit reports, process analysis, etc. can result in change requests. Quality plan and metrics are output of the Plan Quality Management process while quality control measurements are output of the Control Quality process.

PMBOK reference: (8.2.3, pg. 296)

258: C

Rolling wave planning is an iterative technique where the near future is defined in detail while the farther future is held at a higher level of detail. This approach will provide flexibility to plan details when enough information becomes available.

A well-defined scope statement and a detailed work breakdown structure, both will be difficult to achieve with a fuzzy scope and a high degree of uncertainty. Similarly, predictive life cycle will not be effective when dealing with unclear scope and high uncertainty.

PMBOK reference: (6.2.2.3, pg. 185)

259: A

Defining activities, estimating activity durations, and developing schedule are a one-time effort. After that, throughout the rest of the project life cycle, the schedule has to be controlled, work performance information has to be generated, compared against baselines, and reported. If a change occurs, the change request has to be processed and approved, and the baseline has to be updated. So it is the Control Schedule process that takes most of the effort.

PMBOK reference: (6.6, pg. 222)

260: B

It does not matter if the stakeholders have a negative or positive impact on the project; their needs must be met based on their level of influence, power, and alignment of their interest with the project's objectives. The other three are correct statements.

PMBOK reference: (Key concepts for project stakeholder management, pg. 504)

261: C

Each person has different communication needs so the most effective step the project manager can take in this scenario is to understand the communication needs of the new sponsor and update the communication plan to reflect that. With a new role, understanding project details in a meeting or self-accessing project repository will be the last thing on new sponsor's mind. Both approaches will likely prove ineffective. Sending project status report without an understanding of the type of communication and how frequent communication the sponsor is expecting will be ineffective.

PMBOK reference: (13.4, pg. 530)

262: D

Project audit requirements, acceptance criteria, and team performance appraisal guidelines, all impact the project or phase closure work. Marketplace conditions is not an organizational process asset but rather it is an enterprise environmental factor. Even if it was an organizational process asset, it is too late for marketplace conditions to have any impact on the Close Project or Phase process.

PMBOK reference: (4.7.1.8, pg. 126)

263: C

Pareto chart is used for classifying and sorting highest frequency factors. What-If scenario analysis helps in looking at the impact of various options on the results. Fast tracking compresses the schedule. Resource leveling puts the resources to best use. In case of a very expensive resource, you want to minimize the non-productive time of the resources and keep the person fully engaged. Resource leveling can help in increasing resource utilization.

PMBOK reference: (6.5.2.3, pg. 211)

264: B

Face-to-face interaction is the most effective method to build trust which helps in managing project knowledge. Once trust has developed then virtual interaction can be taken up as an ongoing method. Meetings as the answer is not a very strong choice as these can be done face-to-face or virtual. Active listening helps but does not directly build trust.

PMBOK reference: (4.4.2.2, pg. 103)

265: B

Daily stand up is not a meeting used during the project closeout process because this meeting is about what work was completed during the previous day and what work is planned for the next day. All the other three are types of meetings that may be held during project closeout process.

PMBOK reference: (4.7.2.3, pg. 127)

266: D

In terms of schedule performance, Schedule Variance (SV) is the difference between Earned Value (EV) and Planned Value (PV).

SV = EV - PV
SV = 127,200 - 143,000
SV = - 15,800 (negative value means behind schedule)

The Schedule Performance Index (SPI) = EV / PV
SPI = 127,200/143,000 = 0.89 which is less than 1.

Hence, the project is behind schedule.
PMBOK reference: (6.6.2.1, pg. 226)

267: C

Agile lifecycle is well suited for a project with a high degree of change and high frequency of deliveries. If the project has a high degree of change but low frequency of delivery then iterative lifecycle is appropriate. Select incremental lifecycle when the frequency of delivery is high but the degree of change is low and select predictive when both the frequency of delivery and degree of change are low.
PMBOK reference: (The Agile Guide, figure 3-1, pg. 19)

268: B

The project manager is following the Halo Effect. Just because a contractor did a really good job with office plumbing project does not mean this contractor is qualified to work on high-pressure gas pipeline project with totally different technical, quality, delivery, and other requirements. So the project manager missed the qualification of the seller. Bidder's conference happens when multiple prospective sellers are involved. The invitation to the seller is the request for proposal; it may not be called as such in this case. Independent estimate is not required. When only one seller is being invited, the buyer is well aware of the costs involved otherwise multiple sellers would have been invited.
PMBOK reference: (12.1.3.5, pg. 478 and 12.2.2.4, pg. 487)

269: B

The risk score is calculated by multiplying the probability of occurrence with the impact. If the probability of occurrence is very high and the risk score is low it means the impact is very low. Same will be the case when the probability of occurrence is very low and the impact is very high, it will result in low-risk score.
PMBOK reference: (Figure 11-5, pg. 408)

270: C

The most common problem related to implementing risk responses is that a documented risk response is not executed when the risk occurs. This happens because a risk owner does not put in the required effort to respond to the risk. Risk audit happens as part of the Monitor Risks process. Documenting a risk response and assigning an owner to a risk response happen in the Plan Risk Responses process.

PMBOK reference: (11.6, pg. 450)

271: D

The ability to make things happen is called political trait. Being intelligent and smart is intellectual, able to understand and build systems is systemic, and the ability to understand and manage people is a social trait.

PMBOK reference: (3.4.5.2, pg. 66)

272: C

Stakeholder engagement assessment matrix monitors engagement of stakeholders by tracking the changes in the level of engagement of each stakeholder. Stakeholder engagement plan lists the actions needed to get stakeholders involved at an appropriate level. Stakeholder register has the stakeholder classification data. Communication management plan provides the plan of various communications.

PMBOK reference: (13.4.2.3, pg. 534)

273: A

The project team and project management plan are developed after the project charter has been approved. Meeting management is an interpersonal and team skill; it helps in productive meetings with valuable outcomes. Organizational process assets (OPA) include organizational standards, policies, procedures, governance framework, templates, and guides, as well as historical information and lessons learned repository and thus will be most helpful at this stage.

PMBOK reference: (4.1.1.4, pg. 79)

274: D

The seller is charging for the time a resource spends on the contract/project, therefore this must be a time and material contract. In cost reimbursable and cost plus fixed fee contracts, the actual cost of the resources will be reimbursed not a negotiated price.

PMBOK reference: (12.1.1.6, pg. 472)

275: A

Assigning probability and impact values is done as part of the risk probability and impact assessment. There is no mention of any risk categorization being done in the given scenario. The probability and impact matrix is a grid used for mapping probability and impact. Risk analysis is a

very general term in this case and so it is a weak choice.
PMBOK reference: (11.3.2.3, pg. 423)

276: D
It is the project team working or executing the project that needs the list of factors; what will the sponsor and end users can do with that list? They would rather see the steps the project manager is taking to bring the project back on track. In order to add new activities or redevelop the schedule, an approved change request is required. Therefore, a change request to update the schedule baseline should be created.
PMBOK reference: (6.6.2.1, pg. 227 and 6.6.3.3, pg. 229)

277: D
Product life cycle is always sequential and cannot be iterative or overlapping. Both the project and product life cycle have a varying duration based on various factors that change over time. A product life cycle spans multiple project life cycles and not the other way around. The correct answer is that the project life cycle provides the basic framework for managing the project while product life cycle represents the evolution of the product.
PMBOK reference: (1.2.3.5, pg. 16 and 1.2.4.1, pg. 19.)

278: A
Procurement specialist or a member of the procurement team will take the lead role because they are trained and experienced in ensuring a good outcome for both parties. The individual usually has the authority to sign the contract.
PMBOK reference: (12.2.2.5, pg. 488)

279: A
The receiver of the message is the one who decodes the message and is also called a decoder. In this case, the project manager, who received the message, is the decoder. Vendor's representative is the encoder or sender and letter is the medium through which the message has been sent.
PMBOK reference: (10.1.2.4, pg. 371)

280: C
Schedule Performance Index (SPI) = Earned Value / Planned Value
Earned Value of a project when it has been completed is Budget At Completion (BAC). Similarly, Planned Value of the project at the end is also BAC. So,
SPI = BAC / BAC = 1.0
PMBOK reference: (7.4.2.2, pg. 263)

281: D

The question is asking about the present value of the return. The formula is:

$PV = FV / (1 + i)^n$

$PV = 500{,}000 / (1 + 0.06)^5 = 373{,}629$ which is approximately 370,000

PMBOK reference: (1.2.6.4, pg. 34)

282: A

Manage quality process is not performed to control, inspect, or measure quality. The purpose of manage quality process is to convert the quality management plan into actions so that the organization's quality policies are implemented. This helps in a higher probability of meeting the project's quality objectives.

PMBOK reference: (8.2, pg. 288)

283: C

It is not functional as it is clear from the scenario that the project is in a matrix organization. It cannot be a weak matrix organization since any escalation will be to the project manager's own functional manager which is not the case here. It cannot be project-oriented as all resources report directly to the project manager. Only in the strong matrix environment, the project manager will have that kind of authority to escalate the issue and directly approach a functional manager's director. Therefore this can occur in a strong matrix organization.

PMBOK reference: (Table 2-1, pg. 47)

284: B

Library services, web searches, and reading published articles are examples of information management which is one of the tools and techniques in Manage Project Knowledge process. These are not organizational process assets because these are not related to organizational processes.

PMBOK reference: (4.4.2.3, pg. 103)

285: D

Since the project manager is reviewing a large number of errors and trying to see what are the root causes of those errors, he is trying to manage quality where root causes are identified by not just looking at the quality control measurements but also quality plan, policies, and procedures. It is not brainstorming, decision making, or change control.

PMBOK reference: (8.2.2.4, pg. 293)

286: B

Work breakdown structure (WBS) dictionary is a document that provides detailed information about a WBS item or work package. Besides other information, it contains the cost estimates, resources required, responsible organization, and account codes. So WBS dictionary will help the project accountant identify the cost center of that resource.

PMBOK reference: (5.4.3.1, pg. 162)

287: C

WBS ID will be defined during the initial activity definition because work packages are decomposed to define activities. Predecessor activities will only be identified once activities are sequenced. Duration and start dates will be known when activity durations are estimated in a later process.

PMBOK reference: (6.2.3.2, pg. 186)

288: B

SWOT stands for Strengths, Weaknesses, Opportunities, and Threats. It is a technique used for identifying risks and understanding its dynamics.

PMBOK reference: (11.2.2.3, pg. 415)

289: A

Such a review is called an audit. It is a planned pre-defined process to review the procurement process and its results and understand what went well and where were the weaknesses. These observations are then brought to the project manager's attention and recommendations are made for improvement. The negotiated settlement is an agreement on a dispute.

PMBOK reference: (12.3.2.5, pg. 498)

290: A

This is called gold plating i.e. adding features or functions that are beyond requirements or upgrading a product when it is not required. It is a kind of scope creep and may or may not bring the value but will likely result in higher risks to the project.

PMBOK reference: (5.6, pg. 168)

291: B

Configuration management system contains the list of all items that are under change control so if there is any change to any of those items; this system provides how the change is to be made including the process of going through the change and updating the item.

PMBOK reference: (4.6.2.2, pg. 118 and pg. 701)

292: A

Labor costs, material costs, and equipment costs are all included in the cost baseline but management cost is usually put as an overhead on the project. This means that it is a set number or percentage that is booked against the project but does not form part of the cost baseline.

PMBOK reference: (7.3.3.1, pg. 254)

293: D

The focus of the project manager should be to resolve the issue. Conflicts should be addressed early so asking the team members to ignore the issue can make it a bigger conflict later in the project. Though issues should usually be discussed in private, the project manager is involved now so he/she has to address it. Change requests are only created for items that are being tracked through the configuration management system and need to be modified. The project manager should try to understand what the disagreement is so that he/she can work with the team members to come up with a solution in a collaborative environment. So, this is the best choice.

PMBOK reference: (9.5.2.1, pg. 348)

294: A

Work Performance Data is an input to the Monitor Communications process which is then analyzed and results in Work Performance Information as an output. It includes information on how well the project communication was done compared to the planned communication and measures how effective the communication has been.

PMBOK reference: (10.3.3.1, pg. 392)

295: C

The project charter is not an input, output or tool and technique of the Direct and Manage Project Work process. Expert judgment and project management information system are tools and techniques. Deliverables, work performance data, change requests, issue log, and project management plan updates are output. Approved change requests which include approved corrective actions and approved preventive actions are input to the process.

PMBOK reference: (4.3, pg. 90)

296: B

These are the functions performed by the configuration control and integrated change control system. Configuration control is focused on specifications of both deliverables and the processes while change control is about managing changes to documents, deliverables, and baselines. Control chart has no role in change request processing. There is nothing called configuration chart in this context. Change control board is part of change control but this covers only a portion of the work mentioned in the above scenario.

PMBOK reference: (4.6.2.2, pg. 118)

297: C
Optimistic estimate = 3 hours
Pessimistic estimate = 12 hours
Most Likely estimate = 10 hours.
The formula for three point estimation using triangular distribution is:
E = (O + M + P) / 3 = (3 + 10 + 12) / 3 = 8 hours
PMBOK reference: (6.4.2.4, pg. 201)

298: D
Risk identification is a continuous process throughout project life cycle. If a risk is identified, no matter by whom, it should be recorded on the risk register and analyzed. If it requires a response, then a response should be prepared.
PMBOK reference: (11.7.2.3, pg. 457)

299: D
Least flexible activities in a schedule are the activities on the critical path. Actually, these are non-flexible activities because any change in these activities will change the end date of the schedule. Therefore, you are using the critical path method. PDM in itself does not show the flexibility of activities without critical path information though it shows the relationship between activities. Three-point analysis uses three estimates to find the duration of each activity and does not show which activities are the least flexible.
PMBOK reference: (6.5.2.2, pg. 210 and 6.6.2.2, pg. 227)

300: C
Controlling PMO can provide the level of control and influence to have projects go through mandatory audits and gate reviews, and centralized reporting without managing the projects. Supportive PMO works in a supportive role and as a project repository. Directive PMO manages the project directly. There is no PMO type called as managerial.
PMBOK reference: (2.4.4.3, pg. 48)

301: A
The project manager working alone cannot effectively engage stakeholders throughout the project life cycle. Project team members should be on the lookout and identify if they find someone who is being impacted by the project or someone who can influence the project. They should always understand stakeholders' needs and expectations.
PMBOK reference: (13, pg. 505)

302: D
First-time risk probability and impact assessment is under planning process group and happens during the Perform Qualitative Risk Analysis. Since there is a change in the probability and impact of an identified risk, it must be the Monitor Risks process.
PMBOK reference: (11.7, pg. 453)

303: B
Opportunity is positive, 40% x (+ 10,000) = + 4,000
Threats are negative, 70% x (- 13,000) + 20% x (- 5,000) = - 11,100
So the contingency reserve should be + 4,000 - 11,100 = 7,100 (since it is negative)
PMBOK reference: (11.4.2.5, pg. 435)

304: B
Work is produced in Direct and Manage Project Work process while work and project performance are reviewed in the Monitor and Control Project Work process.
PMBOK reference: (4.3, pg. 90 and 4.4, pg. 95)

305: D
Budget At Completion (BAC) = 1,000,000.
Actual Cost (AC) = 650,000.
Without knowing the Cost Performance Index or Cost Variance, the earned value cannot be determined. It can be 650,000 if CPI = 1.0
It cannot be the cost variance since CV = EV - AC.
Though it is a design-build project, there is no mention of this expense being the design cost. So this choice is also incorrect.
650,000 have been spent and cannot be recovered. This money is called the sunk cost.
PMBOK reference: (X3.3.5, pg. 671 and 7.4.2.2, pg. 261)

306: C
It means variables are closely related to each other. A change in one variable will result in a change in the other variable.
PMBOK reference: (8.2.2.4, pg. 293 and 8.3.2.5, pg. 304)

307: D
A portfolio has an organizational scope that changes with the strategic objectives of the organization. Therefore, any change in strategy or enterprise environmental factors may result in the change of the portfolio scope. Projects and programs may get added to the portfolio when these are to be worked on or taken out of the portfolio when these are completed or canceled. Subsidiary portfolios may be created for better tracking of

performance results. Portfolio management also includes some operational work.
PMBOK reference: (Table 1-2. pg. 13)

308: B
According to the interactive communication model, a communication is confirmed to have happened when the encoded message was sent and received and feedback was then received back. Project manager's email of the issue only covers the first half of communication. It does not say if the sponsor received the communication and confirmed. A minutes of meeting document is the message but was not sent to anyone in this example. Project progress report in the company's newsletter is a one-way communication. There is no indication that it was read. Team member's performance improvement is the correct answer because the training (message) was given (sent) to the team member (receiver) who then improved his performance (feedback) after getting back to work.
PMBOK reference: (10.1.2.4, pg. 372)

309: B
Reserve analysis is a tool and technique and not an input to the Determine Budget process. All the other three are inputs to the process.
PMBOK reference: (7.3, pg. 248)

310: A
The developer making a change or adding new information to the report without any prior approval or discussion is an example of scope creep even when the assumption is that it enhances benefit realization or helps exceed the customer expectations. Scope creep can happen for any reason, one of which is, when the team starts adding minor things into the scope because they feel it is not taking any extra time or money. Adding scope without approval is a very risky approach to exceed expectations and is not recommended. When the project team's actions result in scope creep, it is also referred to as gold plating.
PMBOK reference: (5.6, pg. 168)

311: A

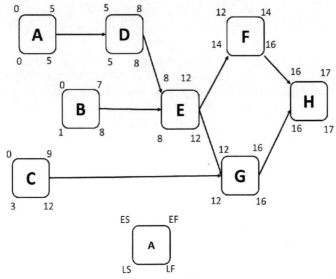

The solution is shown in the figure. The late start of activity C is 3, the duration of activity A is 5, and the late finish of activity B is 8.

PMBOK reference: (6.5.2.2, pg. 210)

312: D

Plan Procurement Management is the process where the procurement management plan is developed and bid package is prepared. After that in the Conduct Procurements process, sellers' responses are solicited, a seller is selected and the contract is awarded.

PMBOK reference: (12.2, pg. 482)

313: C

Crane A: 400 per 8-hr means 400/8 = 50 per hour. So 50x400 + 100x400 + 6000 = 66,000

Crane B: 80x400 + 80x400 + 2000 = 66,000

Both cranes cost is the same for 400 hours so any of these two can be selected.

PMBOK reference: (9.2.2.5, pg. 325)

314: D

Residual risks are the left-over risks after the implementation of risk response while secondary risks are the risks that arise due to the implementation of risk response. Both residual risks and secondary risks can be response planned for and can be responded to using contingency reserve.

PMBOK reference: (11.5.3.3, pg. 448)

315: A
Work will stop immediately but you should go through the handover of deliverables to the sponsor/customer/operations and then release the resources to complete the Close Project or Phase process. Project termination decisions are rarely made because of project team's performance. The decision likely is due to misalignment of project objectives from a changed business direction or due to lack of funding.
PMBOK reference: (4.7.3.4, pg. 128)

316: A
Project scope statement will not have the list of activities that must be completed to achieve the project's objectives. That list is created from WBS work packages separately during the Define Activities process. However, product scope description and project exclusions, both are identified in the project scope statement. List of deliverables and acceptance criteria is also a part of this artifact.
PMBOK reference: (5.3.3.1, pg. 154)

317: A
List of identified risks is just one piece of information on the risk register. There is no check-in and check-out risks that happen during project risk management. Not all risks require responses only the ones that are significant need to have a response planned. It is a document that contains all of the outcomes of the risk management process including analysis, response planning, watch lists, expected monetary value, etc.
PMBOK reference: (11.2.3.1, pg. 417)

318: A
In a joint application development (JAD) session, requirements are gathered and documented by the development team along with business subject matter experts. The project manager may or may not participate in the JAD sessions. The business analyst will likely but not necessarily participate in a JAD session. Project sponsors do not participate in JAD or other requirements gathering sessions.
PMBOK reference: (5.2.2.6, pg. 145)

319: B
Approved changes to the schedule baseline happen in the Direct and Manage Project Work process. Minimizing changes to the project schedule in itself is not a benefit. Measuring schedule variances from the schedule baseline are only one part of maintaining the baseline. Maintaining the schedule baseline is the main benefit and it includes measuring the variance.

PMBOK reference: (6.6, pg. 222)

320: A

Gathering the requirements is not a part of the kick-off activity. In fact, the kick-off meeting should never be used to gather requirements. The purpose of the kick-off meeting is to communicate project objectives, gain the commitment of the team, get the stakeholders involved and get them excited about the project, and make the roles and responsibilities clear to all the stakeholders.

PMBOK reference: (4.2.2.4, pg. 86)

321: A

Customer's refusal to accept a deliverable is a significant issue that requires appropriate effort is put in place to problem solve the issue. So the project manager should review the acceptance criteria, the deliverable and customer's objection as well as the team's arguments in order to resolve the issue. Confronting approach is also a choice but without the knowledge of why the deliverable was rejected in the first place, it cannot be used. A change request cannot be submitted without knowing what is to change and why the change has to happen. Though customer's interests are always to be protected, knowledge of what has been missed, if any, is important before asking the team to make the change.

PMBOK reference: (9.5.2.1, pg. 348)

322: D

The start-to-start relationship means the second task starts after the start of the first task. Since there is a 5 days lag, the second task will start 5 days after the start of the first task.

PMBOK reference: (6.3.2.3, pg. 192)

323: B

Performance measurement baseline is not derived from the schedule baseline. Though both seem to go hand in hand, they are separate in essence. The cost estimates which are accumulated into control accounts and further into cost baseline relate to the schedule activities, and so it can be displayed in the form of an S-curve.

PMBOK reference: (7.3.3, pg. 254)

324: C

Though lessons learned are generally considered as Project or Phase Close activity, lessons learned should be identified throughout the project life cycle. The formal activity ensures these get recorded and reviewed by the team before putting it as a record. Lessons learned earlier in the project can be applied later.

PMBOK reference: (4.4.3.1, pg. 104 and 10.3.1.2, pg. 390)

325: B
The project manager should evaluate the impact this request has on the project and if needed make the appropriate changes to the communication management plan. All the other three options require that a proper impact assessment has already been done but there is no indication of that in the question.
PMBOK reference: (10.3.3.2, pg. 393)

326: B
First, identify the key stakeholders from the business case which has an initial list of major stakeholders. This list will grow as you get deeper into the project planning later. Salience model and stakeholder matrix will analyze stakeholders not identify them. The project management plan is created later and does not exist at this time.
PMBOK reference: (13.1.1.2, pg. 509)

327: C
Constructive changes are uniquely identified and documented using a formal communication method. These changes have modified the contract or these will potentially modify the contract.
PMBOK reference: (12.3.2.2, pg. 497)

328: D
Cost plus material fee does not make sense as the material is already a cost that is being reimbursed under the term 'cost'. All other three are valid cost-reimbursable contracts.
PMBOK reference: (12.1.1.6, pg. 472)

329: C
20,000 joints in 250 days means 80 joints per day. Three welders can do 90 at the rate of 30 joints per welder per day. So the number of welders is just about right.
PMBOK reference: (9.2.2.4, pg. 324)

330: A
Fire and theft, injury and life risks all have a negative outcome. Overall project risk is the overall uncertainty of the project outcome. This includes the combined effect of individual risks and impact of stakeholders, and it can have a positive and negative outcome.
PMBOK reference: (pg. 397)

331: C

The issues being faced by the project manager show that meetings are not in control or it could be that the team members are not really sure what they are to do in the meeting. Best approach is to set ground rules for the meeting in the team charter. For example, inform the project manager if you are late or going to be absent, do not leave the room in the middle without letting know, no calls or texting during the meeting, etc.

PMBOK reference: (9.1.3.2, pg. 320)

332: B

During the Direct and Manage Project Work process, approved changes are implemented, work performance data is collected, and technical and organizational interfaces are managed. Work performance reports are created in the Monitor and Control Project Work process.

PMBOK reference: (4.3, pg. 92)

333: A

After quantitative risk analysis is completed, individual risks are prioritized and top priority risks are later reviewed for response planning. Sometimes risk responses may also be suggested which will be considered during the Plan Risk Response process. The risk register is continuously updated throughout the project and not just at the end of the Quantitative Risk Analysis process. So this cannot be something happening particularly at the end of the Quantitative Risk analysis process.

PMBOK reference: (11.4.3.1, pg. 436)

334: D

Stakeholders can be classified on a stakeholder cube based on power, influence, and interest. They can be classified on a salience model using power, legitimacy, and urgency. Stakeholders can also be classified using the direction of influence. Identifying stakeholders as executives, managers, and staff does not provide any leverage to the project manager and, in reality, could be detrimental to the project as the focus may shift to satisfy executive stakeholders while ignoring the needs of the staff.

PMBOK reference: (13.1.2.4, pg. 512-513)

335: B

Adding scope does not necessarily mean that more risks must be added. Instead, risk identification must be performed to determine if there are any new risks. If new risks are identified, these should be analyzed and response planned if needed.

PMBOK reference: (11.7.2.3, pg. 457)

336: B
Explicit knowledge can be easily recorded using words, pictures, and numbers. Tacit knowledge is personal in nature and difficult to express. Beliefs, insights, and experience are examples of tacit knowledge. Though it is recorded knowledge, it is a weak answer.
PMBOK reference: (4.4, pg. 100)

337: D
A quality audit is an independent review to check the adequacy and efficiency of policies and procedures as well as to see if the project activities comply with the organizational policies and procedures. None of the other choices serve this purpose.
PMBOK reference: (8.2.2.5, pg. 294)

338: B
The question for the right cost may be considered when acquiring resources but the release of resources for use will not be impacted by the cost. However, release for use at the right time, at the right place, and in the right amount will be considered.
PMBOK reference: (9.6, pg. 353)

339: A
A project manager is focused on the project goals and hence will take steps that move him/her closer to achieving those goals. Sending an apology note or doing a performance review first does not help with the objectives. Increasing project communication does not solve the problem viz. not regularly updating the issue log. Sponsor is worried seeing issues have stayed open for a long time so project manager should review those open issues, get them updated and resolved.
PMBOK reference: (10.3.3.4, pg. 393)

340: D
Cost estimates are the least likely to be a source of conflict among the four choices. Most conflicts occur due to the shortage of resources, scheduling priorities, and personal work styles.
PMBOK reference: (9.5.2.1, pg. 348)

341: A
High-level estimation is usually done since changes continue to occur throughout the project. A detailed estimate is only done for the next iteration while high-level estimate may get revised for the remainder of the project to save time and estimation effort.
PMBOK reference: (Considerations for agile/adaptive environments, pg. 234)

342: D
Project manager, project team, sponsor, the performing organization, and the customer, all have a role to play in the Manage Quality process. There may be specific responsibilities assigned to individuals in traditional project management but, everyone contributes to the Manage Quality process.
PMBOK reference: (8.2, pg. 290)

343: B
The project cost performance is improving is an example of trend analysis based on the given data. Cost performance index from 0.96 to 1.02 to 1.05 is an upward/improvement trend. It is also true that the project is under-budget but that will be called variance analysis.
PMBOK reference: (4.5.2.2, pg. 111)

344: D
Change log is the only input, among the four choices, to the Manage Stakeholder Engagement process. Among various plans, only the stakeholder engagement plan, risk management plan, change management plan, and Communications Management Plan are the input.
PMBOK reference: (Figure 13-7, pg. 523)

345: A
The accuracy of the business case and other information on benefits management may be recorded as part of project documents update during Close Project or Phase process. The Control Costs process tracks actual costs against cost baseline and does not check the accuracy of the business case. The Develop Project Charter process is too early to check the accuracy of the business case as nothing has been worked on and delivered.
PMBOK reference: (4.7.3.1, pg. 127)

346: D
Assume 'm' is the number of months.
Then,
Buy option: 150,000 + 5,000 x m
Rent option: 5,000 + 10,000 x m
Solving for m, 150,000 + 5,000 m = 5,000 + 10,000 m
m = 29 months
PMBOK reference: (12.1.2.3, pg. 473)

347: A
Total Quality Management is one of the quality improvement initiatives. The purpose is to find and modify methods that will create a continuous improvement environment for the products, services, and business

practices and thus improve both project and product quality.
PMBOK reference: (pg. 275)

348: B
Halo effect is a cognitive bias that results in generalizing a person's performance in one area and applying it to another area. So a programmer getting promoted to project manager because of successful performance in the programming area is a good example of that. When a project team member lacks the competency, project performance can suffer.
PMBOK reference: (9.1.3.1, pg. 319)

349: B
Since you are having problems with project B, you need to find out what challenges were faced by the previous project and how were those handled. So you should do a review of project documentation and lessons learned of that project and also speak to its project manager, if possible. The issue is not that you cannot manage two projects at the same time but you are having problems controlling one project. So putting one project on hold or not starting another project, both are not the right answers. Scope control is as much required as cost, schedule or quality control on a project. Though it is important to define requirements as completely as possible, it may not be easy to do that without reviewing previous project files.
PMBOK reference: (4.3.1.5, pg. 94)

350: C
Transformational leadership style is to inspire and motivate the team, encourage idealized behavior and innovation. Allowing the team to make their own decisions and set goals is Laissez-faire style while focusing on goals, feedback, and accomplishment to determine rewards is transactional style. Servant leader style focuses on the team's growth and development, collaboration, and relationships.
PMBOK reference: (3.4.5.1, pg. 65)

351: D
Having a clear agenda that states the objectives of the meeting creates a focus in the meeting. Advising all in attendance to discuss one topic at a time is a partial solution to the problem. The number of people and mandatory participation in the meeting is not related to the issue here.
PMBOK reference: (10.2.2.6, pg. 386)

352: C
Since this is a change request, it should be a formal written communication. Change request will impact project plan and baselines once approved hence they have the potential of affecting the project goals. Being

in written form, formal communication brings clarity and confirms the agreement by the parties.

PMBOK reference: (4.6, pg. 115 and 10.2.1.2, pg. 382)

353: A

Job shadowing is an observation/conversation technique used for collecting requirements where the observer gets hands-on experience of the product or service to see what the customer/user experiences. Nominal group technique is used along with brainstorming and includes voting on brainstormed ideas. Interviews are formal or informal question-answer sessions to collect requirements. Facilitation is guiding a group to address the topic of discussion.

PMBOK reference: (5.2.2.6, pg. 145)

354: A

A handoff of work, product, service or result from one phase to another will identify the transition. The deliverables could be the one being handed off to the next team but deliverables do not identify transition; these identify completion of work within a phase. Project reports and milestones could show phase end but do not identify phase transition.

PMBOK reference: (4.7.3.2, pg. 127)

355: D

The purpose of phase initiating processes is to keep the project aligned to the business goals and meet the business need. By reviewing the project charter and stakeholders list, the project gets realigned to the business need. Changes to the project charter are rare but this is the perfect time to see that business objectives of the project have changed and require an update to the project charter. Previous phase closure would already have happened that is why new phase is being initiated. Following processes for the purpose of following processes is not a good reason.

PMBOK reference: (4.1, pg. 75)

356: A

In order to find the root cause of certain issues, root cause analysis has to be performed. Fishbone diagram is a very effective technique for this purpose. All other three options require that reasons for non-conformances are known before any step can be taken.

PMBOK reference: (8.2.2.4, pg. 293)

357: D

The business case for the project cannot have affected the development of the plan because it is not an input to Develop Project Management Plan process. The templates, lessons learned, and change management policies

affect the development of the plan.
PMBOK reference: (4.2.1.4, pg. 84)

358: C
A histogram will show the types of issues occurring and their frequency. Affinity diagram organizes defects or causes into groups. Matrix diagram shows the strength of relationships among causes while scatter diagram shows the relationship between two variables.
PMBOK reference: (8.2.2.4, pg. 293)

359: B
Since the work cannot proceed as per plan due to the issue prohibiting the completion of planned work, a change request would need to be submitted. The project performance report is created in the Monitor and Control Project Work process and takes work performance information from various control processes which in turn receive work performance data as an input from Direct and Manage Project Work process. Technical testing of the completed deliverable is part of the Control Quality process. Customer's review of deliverable happens as part of the Validate Scope process which occurs after deliverable is completed and verified.
PMBOK reference: (4.3.3.4, pg. 96)

360: C
Control charts do not show relationships between two factors. Scatter diagram can be used to see the relationship between the two factors. All other options are attributes of control charts.
PMBOK reference: (8.3.2.5, pg. 304)

361: B
Quality and grade are often taken as one and the same but these are two different terms. Quality is the degree to which a set of inherent characteristics fulfill requirements while grade is a category assigned to deliverables with same functional but different technical capabilities.
PMBOK reference: (Key concepts for project quality management, pg. 274)

362: B
The project-oriented organizational structure is built with project team reporting directly to the project manager in the hierarchy of the organization. There is no functional manager role in a project-oriented structure. Each team member will have one reporting line and that is to his/her project manager. Team members work full-time on the project.
PMBOK reference: (Table 2-1, pg. 47)

363: B

A program is a way to meet business needs by coordinating and controlling multiple related projects. The combined goal of all the projects in a program is the goal of the program. These projects may or may not be running concurrently. A program may include a project due to government mandate as well as other projects related to market demand. It may also involve several departments within an organization and may not necessarily be restricted to one department.

PMBOK reference: (1.2.3.1, pg. 11)

364: C

Resource calendars do not contain location and contact information of resources. Those pieces of information are kept on the team roster. Resource availability schedule, time zones, work hours, vacation days, and local holidays are included in the resource calendar.

PMBOK reference: (9.3.1.2, pg. 331)

365: D

The Salience model classifies stakeholders on the basis of their power, urgency, and legitimacy. Stakeholder cube is a three-dimensional model that may use power, influence, and interest as the three factors.

PMBOK reference: (13.1.2.4, pg. 513)

366: A

Customer or sponsor cannot be forced or pressurized to accept deliverables. So asking for help from other stakeholders and forcing acceptance, because these deliverables are as per plan, will not work. If there is a change in the business need, an appropriate step will be to create a change request so that rejected deliverables could be modified to meet the business need. This holds true if the deliverables can be modified or fixed. If the deliverables do not meet the business need, it is time to review if the project is still valid and whether it should be continued or killed.

PMBOK reference: (1.2.4.3, pg. 21)

367: C

Design for X can be used for designing the new braking system to identify an optimum design that satisfies reliability, usability, safety, cost, manufacturing, and other factors. All the other three tools will not generate any valuable information when applied to a new and innovative design.

PMBOK reference: (8.2.2.6, pg. 294)

368: D

The Conduct Procurements process is part of the Executing process group. Control Procurements process happens after the Conduct

Procurements is completed and is part of the Monitoring and Controlling process group. Planning happens before procurements are conducted.
PMBOK reference: (Table 1-4, pg. 25 and 12.2, pg. 482)

369: C
The optimistic estimate is 10 days while pessimistic estimate is 28 days. However, the most likely estimate is 16 days. Using the beta distribution, the formula is:
Expected duration = (optimistic + 4 x most likely + pessimistic) / 6
E = (10 + 4x16 + 28) / 6 = 17 days
PMBOK reference: (6.4.2.4, pg. 201 and 7.2.2.5, pg. 244)

370: D
A well-developed and thought-out communication plan is extremely important in a virtual team environment. Communication challenges may occur due to different time zones, language ability of the team members, information sharing options, or resolving conflicts in a distributed environment. Without a detailed communication plan, use of email and instant messaging may not be effective. Responsibility assignment matrix is helpful in both the virtual and co-location settings but may not be fully effective without proper communication. Knowledge of the local language and customs will help but cannot be considered the MOST effective of all four.
PMBOK reference: (9.3.2.4, pg. 333 and 9.4.2.2, pg. 340)

371: D
Kaizen is a philosophy that improvement to a system, process etc. must occur on a continuous basis i.e. it is all about events focused on improvement of the systems and processes.
PMBOK reference: (The Agile Guide, p. 152)

372: C
Using the current rate of progress is incorrect because resource shortage issue is gone which had affected current performance. A totally new estimate will be a wasted effort since whatever has been the main reason affecting performance has been fixed. The current rate of progress for design work cannot be used as the resource is available now. Therefore, the best choice is to use the originally planned rate of progress to calculate the estimate to complete.
PMBOK reference: (7.4.2.2, pg. 264)

373: D
Gestures, the tone of the voices, and facial expressions help transmit the meaning and understand the argument better than all the other options.

Meaning of the same sentence changes dramatically with the change in gestures, tone, and facial expressions. The subject matter expertise, if brought into as a guide to understand the arguments actually, is a bias that stops the listener from understanding the argument. Facts and fiction do help understand the argument but it's the gestures, tone, and facial expressions that give them the meaning. Time of the day has no bearing on understanding.

PMBOK reference: (10.2.2.3, pg. 383)

374: C

For a multi-year global project, currency exchange rate and inflation will be considered as enterprise environmental factors when estimating costs. Cost of quality is a tool and technique used in the Estimate Costs process. Cost estimation policy and lessons learned repository are organizational process assets used in the Estimate Costs process.

PMBOK reference: (7.2.1.3, pg. 243)

375: C

The purpose of the project charter is to authorize the project manager to proceed with the project; therefore, the project charter gives authority to the project manager to engage organizational resources on the project. The business case has already been created and is an input to the Develop Project Charter process. Creating a project charter precedes the approval of project charter otherwise there is nothing to be approved. This is not a reasonable answer. Creating a project charter helps with stakeholder identification indirectly and is not the main purpose or key benefit of it.

PMBOK reference: (4.1, pg. 75)

376: B

Forecasting methods is not a tool or technique used in Monitor Communications process. All the other three are tools and techniques of Monitor Communications process.

PMBOK reference: (10.3, pg. 388)

377: C

The related leadership trait is to guide and collaborate using relational power. Do the right things is a leadership behavior opposite to do things right behavior of management. Focus on long-range vision is a leadership trait compared to management behavior of focusing on short-term goals.

PMBOK reference: (3.4.5, pg. 64)

378: B

Managing is not an engagement level of a stakeholder. All the other three are engagement levels of stakeholder including resistant and

supportive.
PMBOK reference: (13.2.2.5, pg. 521)

379: B
The two purposes of managing both tacit and explicit knowledge are reusing existing knowledge and creating new knowledge. Both are part of knowledge management which may use the technique of information management. Conducting lessons learned and updating project documents will happen in order to achieve those two objectives but these cannot be the objectives.
PMBOK reference: (4.4, pg. 100)

380: C
The purpose of using earned value management is to measure the performance. It provides us with variances from the plans and schedule. Performance indices provide us with the basis to forecast the future performance.
PMBOK reference: (7.4.2.2, pg. 261)

381: C
Precedence diagramming method shows four different types of relationships or dependencies between various activities in a graphical format which is not evident in other types of network techniques. PDM does not show progress at any point in time. Whether it is most commonly used or not is not an advantage or disadvantage so this answer is incorrect. It can show project start and finish dates but other methods also show that information so it cannot be the advantage over the other methods.
PMBOK reference: (6.3.2.1, pg. 189)

382: D
Risk response planning includes deciding on the response strategy and assigning an owner to each risk that needs to be responded to. The response strategy was decided but no owner was assigned which resulted in lack of an action plan to respond to the risk.

Thanking manager in the email which is about the project team's performance seems flattering and out of context. Fixing project problems especially when it is impacting the whole organization does not require permission of the manager; it is the responsibility of the project manager. Emergency issues, like the one mentioned, do not need to go through the integrated change control process. The purpose of the integrated change control process is not to enforce process implementation but rather control changes to the project. The manager is disappointed that the risk was prioritized, response strategy decided, but no owner was identified and no

action plan was created. This is a project management failure.
PMBOK reference: (11.5.3.3, pg. 448)

383: B
Shipping product order received through the internet would be difficult to qualify as a project even though it is a larger than usual order. Shipping orders is a well-defined repeated process. There might be a start but there really is no defined end. There is also no unique output from shipping. In fact, the whole process can be put down as a standard operating procedure where each step is well defined. All other three are temporary in nature with a unique output and can be called a project.
PMBOK reference: (1.2.1, pg. 5)

384: A
In order to define the scope of a project, requirements should already have been gathered and documented. The requirement documentation becomes an input to the Define Scope process. At the start of the Define Scope process, requirements traceability matrix contains only the list of gathered requirements, and its purpose is to link those requirements to the business needs so it may get updated as part of the output of the process. The project scope statement is an output of the process while product analysis is a tool and technique.
PMBOK reference: (5.3, pg. 150)

385: C
Risk register contains all the identified risks but the project charter which is a document created earlier during the Develop Project Charter process as part of initiating has overall project risks. The risk management plan is part of the project management plan and it does not contain a list of risks.
PMBOK reference: (4.1.3.1, pg. 81)

386: B
Since no resources are available, the schedule cannot be crashed but the review has shown that most dependencies built between activities are of discretionary type and not mandatory so it means that the schedule can be fast tracked by changing the schedule to perform activities in parallel. Fast tracking would be the best option. Removing non-critical activities will not affect the schedule end date since the end date is driven by the critical activities. It does not make sense to define activities as non-important and major.
PMBOK reference: (6.3.2.2, pg. 191 and 6.6.2.6, pg. 228)

387: C

Since the work was completed as specified and deliverables were accepted by the buyer, the work should be considered complete and you should proceed with closing the contract. The level of customer satisfaction cannot impact the completion and closure of the project. It is too late to cancel or put the contract on hold as the work is already complete.

PMBOK reference: (12.3.3.1, pg. 499)

388: C

This process is performed periodically throughout the project when a deliverable is ready for formal acceptance. Deliverable acceptance should be done as soon as a deliverable is completed so that the cost of change is kept at minimum instead of waiting till the end of the project. The other two options are invalid.

PMBOK reference: (5.5, pg. 163)

389: D

Scheduling expertise is the least likely to be considered during the Close Project or Phase process as it is a closing process and not the planning or monitoring and controlling process. Audit expertise can help go through the project or phase audit, legal expertise can ensure all procurement conditions are fulfilled, and regulations expertise can ensure all legislation and regulatory requirements have been met.

PMBOK reference: (4.7.2.1, pg. 126)

390: B

Hiring a truck to move material closer to the site cannot be called cost of quality unless moving closer to the site is to improve or sustain the quality of the material. All others are examples of the cost of quality which includes the cost to prevent errors, cost to assess quality, and cost to fix errors.

PMBOK reference: (Figure 8-5, pg. 283)

391: B

Sensitivity analysis checks the impact of changing one variable only while all other variables are kept constant. It evaluates which individual project risk has the biggest impact on the project. The results can be displayed in a Tornado diagram.

PMBOK reference: (11.4.2.5, pg. 434)

392: A

The purpose of resource histogram is to see how much work has been assigned to the resource over a period of time. Since assigning of work to resources is part of planning, resource histograms are created in the

Develop Schedule process as part of establishing schedule data. Plan Resource Management and Acquire Resources processes need project schedule as an input. Estimate Activity Resources process also happens later as it needs the resource management plan.

PMBOK reference: (6.5.3.3, pg. 220)

393: C

In a Project-oriented organization and in a PMO structure, the project manager has full control over project resources. In a functional organization, the project manager works as a project coordinator and has little authority and control over project resources. There is no organization type called as functional matrix defined in the PMBOK guide.

PMBOK reference: (Table 2-1, pg. 47)

394: D

The breakeven point can be found out by comparing total cost of buying against total cost of leasing for the months excavator is used. Therefore,

20,000 + 350,000 = 10,000 + 10,000 x months
370,000 - 10,000 = 10,000 x months
months = 360,000 / 10,000
months = 36

So, a minimum 36 months of use will justify buying instead of leasing.

PMBOK reference: (12.1.2.3, pg. 473)

395: A

Once the costs have been estimated, the Determine Budget process aggregates the estimated costs of the individual activities and work packages. The total cost of the project is established and the budget is approved after adding contingency and management reserves to it.

PMBOK reference: (7.3, pg. 248)

396: A

There are two techniques that can be used to compress a schedule. Fast-tracking and crashing. Fast-tracking the schedule is done by putting the activities is parallel and crashing the schedule is achieved by adding more resources so that the work can be completed earlier. Since the scope cannot be reduced, crashing is the technique to be used by engaging more resources instead of fast-tracking which will increase the chances of failure. Analyzing and forecasting schedule does not compress the schedule but only establishes the project status.

PMBOK reference: (6.5.2.6, pg. 215 and 6.6.2.6, pg. 228)

397: B

Timeboxing helps in reducing scope creep which may result in faster delivery with higher quality and lower cost. Timeboxed iteration is an iteration where the duration of the iteration is fixed and work is carried on. Once the duration ends, the iteration is terminated whether work was completed or not. This helps in focusing on high priority and high-value features and functions and helps in reducing scope creep.

PMBOK reference: (6.1.3.1, pg. 182)

398: D

Rewards decisions can be made formally or informally while managing the project team. All the other three are correct statements.

PMBOK reference: (9.4.2.5, pg. 341)

399: D

The manual bottom-up summation is the most common method used by project teams for forecasting the project's performance. The other three methods require some statistical analysis and will be used based on the result of the analysis.

PMBOK reference: (7.4.2.2, pg. 264)

400: D

Organizational process assets include the risk breakdown structure and risk management templates, policies, and procedures. Policies and procedures cannot be updated through projects though recommendation for an update can be made. So 'risk breakdown structure' and 'risk management templates' is the correct answer.

PMBOK reference: (11.7.3.5, pg. 458)

7 - ANSWERS & EXPLANATIONS TEST 3

401: A
In the Initiating process group, the project charter is developed and the stakeholders are identified and recorded on the stakeholder register. Both processes, Develop Project Charter and Identify Stakeholders, are the only processes that belong to Initiating process group.
PMBOK reference: (1.2.4.5, pg. 23)

402: B
Risk appetite is the degree of uncertainty an organization or an individual is willing to accept for getting a reward. The degree of risk someone will be able to withstand is risk tolerance.
PMBOK reference: (Risk appetite, pg. 720)

403: B
Asking what and why is a characteristic of a leader. Asking how and when, doing things the right way, and focusing on the bottom line are characteristics of a manager.
PMBOK reference: (3.4.5, pg. 63)

404: A
The project manager is using the transactional leadership style where the focus is on the goals and feedback. It is also called management by exception since the project manager will only intervene in the decision making if the alignment with project goals is in jeopardy. In laissez-faire, the team sets up its goals and makes decisions. In transformational, the focus is on inspiration and encouragement for higher creativity. In charismatic, the ability to inspire due to high enthusiasm and convictions is the approach.

PMBOK reference: (3.4.5.1, pg. 65)

405: A

The purpose of the Validate Scope process is to formalize the acceptance of the deliverables. Therefore, accepted deliverables will be an output of the Validate Scope process. Verified deliverables from the Control Quality process are an input to the Validate Scope process. Change requests can only be created but are not evaluated and accepted in this process. Signed statement of work can be an input as part of scope baseline but is not an output.

PMBOK reference: (5.5.3.1, pg. 166)

406: C

This is best handled with a quality audit of the plan and quality control measurements against the company policies. A quality audit can identify nonconformances, gaps, and shortcomings. As you have already explained to the sponsor that all test results are good, repeating the same will not likely have any effect. Retesting without any valid reason will be waste of time and money. Getting help from the senior manager is a vague approach as no clear direction has been mentioned as to what type of help will be sought.

PMBOK reference: (8.2.2.5, pg. 294)

407: C

Scheduling software tools, work authorization systems, information distribution systems, configuration management systems, and interfaces to other online automated systems are all part of the project management information system. These are not organizational process assets or deliverables. Organizational systems as the answer is too general so it is a weak choice.

PMBOK reference: (4.3.2.2, pg. 95)

408: D

Evaluate program and project proposal to derive maximum value out of the investment is the main goal of portfolio management. The focus on creating a balanced portfolio helps in achieving the strategic goals of the organization. All others are the responsibilities of the project management office.

PMBOK reference: (1.2.3.3, pg. 15)

409: B

First, establish the scheduling method and then select the scheduling tool to be used. Afterward, an appropriate model will be selected to develop the schedule. The schedule will get more data as project data is created or becomes available otherwise. For example, if the precedence diagramming method is selected as the scheduling method, then the tool can be Microsoft Project, and the model can come from a template or a previous project in Microsoft Project. The template or the previous Project is populated with the project scheduling data to develop the schedule.

PMBOK reference: (Figure 6-2, pg. 176)

410: C

Competency can be the issue if significant errors are noted in the work done by a resource. Resource allocation and authority do not result in a high error rate. Resource programming is not a term in this context.

PMBOK reference: (9.1.3.1, pg. 319)

411: C

Unless it was written in the contract that the final deliverable, the new chemical mixing machine, will be used for one year before acceptance, this might be a wrong approach according to the contract. There could be a support or warranty period defined in the contract that says that for one year the product will be maintained by the manufacturer at no cost to the customer.

PMBOK reference: (4.7.2.3 and 4.7.3.2, pg. 127)

412: B

Analyze communication requirements of stakeholders' is not a part of stakeholder analysis. This will be done as part of developing the communication management plan. All other choices are explored as part of stakeholder analysis.

PMBOK reference: (13.1.2.3, pg. 512)

413: A

The project budget is the Budget At Completion (BAC) which is 700,000. This is also called the cost baseline. The rest of the information is not needed to answer this question.

PMBOK reference: (7.4.2.2, pg. 261)

414: B

Resource optimization helps engage resources at or below their availability level so it may remove over-allocation of resources. Resource leveling can result in the change of the schedule critical path. Resource optimization does not reduce the impact of the low skill level of resources.

PMBOK reference: (6.5.2.3, pg. 211)

415: C

Once the contract is terminated, one of the first things to do is to transition the final or intermediate product, service, or result to the buyer. There is no need for negotiations as the decision to terminate has already been made. A dispute may or may not result from contract termination so it cannot be said that disputes will be triggered. Final report preparation is one of the last activities done in the Close Project or Phase process.

PMBOK reference: (4.7.3.2, pg. 127)

416: B

Quality control compares the results of quality measurements with the quality standards set in the quality plan while quality assurance audits the quality control measurements and quality plan against the company quality policies and procedures.

PMBOK reference: (8.2, pg. 289 and 8.3, pg. 298)

417: C

Safety measures' is a characteristic of the cost of conformance. All other three are characteristics of the cost of nonconformance.

PMBOK reference: (Figure 8-5, pg. 283)

418: D

The Monitor and Control Project Work process is concerned with the monitoring of the implementation of approved changes. Approving and rejecting changes happens in the Perform Integrated Change Control process while implementation of approved changes is done in the Direct and Manage Project Work process.

PMBOK reference: (4.5, pg. 107)

419: A

A project charter is not a contract as there is no consideration or benefit exchanged that arises from it. Even in the case of external projects where there is a contract, a project charter will be an internal agreement within the organization to ensure successful delivery of the project as per contract. All the other three are characteristics of a project charter.

PMBOK reference: (4.1, pg. 77)

420: C

The total duration of the critical path is $3+2+3+5+6+12+1+10 = 42$ days.

Duration of the critical path to deployment completion = 32 days (excludes post-deployment support)

Activity 6 which is late by 6 days gets the delay added to the critical path while activity 5 completed 1 day earlier gets the time saving deducted from the critical path. $32 + 6 - 1 = 37$ days is the minimum time it will take to deploy the project. Post-deployment support will happen after deployment.

PMBOK reference: (6.5.2.2, pg. 210)

421: D
Project funding requirements can be incremental or lump sum. For example, payments done on a monthly basis or at specific intervals will be incremental. If the payment is to be made just once, let say, at the start of the project, it will be a lump sum payment. Contingency and management reserve are part of the project budget but management reserve is not included in the funding provided to the project. Other two options are invalid.
PMBOK reference: (7.3.3.2, pg. 256)

422: C
In general, conflicts should be resolved in private in a project. This increases the chance of getting to a resolution faster, parties will be more willing to compromise, and it will be cost effective.
PMBOK reference: (9.5.2.1, pg. 348)

423: A
Project stakeholders' risk appetite and threshold have a direct impact on the responses created to manage the risks. A high appetite means responses may not be too stringent while low appetite requires very well thought out and tight risk responses. Risks identification, cost of risks, and expected monetary value, all three are not impacted by project stakeholders' risk appetite.
PMBOK reference: (11.5.1.3, pg. 441)

424: B
You should compare the performance baselines with the work performance data and calculate variances. This will generate work performance information. It will also lead to forecasting the remaining part of the project. Afterward, areas of improvement can be identified, corrective actions can be suggested, and also information can be sent to the project sponsor.
PMBOK reference: (7.4.3.1, pg. 268)

425: D
Whether it is a non-technology or a technology project, the configuration management helps in ensuring project items remain consistent and operable. The configuration management plan is part of the project management plan so 'through the project management plan' is too general and a weak answer. Change control board is a tool for approving, rejecting, or deferring changes as part of change management. The control chart is irrelevant in this scenario.

PMBOK reference: (4.6.1.1, pg. 116 and 4.6.2.2, pg. 118)

426: B

There is no estimation required for milestones. Milestones are either complete or incomplete since they have zero duration. Milestones can be defined because they are required by contract or these may be set up optionally based on historical information for better project tracking.

PMBOK reference: (6.2.3.3, pg. 186)

427: B

She can get a head start by using a WBS from a similar previous project as a template then modify it to fit the new project. A work package is the lowest level where cost and time estimates can be prepared. So it drilling down 2-3 levels only will defeat the purpose of creating work packages. Skipping the WBS entirely or asking users to prepare WBS is a bad practice. WBS should be prepared by the project team.

PMBOK reference: (5.4.2.2, pg. 159)

428: B

Project management process groups are independent of the project phases. A project phase is a collection of logically related project activities. Project management process groups are repeated in each phase but may also continue from one phase to another. For example, a design phase will be initiated, planned, executed, controlled and closed. Then a construct phase will be initiated, planned, executed, controlled, and closed.

PMBOK reference: (Figure 1-5, pg. 18 and 1.2.4.5, pg. 23)

429: B

The reason for taking up a project is that there is a business need. Therefore, performing the needs assessment to understand business goals and objectives, issues and opportunities, and recommending proposals to address them, has to be the first piece of work done to decide which project is selected for implementation. The other three options follow the needs assessment.

PMBOK reference: (1.2.6.1, pg. 30)

430: C

Project team directory can be used to record the team members and their roles and responsibilities. Resource calendar identifies the work start and end dates and other scheduling information for resources. Resource management plan guides on how resources are to be categorized, acquired, developed, managed, and released. Resource breakdown structure is the hierarchical representation of resources by category and type.

PMBOK reference: (9.3.3.2, pg. 334)

431: B

All bidders should be treated equally and fairly. No one should be given preferential treatment because they are first-time bidders or have been bidding for a long time, have worked on several contracts before, or any other reason. Therefore, the incorrect statement about vendor conferences is that "First-time bidders should be given extra attention to encourage them to bid."

PMBOK reference: (12.2.2.3, pg. 487)

432: D

Facilitation is the interpersonal skill that a project manager uses in most of the project processes. As per PMBOK guide 6th edition, facilitation is used in 9 processes while active listening and leadership are used in 3 processes and decision making is used in 1 process only.

PMBOK reference: (Table X6-1, pg. 690)

433: D

The Cost Variance (CV) and Earned Value (EV) are not indices. Cost Planned Index, Schedule Planned Index, Cost Planning Index, and Schedule Performing Index, do not exist. The correct answer is the Cost Performance Index (CPI) and Schedule Performance Index (SPI).

PMBOK reference: (7.4.2.2, pg. 263)

434: D

Make active use of progressive elaboration. Create an overall high-level plan, and then do a more accurate cost estimate and detailed plan for the nearest future. As the project progresses, go through detailed planning of the next time period. This way you can save time in initiating and planning the project and can move to executing rather quickly. Expert judgment does not speed up the process but it helps in creating an effective result. You cannot move from project charter into executing directly. You need to have a plan.

PMBOK reference: (6.2.2.3, pg. 185 and pg. 565)

435: B

In a functional organization, all work is assigned by the functional manager. Sponsor or project team members do not have the authority to assign work. Project manager assigns work in Project-oriented organization. In strong matrix organizations, the project manager may assign work based on how much time a resource has been allocated to the project by the functional manager.

PMBOK reference: (Table 2-1, pg. 47)

436: D
Upper and lower control limits can be calculated by finding out the mean and the given standard deviation. Mean or average is 352 and standard deviation is given as 49.
So upper control limit is 352 + 3 x 49 = 499 and lower control limit is 352 - 3 x 49 = 205
PMBOK reference: (8.3.2.5, pg. 304)

437: D
Project team members are acquired/engaged and developed during execution of the project or phase. Therefore you are in the Develop Team process which belongs to Executing Process Group.
PMBOK reference: (9.4, pg. 336)

438: B
Cost-benefit analysis is to determine the best corrective action in terms of cost in case of project deviations. Trend analysis is used to forecast the future performance based on past results. Root cause analysis tries to find the main reasons for a problem and variance analysis checks the difference between the plan and actual results.
PMBOK reference: (4.5.2.2, pg. 111)

439: B
Comparing sample results and measurements with the standards or metrics is part of the Control Quality process. Manage quality is about ensuring the quality management plan and quality management activities are following organizations' quality policies and procedures. There are no processes called perform quality sampling or perform quality inspection.
PMBOK reference: (8.3.3.1, pg. 305)

440: C
In order to measure Six Sigma performance, defects found are reported against how many samples were checked so stating the quality results in terms of defects per million is correct. Upper and lower specifications only provide what is the range within which results are acceptable to the customer. It is not possible to measure how many defects were not found while managing or controlling quality on a project. A Sigma is the standard deviation of the data so saying how many sigmas found is illogical in this context.
PMBOK reference: (8.2.2.8, pg. 296)

441: C
Work performance data does not exist when the Plan Procurement Management process is being conducted. It is an input to the Control

Procurements process. Scope baseline is an input to the Plan Procurement Management process which includes the project scope statement and work breakdown structure.
PMBOK reference: (Figure 12-2, pg. 466)

442: A
The checklist is the best tool among the four choices given. It lists all steps to be performed in a sequence which can be followed by different teams and individuals working in different areas. A quality management plan is a weak choice as it discusses how quality will be planned, managed, and controlled. Work breakdown structure and WBS dictionary help in breaking down project work but do not address the quality directly.
PMBOK reference: (8.2.2.1, pg. 292)

443: D
Optimal Cost of Quality is the correct choice because it compares the benefits and costs of different options and in this case, verifies if the gain from improving quality is equal to or lower than the incremental cost to achieve that quality.
PMBOK reference: (8.1.2.3, pg. 282)

444: D
When a project is canceled, the incomplete deliverables are to be handed over to the customer. This happens in the Close Project or Phase process because the process will be executed whether the project was completed or canceled. In the Control Scope process, the deliverables being developed are checked against specifications. In the Validate Scope process, the customer is asked to formally accept the deliverable only after verification is done by the Control Quality process. There is no process called as Cancel Project or Phase process.
PMBOK reference: (4.7.1.4, pg. 125)

445: B
It appears that the team is afraid that you can damage their performance review and impact their bonus. In other words, they think you have coercive power. Formal power may or may not carry with it coercive power so this is a weak choice. Referent power relates to admiration or respect and pressure-based power refers to reducing the number of choices to get compliance. Both of these powers are not what the project team is considering.
PMBOK reference: (3.4.4.3, pg. 63)

446: C
If negotiations have failed then the next logical approach is to try

mediation by asking a third party to help reach an agreement. Negotiation has already been tried so it is the wrong choice. If mediation fails, then arbitration or litigation can be taken up.

PMBOK reference: (12.3.2.2, pg. 497)

447: A

Requirements traceability matrix is the specific tool that links product requirements from their origin to the deliverables that satisfy them. It helps to ensure that each requirement adds business value by linking it to the business and project objectives. A requirements documentation lists all the requirements but does not show the link between the requirements and the deliverables.

PMBOK reference: (5.2.3.2, pg. 148)

448: B

The two types of non-event risks are variability risks and ambiguity risks. Variability risks are uncertainties related to some aspects of the project, for example, lower than expected productivity, higher snowfall in winter, etc. Ambiguity risks are due to unknown future, for example, deploying new and innovative technology.

PMBOK reference: (Non-event risks, pg. 398)

449: A

The warning sign is called a risk trigger which identifies that either a risk has occurred or is imminent. Risk Threshold is the level of risk beyond which stakeholders and organization require that a risk response is planned.

PMBOK reference: (11.5.1.2, pg. 440)

450: C

This process breaks down the quality management plan into specific steps to ensure organizations' quality policies have been incorporated into the project. The quality requirements of the project are audited and the results of quality control measurements are reviewed to ensure the requirements are adequate.

Quality of deliverables and comparison of quality control measurements against the plan happens in the Control Quality process. Audit guidelines are established in the quality management plan.

PMBOK reference: (8.2, pg. 288)

451: C

The seller selection criteria should be reviewed to select the seller for the award of the contract. The other three choices can be considered if one or all of these are part of the seller selection criteria.

PMBOK reference: (12.2.1.3, pg. 485 and 12.2.3.1, pg. 488)

452: B
Knowledge can be captured in a lessons learned register using videos, photos, audio, and other ways. Challenges and problems including recommendations and proposed actions are recorded on a lesson learned register. This information is not part of project performance report and is not consider work performance data. There is no mention of a computer hard disk as a method of recording the information.
PMBOK reference: (4.4.3.1, pg. 104)

453: C
Establishing project phases helps in better control of the project work. It also gives an opportunity to assess project performance and take appropriate corrective or preventive actions in the next phases. Based on funding conditions or timing, project phases allow split of work that can benefit from focused planning. However, faster delivery is generally not a factor considered when phases are established though it may provide interim deliverables at phase end.
PMBOK reference: (1.2.4.2, pg. 21)

454: C
When the project is behind schedule, the Schedule Variance (SV) is negative i.e. Schedule Performance Index (SPI) will be less than 1.
Since SPI = EV/PV, it means Earned Value (EV) is less than the Planned Value (PV).
PMBOK reference: (Table 7-1, pg. 267)

455: C
Once a defect has been repaired it should be reviewed to verify that the defect has been repaired and it conforms to the documented standard. Stakeholders' satisfaction though important is not something against which the 'defect repair' will be compared. Project charter only gives a high level of scope. Use of Pareto chart is invalid in this situation.
PMBOK reference: (8.3.2.3, pg. 303)

456: A
The project management plan during its development can be updated as many times as needed. No change request is required as there is no baseline or controlled document to update.
PMBOK reference: (4.2, pg. 83)

457: C
He forced the decision instead of using other techniques. If he had

listened to both arguments, understood the root cause and then provided a solution, that would have been problem-solving. If the decision was made taking some of each person's argument, it would be called compromising. If the project manager had not made a decision, then it would have been a withdrawal.

PMBOK reference: (9.5.2.1, pg. 349)

458: A

It is the most fundamental work breakdown structure components that represent verifiable products, services or results. Though deliverables also represent verifiable products, services or results; this is a weak choice because the WBS components encompass all fundamental components that makeup deliverables. A WBS has multi-level details including deliverables, work packages, and WBS components under one planning package or control account.

PMBOK reference: (5.4.2.2, pg. 160)

459: D

Benchmarking technique does not measure project performance against the plan. Using the actual or planned project practices, benchmarking technique identifies the best practices, generates ideas for improvement, and provides a basis for measuring the performance.

PMBOK reference: (8.1.2.2, pg. 281)

460: C

There are no techniques used in project management for conflict resolution called as schmooze, flatter, or ignore. The only valid choice among the four options is 'compromise, accommodate, collaborate, and force.'

PMBOK reference: (9.5.2.1, pg. 349)

461: A

Business case, benefits management plan, and agreements, are all an input to the Develop Project Charter process.

PMBOK reference: (4.1.1, pg. 77)

462: D

Transactional leadership style is similar to micro-management as it focuses on smaller details and monitors the outcome of each decision and step involved. The leader uses this approach to reward or punish based on the outcome at each transaction. The other three approaches focus more on building trust, inspiring, and motivating the team members.

PMBOK reference: (3.4.5.1, pg. 65)

463: D
The benefits management plan is an input to the Close Project or Phase process to measure whether gains from the project were achieved as planned. The business case is an input to check if the expected outcome from the economic feasibility study occurred. The other two options are incorrect.
PMBOK reference: (4.7.1.5, pg. 125)

464: A
The ceiling is the maximum price the buyer pays to the seller and any costs above the ceiling are borne by the seller. Since the total cost of the project is 260,000 but the ceiling was set at 240,000, the buyer will only pay 240,000 to the seller.
PMBOK reference: (12.1.1.6, pg. 471)

465: C
This is an example of statistical sampling where a few random tests or samples are taken and compared against the standard. The result of this sampling is taken as a result for the population. For example, if 100 random calls were made, and 90 of those say they received the flyer then it's assumed that 90,000 out of 100,000 households received the flyer.
PMBOK reference: (8.3.2.1, pg. 303)

466: B
Statement of work is a fully detailed scope of work providing sufficient information to the seller so that work can be completed successfully. It contains other information such as period and place of performance, desired results, deliverable specifications and quantity, payment schedule, warranty, and so on. Therefore, statement of work is not a high-level brief document that helps in negotiations and modifications during contract administration stage.
PMBOK reference: (12.1.3.4, pg. 477 and 12.2.3.2, pg. 489)

467: B
Although it seems that requirement gathering or project planning should be the next step, the first thing the project manager should do is to understand the purpose of the project, its objective and expected results. This is helpful in two ways; one, you validated that the project charter and, two, you developed a connection/relationship with the stakeholders especially with the sponsor.
PMBOK reference: (4.1, pg. 77)

468: C
If the contract has any term that is against the law of the land, then such

a contract is not legally binding and is unenforceable. Seller unable to perform the work, the buyer not making the payments, or contract unacceptable to the legal counsel, do not make the contract invalid.

PMBOK reference: (Key concepts..., pg. 461 and 12.2.3.2, pg. 489)

469: A

Since your manager has refused you resources, it means the resources and you both work for the same manager. This is a characteristic of a functional organization. If the resources were coming from different managers it would have been a matrix organization.

PMBOK reference: (Table 2-1, pg. 47)

470: D

Once the work breakdown structure is completed to the work package level, then the activities will be defined. Afterward, these activities will be sequenced, and then the durations will be estimated. So it is too early to talk about estimating durations.

PMBOK reference: (6.4, pg. 195)

471: A

Fishbone diagram is also known as the Ishikawa diagram, Cause-and-Effect diagram, and why-why diagram. All the other three are different types of diagramming methods.

PMBOK reference: (8.2.2.4, pg. 293)

472: D

Since not all identified risks are response planned so the risk audit does not look at all identified risks to check if these were planned or not. However, all the other three options may be the objectives of risk audit.

PMBOK reference: (11.7.2.2, pg. 456)

473: A

"As an office assistant, I need to access the supplies cabinet, so I can check which supplies are running out" is an example of a user story. A user story has three components: what is the role, what is to be done, and what is the benefit.

PMBOK reference: (5.2.2.6, pg. 145)

474: D

The first option is to see if the schedule can be compressed either by adding more resources and/or fast tracking by running activities in parallel. Any of the other options can be pursued after this is done. Asking resources to work overtime is one way a schedule can be crashed. So this is not the best answer. Cutting the scope or informing the customer that

deadline cannot be met are other options that can be looked at if compression does not produce the required result.
PMBOK reference: (6.6.2.6, pg. 228)

475: B
These types of risks are called secondary risks because they arise as a direct result of implementing a risk response. They are known risks but so are all the other risks recorded on risk register. There is no such term as responded risks defined in PMBOK guide.
PMBOK reference: (11.5, pg. 439)

476: B
You have to find out % Variance at Completion (%VAC).
%VAC = ((BAC - EAC) / BAC) x 100 where,
BAC = Budget at Completion. Since Earned Value is 200,000 and project is 50% complete. This implies
EV = 0.5 x BAC or BAC = 200,000 / 0.5 = 400,000
%VAC = ((400,000 - 500,000) / 400,000) x 100 = -25%
or 25% over the cost baseline.
PMBOK reference: (Table 7-1, pg. 267)

477: D
The contract change control system cannot be defined separately from the terms of the contract. If it is separate then it will not be part of the contract and cannot be enforced by the contract. An agreement is signed at the end of the Conduct Procurements process so there is no contract change control system to use during Plan Procurement Management and Conduct Procurements process. Control Procurements process is the only Procurement Management process where a contract change control system is used.
PMBOK reference: (12.3, pg. 494 and 12.3.3.4, pg. 499)

478: D
Official approval to proceed with the project work is obtained when the project charter is approved by the sponsor. Stakeholder identification goes on throughout the project life cycle. Deliverable acceptance happens at the Validate Scope process which is in monitoring and controlling process group. The project manager usually is assigned at the start of the initiating processes but it does not mean the project is officially being authorized to proceed.
PMBOK reference: (4.1, pg. 75)

479: B
Stakeholder engagement matrix is a technique used for engagement

planning of all stakeholders except the project team. Communications strategy and inspections are not part of this plan. Recognition and rewards are an important aspect when thinking about how the project team will be managed and how they will be rewarded for good performance. Therefore, 'recognition and rewards' is the only choice out of the four that will be considered for the team management plan.

PMBOK reference: (9.1.3.1, pg. 319)

480: B

The bottom-up estimating technique generally results in the most accurate estimate among the four techniques given. Top-down estimation is another name for analogous estimation technique, and it is less accurate. The parametric estimate can be fairly accurate depending on the quality and type of data used.

PMBOK reference: (6.4.2.5, pg. 201 and 7.2.2.4, pg. 244)

481: D

Using six sigma quality means a maximum of 3.4 defective parts per million is acceptable. Therefore, out of the 10,000 parts, there will be zero parts acceptable as defective parts.

PMBOK reference: (8.2.2.8, pg. 296)

482: C

Total work = 1,000 light fixtures
Total duration = 10 days
Work productivity required = 1,000 / 10 = 100 light fixtures / day
Work hours in a day = 8 hours
Work productivity required per hour = 100/8 = 12.5 light fixtures/hour
Number of electricians = 2
Work productivity per electrician = 12.5 /2 = 6.25 light fixtures/hour
PMBOK reference: (9.2.2.4, pg. 324)

483: C

All the 'projects' are in reality repeated operational activities. Whether an order is 10 or 300,000 has no bearing on how it is processed i.e. it is processed the same way. Though each order has a start and an end date, there is no unique product as an output; it is the same product.

PMBOK reference: (1.2.1, pg. 4)

484: A

Use the integrated change control system to record and assess if a change to the scope is required and what the impact might be and then process that for approval. All other options can only be acted on once an assessment is done and change has been evaluated.

PMBOK reference: (4.6, pg. 113)

485: B
Concerns regarding delays, cost overruns, and quality are called issues and should be recorded and tracked on an issue log. An issue log is an effective tool to track the evaluation and resolution of issues. Change log tracks the changes to ensure proposed changes go through evaluation and approval while approved changes complete implementation. Assumption log records and tracks assumptions until they are known as facts or no longer exist as assumptions. The risk register is used to track risks during various stages of risk management.
PMBOK reference: (4.3.3.3, pg. 96)

486: D
Resource leveling is not a solution to this problem. In fact, resource leveling may extend the schedule for optimizing resource usage. However, the schedule can be crashed by adding resources and/or can be fast tracked by running activities in parallel. The critical path can also be shortened by removing an activity from the critical path, if possible.
PMBOK reference: (6.6.2.6, pg. 228)

487: D
This information is part of the final report of the project created in the Close Project or Phase project. The benefits management plan and business case are created before the start of the project so these documents do not contain evidence that the project objectives have actually been met. Quality reports provide information that can be used by various processes to take corrective actions to achieve the project quality objectives.
PMBOK reference: (4.7.3.3, pg. 127)

488: B
An email that does not follow any specific pattern and it is written in an unofficial spontaneous manner is an informal written communication. Sometimes it can be a formal written communication if a template is used to send a formal message.
PMBOK reference: (Informal, pg. 361)

489: C
The probability is 70% and the impact to the schedule is 10%.
So, 0.7 x 0.1 = 0.07 is the value of risk.
PMBOK reference: (11.3.2.3, pg. 423)

490: D
The Develop Project Charter process is performed only once at the start

of the project. It may be rarely repeated at pre-defined points, for example, at the start of a new phase when each phase is being formally initiated.

PMBOK reference: (1.2.4.4, pg. 22)

491: C

You will need project communications that were distributed to stakeholders according to the communication management and stakeholder engagement plan. For stakeholder management, the project charter is only needed when identifying stakeholder. Change log is an input to Manage Stakeholder Engagement process to communicate change requests and their status to stakeholders. The project schedule is an input to Plan Stakeholder Engagement process because it contains information on activities relationships to stakeholders.

PMBOK reference: (13.4.1.2, pg. 532)

492: D

The final report is an output created in the Close Project or Phase process and so it cannot be reviewed as an input to the process. Risk report is an input to ensure there are no open risks. Quality reports are an input to confirm all quality assurance issues have been managed. Contracts provide the requirements for formally closing the procurements.

PMBOK reference: (4.7.1.3, and 4.7.1.6, pg. 124-125)

493: D

The business case and project charter are not modified. The change to those two documents is only needed if there is a significant change to the project objectives. In that case, the project will likely be terminated. Approved changes cannot be tracked against the cost and schedule baselines if the baselines have not been impacted. Work authorization system sequences and authorizes work. The work has to be included in the project plan before it can be performed. Therefore, approved change requests have to be implemented through the Direct and Manage Project Work process.

PMBOK reference: (4.3.1.3, pg. 92)

494: D

Though all four options are helpful in making the presentation successful but asking for specific support at the end will help the most. This can only happen if the project manager is well aware of the needs and objectives of the project and the team as well as the expectations of the audience.

PMBOK reference: (10.2.2.3, pg. 384)

495: B
Assumptions log is not one of the documents updated as part of the Implement Risk Responses process. However, it may get updated during Monitor Risks process. Issue log, risk register, and project team assignments are likely to be updated as part of the Implement Risk Responses process.
PMBOK reference: (11.6.3.2, pg. 452)

496: C
Schedule Performance Index (SPI) = 1.06 and Schedule Variance (SV) = 10,000 only tells us that we are ahead of schedule but does not provide us the complete picture. We need to know the actual cost and earned value to calculate what is being asked by the finance representative by using the formula:
Cost Variance (CV) = Earned Value (EV) - Actual Cost (AC)
PMBOK reference: (7.4.2.2, pg. 262)

497: A
The statement of work is not a type of contract itself but it is a component of contracts. All the other three are types of contracts.
PMBOK reference: (12.1.1.6, pg. 471)

498: B
The problem is with deliverables being produced late so there is no need to involve the team leader of the receiving team. Even if the second team is still able to produce their deliverables in time, the issue needs to be addressed, since late deliverables of the first team are affecting the second team's schedule. The best approach is to discuss with the first team leader why the deliverables are being produced late and what can be done to fix that. This should preferably be done in private using a collaborative approach.
PMBOK reference: (9.5.2.1, pg. 348)

499: C
The fixed price would be the riskiest contract in this case where it is a very large multi-million dollars contract where the scope and specifications of deliverables may not be well defined.
PMBOK reference: (12.1.1.6, pg. 471)

500: B
A stakeholder is someone who is impacted by the project or can influence the project so the stakeholder cannot be removed from the project. Discouraging right at the start that very few changes will be entertained will damage the relationship as this message shows that it is more important to reduce the number of changes than completing

deliverables that give the value expected by the stakeholders. The best approach is to involve the stakeholder actively earlier in the project so that changes get proposed and processed in the early stages when the impact of the change is lower.

PMBOK reference: (13.3, pg. 524)

501: B

Storytelling, communities of practice, conferences, and networking are all examples of knowledge management tools and techniques. All the other three options are incorrect.

PMBOK reference: (4.4.2.2, pg. 103)

502: B

Level of precision is typically not a concern when planning for schedule management. However, when planning for cost management, rounding up and down the cost can result in significant difference and that is why a certain level of precision is established in the cost management plan.

PMBOK reference: (6.1.3.1, pg. 182)

503: D

It cannot be said that the internal team's estimate must be incorrect. It may or may not be correct but bidders would not know what the internal estimate is for the work so it cannot be a reason. All the other are valid reasons for a low number of bid submissions.

PMBOK reference: (12.2.1.3, pg. 485 and 12.2.2.3, pg. 487)

504: D

You do not have any power and have very low interest in the project. So she should classify you as a stakeholder with low power and low interest.

PMBOK reference: (13.1.2.4, pg. 512)

505: C

Rolling wave planning technique is not a sequential technique. It is an iterative technique for decomposing work and can also be called as a type of progressive elaboration.

PMBOK reference: (6.2.2.3, pg. 185)

506: A

This is because expected monetary value is not the cost of the risk impact but the probabilistic value of the risk. The project manager is happy with the outcome because the risk event was expected to be of much higher cost than 15,000. There is no indication of being under budget or ahead of schedule in the scenario so these are not the correct choices.

PMBOK reference: (11.4.2.5, pg. 435)

507: A
Change log is the input to the Manage Stakeholder Engagement process while change request is the output of the process. Work performance data and assumption log are neither the input nor the output of the process.
PMBOK reference: (Figure 13-7, pg. 523)

508: B
Acquiring resources is done in the Acquire Resource process. In Control Resources process, resources are released for use at the right time, at the right place and in the right amount; resource expenses are monitored, and any resource shortage or surplus is dealt with.
PMBOK reference: (9.6, pg. 354)

509: D
Trend analysis is a type of analysis where organizational models are validated using data from the project. Regression analysis is where interrelationships between various project variables are reviewed for their contribution to the project outcomes. Schedule analysis includes different techniques used for developing and refining the schedule. There is no technique called model analysis identified in PMBOK guide.
PMBOK reference: (4.7.2.2, pg. 126)

510: C
Only the Develop Project Charter process is in the Initiating process group. All other processes, mentioned as choices, are part of the Planning process group.
PMBOK reference: (4.1, pg. 75)

511: C
Reconciling the cost estimate with the approved budget happens in the Determine Budget process. The process involves aggregating the cost of the project and reconciling with the approved budget to confirm that enough funds are available.
PMBOK reference: (7.3.2.5, pg. 253)

512: D
Monitor Communications process does not include the identification of new stakeholders. All the other three are objectives that can be achieved through this process.
PMBOK reference: (10.3, pg. 388 and 10.3.3.2, pg. 393)

513: A
Functional manager and portfolio manager will be highly concerned with the department's overall strategic goals. Therefore, she cannot be any

of these two. The program manager will be more concerned about her role's commitment i.e. program commitments than the department's strategic goals. She has invited the three project managers in her program to discuss projects' progress.

PMBOK reference: (Table 1-2, pg. 12)

514: B

Reduction of scope is not part of crashing the schedule or even fast-tracking the schedule. However, the schedule can be crashed by adding more resources, asking resources to work overtime, and/or providing an incentive to the vendor for early delivery of work.

PMBOK reference: (6.5.2.6, pg. 215)

515: A

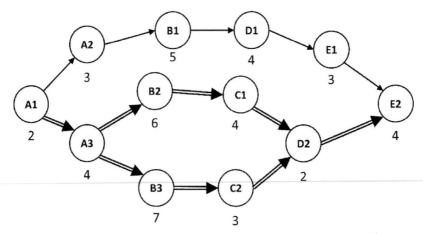

There are two critical paths, as shown in the figure, with a duration of 22. The critical path is the longest path from start to finish.

PMBOK reference: (6.5.2.2, pg. 210)

516: C

Informing stakeholder that the information is being sent as per communication plan does not resolve the complaint so this is not a good choice. Asking stakeholder to review the documentation in the project repository is like asking a customer to a bookstore looking for a specific book to go and find it among thousands of books in the store. Reviewing stakeholder's information needs is the right step followed by updating the project communication management plan if needed. Just sending the plan for review does not do any good.

PMBOK reference: (10.3.3.2, pg. 393)

517: B
TCPI = (BAC - EV) / (EAC - AC) where,
TCPI = To Complete Performance Index
BAC = Budget At Completion
EV = Earned Value
EAC = Estimate At Completion
AC = Actual Cost
ETC = Estimate To Complete

EAC = AC + ETC ---> EAC - AC = ETC = 200,000 given
EV = 60% of BAC = 60% of 500,000 = 300,000
BAC - EV = 500,000 - 300,000 = 200,000
Therefore, TCPI = 200,000 / 200,000 = 1.0
PMBOK reference: (7.4.2.3, pg. 266)

518: B
Business need is well explained in the business case along with some discussion on the implementation approach. Statement of work and project management plan do not contain these pieces of information. Typically there is no mention of business need in the project charter.
PMBOK reference: (1.2.6.1, pg. 31-32)

519: B
To Complete Performance Index describes how the rest of the work needs to be done to meet the originally planned target date and budget. So a TCPI above 1 means performance needs to improve, in this case, 10% above the originally planned performance.
PMBOK reference: (7.4.2.3, pg. 266)

520: B
Corrective and preventive actions are not processes. Integrated change control process (which is part of the monitoring and controlling process) will be used if a change has been identified. In this case, control scope process will be used to review the work package, find the scope variance, and how it impacts schedule or cost, and then integrated change management will be performed, if needed.
PMBOK reference: (5.6.3.1, pg. 170)

521: A
Upgrade of the application every two to three years seems like an operational activity but it is, in fact, a project. The reason is that,
1) Each upgrade will have a definite start and an end
2) Each upgrade will result in a unique product (new features, functionality, security, etc.)

3) Each upgrade creates some business value
PMBOK reference: (1.2.3.4, pg. 16)

522: A
The currency exchange rate is not only considered when using team members from other countries. It will also be important when physical resources from other countries are being acquired, imported, exported, or used. All the other three options are true.
PMBOK reference: (7.1.1.3, pg. 236-237)

523: B
Analogous estimation uses historical data from similar projects to estimate. Since this is a leading edge product there is no previous similar project so this technique may not be effective. Parametric estimation method is also not good for estimating an innovative project as it needs historical data and data from other variables which will not be available. The best technique, in this case, is three-point estimate which is very effective when dealing with high uncertainty.
PMBOK reference: (7.2.2.5, pg. 244)

524: A
Schedule compression is the technique that is used for reducing the schedule. The schedule can be fast-tracked or crashed. Resource optimization, critical path method, and Monte Carlo simulation can help understand the impact but are not the specific techniques used for this purpose.
PMBOK reference: (6.6.2.6, pg. 228)

525: D
Best action is to recommend a change to the company's training policy to allow training of the temporary project resources. This will not just help the current project but future projects too. Waiving training is the same as having untrained resources and the result of that is already evident from a high number of defects. So that is an incorrect approach. If internal trained programmers were available for project work that would have been the first choice. The reason to hire temporary programmers was that internal resources were not available. Training the temporary resources on coding standards is against the company policy whether the formal training is conducted or a brief presentation is provided.
PMBOK reference: (8.2.2.5, pg. 294)

526: A
These documents are all project documents and will be stored as such. Though these documents can be used by future projects as a source of

historical information and/or lessons learned study, they will still be identified as project documents. Project or phase closure documents consists of formal documentation indicating project completion or termination and the reasons thereof as well as the formal procedure of handing over completed and incomplete deliverables.
PMBOK reference: (4.7.3.4, pg. 128)

527: A
Work breakdown structure, which is a part of the scope baseline, is needed for defining activities. Cost can only be estimated after the activities are defined. Parametric estimating is a technique and not an input to the Estimate Costs process. Sponsor's commitment does not have any impact on the estimate. Resource breakdown structure is not used in estimation and is irrelevant.
PMBOK reference: (7.1.3.1, pg. 239)

528: C
When the revenue from improvements becomes equal to the incremental costs to achieve those improvements, optimal quality has been reached. Costs to improve quality further do not increase the revenue at the same rate. This means more money will be spent improving the quality than what will be gained from that improvement.
PMBOK reference: (8.1.2.3, pg. 282)

529: C
The scenario talks about agreement around a discussion. The body language acknowledges that the team member disagrees with the project manager's proposal. Though the message was transmitted the question is asking about disagreement of the team member so this is not the best answer. There is no negotiation and distribution in this case.
PMBOK reference: (10.2.2.3, pg. 384)

530: B
Issue log is not an input to the Direct and Manage Project Work process. All the other three are input to the process.
PMBOK reference: (4.3, pg. 90)

531: C
Communication activity is not a tool and technique of the Manage Communications process. All others are tools and techniques used in this process.
PMBOK reference: (Figure 10-5, pg. 379)

532: C

The scope management plan provides how the project and product scope will be managed and controlled. Scope control plan and scope validation plan do not exist separately but are included in the scope management plan and address their relevant areas.

PMBOK reference: (5.6.1.1, pg. 169)

533: A

A scope management plan includes the processes to prepare a project scope statement, enable the creation of WBS, establish how scope baseline will be approved and maintained, and specify how formal acceptance of the completed project deliverables will be obtained. Requirements are recorded in the requirements documentation, while deliverables and their acceptance criteria are defined in the project scope statement. The requirements prioritization process is part of the requirements management plan.

PMBOK reference: (5.1.3.1, pg. 137)

534: A

Project manager uses available knowledge and current performance to forecast the project. In order to use earned value to forecast, the project manager needs all the available knowledge. He knew current trend from earned value but now uses available knowledge to predict that the current trend will continue. There is no use of interpersonal skills or problem-solving in this scenario.

PMBOK reference: (7.4.2.2, pg. 264)

535: C

There is no value in adding an issue to the lesson learned document without the solution. Similarly, creating a change request document without knowing what the change is useless. Also, the work is already stopped so issuing a notification does not produce any value. The best option is to inform the sponsor and affected stakeholders about the issue and provide a target resolution date. This is important to avoid surprises to the stakeholders which may damage the trust and relationship with the project manager.

PMBOK reference: (4.3.3.3, pg. 96)

536: D

The terms of the payment are part of the contract and fixed unless changed through a change request. These will not be negotiated for individual payments. All the other options are part of the payment system when payments are being made.

PMBOK reference: (12.3, pg. 494)

537: A
Project charter provides an initial list of stakeholders that will be the starting point to identify all the stakeholders of the project. Stakeholder register is an output of the Identify Stakeholders process so it cannot be the document to see an initial list of stakeholders. Resource breakdown structure and team rosters are limited to project team and resources. Also, both of these documents are created later during project planning.
PMBOK reference: (13.1.1.1, pg. 509)

538: B
Any proposed change requires that it be evaluated before any action can be suggested. Therefore the best option is to ask the customer to send in the details of the scope change in writing so that it can be entered into the change management system and then an evaluation of the proposed change can be done to see how it impacts the project.
PMBOK reference: (4.6, pg. 115)

539: C
Parametric estimation uses the statistical relationship between historical data and other factors to come up with an estimate. So 300 per day for an expert resource would be the use of parametric estimating. Project cost summed up from each activity's estimate is bottom-up estimating. Project cost distributed down to each activity is top-down estimating. Lessons learned from a previous project is analogous estimating.
PMBOK reference: (7.2.2.3, pg. 244)

540: D
The first thing to do is to record this issue on the issue log. It is highly unlikely that the resignation can be rejected and it may be against the local employment regulations. Fast-tracking the schedule requires an assessment of the situation which should have been done already but the question does not provide any such information. Similarly, there may be constraints associated with hiring a new resource so this also has to be evaluated.
PMBOK reference: (4.3.3.3, pg. 96)

541: D
The purpose of the project is included in the project charter and usually is based on the same as in the business case. All other choices get created later in planning processes.
PMBOK reference: (4.1.3.1, pg. 81)

542: A
Rework is an example of internal failure costs while liabilities is an example of external failure costs. Destructive testing is an example of

appraisal costs. Quality control refers to the Control Quality process.
PMBOK reference: (8.1.2.3, pg. 283)

543: A
It is a formal written communication that is shared with project stakeholders as per communications management plan. It is also called the work performance report or progress report and can contain status, graphs, forecasts, and other information.
PMBOK reference: (10.2.1.3, pg. 382 and pg. 361)

544: C
This is an example of the cost of non-conformance which results due to rework, errors, and defects. Cost of quality as a choice is too general.
PMBOK reference: (8.1.2.3., pg. 283)

545: D
Analogous estimating is a less accurate method than the bottom-up estimating technique. However, it is a quick method, costs less, and frequently used.
PMBOK reference: (6.4.2.2, pg. 200 and 7.2.2.2, pg. 244)

546: A
Work performance data will not be an output of this effort. It was the input that was analyzed and the variance was observed. This may lead to the seller's performance evaluation, change requests, and updates to organizational process assets.
PMBOK reference: (12.3.3.4, pg. 499 and 12.3.3.7, pg. 501)

547: D
Stakeholder engagement matrix will likely have no purpose to serve when included in a work performance report. All other three are commonly part of the work performance report as they establish the current status of the project and help provide the trend and forecast.
PMBOK reference: (10.2.1.3, pg. 382)

548: B
Stakeholders have the most impact at the start of the project because at that time the direction of the project, the requirements and the deliverables, and all other attributes are being set. Any change or addition at this stage has a minimum impact on the project's cost and time and thus it is easier to make such changes.
PMBOK reference: (1.5 and Figure 1-3, pg. 549)

549: C
In the Validate Scope process, completed deliverables are submitted to the sponsor for acceptance who will accept or reject the deliverables. Rejection may result in a change request. Therefore, 'accepted deliverables' is the correct answer. Inspection and product analysis are tools and techniques. Work performance data is an input to the process.
PMBOK reference: (Figure 5-15, pg. 163)

550: B
A change request to update performance baselines is the best answer because not only that the extra cost needs to be added to the project cost but also the additional scope is to be added to the project scope. It is possible that a change to schedule baseline may also be needed. A rejection letter may be written once the change is evaluated, reviewed and rejected, and the change is out of the scope of the project.
PMBOK reference: (5.6.3.2, pg. 170)

551: A
From the scenario, the point of change is the award ceremony and the dinner. The event was supposed to further improve the performance but had the opposite effect. One of the best practices in reward management is to reward the whole team when the whole team is working together to achieve goals. Rewards should satisfy and motivate individual team members, so the cultural difference should be looked at while making a reward decision. Awarding one or two people can demoralize other team members who now see their fellow team members as competitors. Development of such a feeling destroys the team environment and performance. So the best option is to review the reward system of the project.
PMBOK reference: (9.4.2.5, pg. 341)

552: A
Risk breakdown structure is not an output of the Monitor Risks process, and so it is not an update to the risk register. Risk register updates can include newly identified risks, updates to outdated or obsolete risks, and updates to planned risk responses. Realized risks are also updated.
PMBOK reference: (11.7.3.4, pg. 458)

553: B
The classification scheme that can help in assessing stakeholders' current level of engagement is unaware, resistant, neutral, supportive, and leading. Engaged, disengaged, neither engaged nor disengaged is too vague to be used as a classification scheme to assess the level of engagement. Unanimity, majority, plurality, and autocratic are methods of decision

making. Proximity, manageability, connectivity, detectability, and propinquity are parameters for risk prioritization in qualitative risk analysis.
PMBOK reference: (13.2.2.5, pg. 521)

554: A
The project scope statement does not contain the work packages. The Create WBS process which comes after the Define Scope process is where work packages are created by decomposing the project scope. All the other three are part of the project scope statement.
PMBOK reference: (5.3.3.1, pg. 154)

555: A
Work breakdown structure (WBS) does not have any information related to project objectives. The project objective is what drives the development of WBS, but it does not appear on the WBS. All the other choices can be derived from the work breakdown structure.
PMBOK reference: (5.4.3.1, pg. 162)

556: C
Experience will not be a criterion to consider when selecting physical resources. However, it will be one factor to consider when selecting the project team members. Availability of the physical resource when needed on the project, the cost to use the physical resource, and the capability or capacity of the physical resource will be used as criteria for selecting physical project resources.
PMBOK reference: (9.3.2.1, pg. 332)

557: D
Trend analysis is not used for risk identification. All the other three tools are used for risk identification as per PMBOK guide.
PMBOK reference: (11.2.2.3, pg. 415)

558: D
The Start-to-Finish relationship is rarely used when developing the precedence network diagrams. This relationship says that once an activity starts only then another activity can finish.
PMBOK reference: (6.3.2.1, pg. 190)

559: A
Pareto chart is not used as a tool and technique for Control Schedule process. All the other three options are tools and techniques used during the Control Schedule process.
PMBOK reference: (6.6, pg. 222)

560: B
Management reserve is not part of the cost baseline so it is not included in the earned value analysis. Value of the completed work is called the earned value, authorized budget assigned to scheduled work is called planned value, and actual cost of work performed is called actual cost.
PMBOK reference: (7.4.2.2, pg.261)

561: D
All this information and more are found in the communications management plan. The stakeholder register does not provide information about the format and type of communication. RACI chart shows the role and responsibilities of the project team members. Performance report shows the project status and forecast.
PMBOK reference: (10.1.3.1, pg. 377)

562: B
Risk ranking is an output of the Qualitative Risk Analysis process where the probability and the impact of each risk have been assessed that leads to the prioritization of risks for further analysis. Expert judgment is a technique that helps in the ranking. Planning risk responses process comes at a later stage after prioritized risks have been quantified. SWOT analysis is used for the identification of risks.
PMBOK reference: (11.3, pg. 419)

563: A
By securing data through password protection on both the laptop and the portable backup device you may stop data leak but you will still lose both in the above scenario so this cannot be a response plan for above situation. This is an example of a secondary risk that arises when a risk response is implemented.
PMBOK reference: (11.5, pg. 439)

564: D
The project sponsor should be managed closely as this stakeholder has high power in the organization and high interest in the project.

The power/interest grid classification is:
High power / high interest - Manage them closely
High power / low interest - Keep them satisfied
Low power / high interest - Keep them informed
Low power / low interest - Monitor them
PMBOK reference: (13.1.2.4, pg. 512)

565: B

The best option to resolve any dispute with the seller is to go through alternative dispute resolution. These techniques are negotiation, mediation, arbitration, and litigation where the preferred one is the negotiation technique.

PMBOK reference: (12.3.2.2, pg. 498)

566: C

Team communication and collaboration becomes more effective when the team is colocated. Both colocation and the virtual team environment require the almost same level of communication from the project manager. Whether colocated or not, team communication is still required. Cost is dependent on the cost of colocation vs. cost of working remotely as well as the cost of communication.

PMBOK reference: (9.4.2.1, pg. 340)

567: C

Global project with team members in different continents is a constraint on project communication. Language and working time are two reasons for that.

PMBOK reference: (Trends..., pg. 311 and 9.4, pg. 338)

568: A

Although documenting each stakeholder's requirements is a good idea, ranking them in terms of favorability to the project will only create friction among various stakeholders. Only stakeholders who are not impacted by the project and cannot influence the project should be removed from stakeholders list. The sponsor can help in classifying stakeholders but cannot advise in concrete terms as to who should be taken care of more than the others. It is the project manager's responsibility to understand the impact and influence and manage them accordingly. The best option is to use traceability matrix and prioritization process to deliver high-value requirements.

PMBOK reference: (5.1.3.2, pg. 137)

569: C

A scatter diagram will show the planned performance on one axis and the actual performance on the second axis. A histogram displays the frequency of defects by category. A control chart shows whether the process is stable or not. A fishbone diagram breaks down the problem to find the root cause.

PMBOK reference: (8.3.2.5, pg. 304)

570: A
The project life cycle is a component of the project management plan, and thus it is an output of the Develop Project Management Plan. Therefore, it generally does not impact the development of the project charter. This is because the charter is to be developed during the initiating process of the project. However, the project life cycle is selected or finalized during the project management plan development, which occurs after the charter is approved. The other three choices impact the project charter.
PMBOK reference: (4.2.3.1, pg. 88)

571: B
Projects may or may not be strategic. There can be projects to meet regulatory or legal requirements or satisfy stakeholder requests. All the other are essential characteristics of a project.
PMBOK reference: (1.2.1, pg. 4-9)

572: C
Anita: Speed is 300 LOC/day but with error rate of 12%, real speed is 264 LOC/day. So time estimate is 100,000/264 = 380 days approximately. The cost is 380 x 40 x 8 = 121,600.

Barry: Speed is 400 LOC/day but with error rate of 10%, real speed is 360 LOC/day. So time estimate is 100,000/360 = 280 days approximately. The cost is 280 x 50 x 8 = 112,800

Cathy: Speed is 500 LOC/day but with error rate of 10%, real speed is 450 LOC/day. So time estimate is 100,000/450 = 220 days approximately. The cost is 220 x 60 x 8 = 105,600

David: Speed is 600 LOC/day but with error rate of 2%, real speed is 588 LOC/day. So time estimate is 100,000/588 = 170 days approximately. The cost is 170 x 100 x 8 = 136,000

Therefore, Cathy costs the least among all the four resources.
PMBOK reference: (9.2.2.5, pg. 325)

573: D
Work performance data is the input to the Control Stakeholder Engagement process. It includes data about the stakeholders and their current engagement level. Work performance information is the output of this process.
PMBOK reference: (13.4.1.3, pg. 532)

574: B
Size of the project team, geographical location of team members, and security and privacy of data, all have an impact on the communication needs of the project. Your experience as a project manager has no bearing on the communication needs of the project.
PMBOK reference: (10.1.3.1, pg. 377)

575: C
The best approach is to face the speaker and maintain eye contact. This way the team member is not only listening but also taking in non-verbal communication that plays a big role in understanding the message.
PMBOK reference: (102.2.3, pg. 384)

576: B
At this stage, he can only provide a rough order of magnitude estimate, also known as the ball-park estimate. It is a very high level and rough estimate in the range of -25% to +75%. The analogous estimate could have been used if there was a similar project in the past and its costs were available. Parametric and bottom-up estimates are fairly accurate estimates but cannot be provided at a high level during initiating.
PMBOK reference: (7.2, pg. 241)

577: C
Change log is an input to the identify stakeholder process. Assumption log and risk register are outputs of the process. Stakeholder mapping is a tool and technique used in the Identify Stakeholders process.
PMBOK reference: (Figure 13-2, pg. 507)

578: A
It is a list of sellers whose qualifications and experiences are found to be competent to perform the work and thus can be invited to bid for the work. Since they are already found to be qualified (prequalified) the bid will not include qualification components but only the price, terms and statement of work.
PMBOK reference: (12.1.3.1, pg. 475 and 12.3.3.7, pg. 501)

579: C
The first thing you should do is initiate a change request that will be evaluated and approved through the Perform Integrated Change Control process. All other options may end up being the recommendations of the review of the change request.
PMBOK reference: (4.3.3.4, pg. 96)

580: D
Stakeholder engagement plan identifies the strategies and actions required to involve and engage the stakeholders. Stakeholder register contains the list of identified stakeholders and their interest and influence on the project. Power/interest grid and salience model are used to classify the stakeholders.
PMBOK reference: (13.2.2.1, pg. 522)

581: A
The cost performance baseline is what is being impacted and will need to be modified once a change request is approved. So cost performance baseline cannot be followed. Change control board is the one that rejects or approves the change request. There is nothing to follow here. Monitoring and controlling process group contains all the processes that relate to monitoring and controlling the project. So the process group cannot be followed but a process can be. So this cannot be the choice. The change's cost estimate has to be followed to implement the change. This estimate will be recommended for approval through the change request and once approved will be used to update the cost performance baseline.
PMBOK reference: (7.4.3.3, pg. 269 and 7.4.3.5, pg. 270)

582: A
Since the project is moving from one phase to another, the work/deliverables created or updated in this phase need to be formally accepted by the sponsor/customer before closing this phase and moving on to the development phase. Quality control of the design was already completed as mentioned in the question. There is no indication in the question that it is a new team or more developers are to be hired.
PMBOK reference: (5.5.3.1, pg. 166)

583: C
Decision tree does not provide any help in identifying hidden risks. It is used for decision making and helps in analyzing various decision options and calculating the expected monetary value of each option.
PMBOK reference: (11.4.2.5, pg. 435)

584: A
Risk exposure is determined by multiplying the probability of a risk with the impact if the risk occurs. Expert judgment and Delphi techniques can help in suggesting the probability and impact scores but do not directly identify risk exposure.
PMBOK reference: (11.1.3.1, pg. 408 and 11.3.2.6, pg. 425)

585: D
The main reason to create and contribute to lessons learned register is to help the project team with the future work packages as well as future project teams. Creating a document to record what worked well and what failed is a futile effort if the information will not be used in the future. Lessons learned register is not a document related to the team's performance assessment. In fact, the project team should keep any individual or team performance issues out of this register. There must a reason why the project management plan requires lessons learned register to be created and maintained and that reason is to help with the future work.
PMBOK reference: (4.3.3.6, pg. 97)

586: B
Incentives and penalties, terms and conditions, and list of deliverables are all required as parts of the contract since these define what is to be delivered, how, by whom, and what if there is a failure. Work breakdown structure is not required and would be least valuable as part of the contract.
PMBOK reference: (12.2.3.2, pg. 489)

587: B
You will collect data which will then be analyzed to find the root cause of the problem. Then a suitable solution is to be selected and implemented. Afterward, you will have to check if the solution actually fixed the problem.
PMBOK reference: (9.6.2.2, pg. 356)

588: B
Expert judgment is not a technique used in the Control Schedule process. All the other three are tools and techniques of the Control Schedule process.
PMBOK reference: (6.6, pg. 222)

589: C
The tool that is used for verifying whether steps in a process have been completed is called a checklist. Quality control measurements are the work performance data collected when quality control tests are performed. Quality metrics are the expected result against which quality control measurements are compared. A quality report is the output of quality audit, process analysis, or other analyses.
PMBOK reference: (8.2.2.1, pg. 292)

590: C
Late start and late finish dates of an activity can be calculated by using the backward pass while going through critical path analysis of the network diagram.

PMBOK reference: (6.5.2.2, pg. 210)

591: B
Organizational Process Assets (OPAs) are the input to the Develop Project Charter process. All other choices are created much later in the project. OPAs can include organizational policies and procedures, templates, historical information, etc.
PMBOK reference: (4.1.1.4, pg. 79)

592: A
Opportunity cost is not a criterion used for selecting projects as it is a measure of the second best choice. The benefit-cost ratio of 1.3 is not comparable with internal rate of return and net present value as it does not include the time factor. Project with the highest internal rate of return should be selected.
PMBOK reference: (1.2.6.4, pg. 34)

593: A
Though all four choices have a component of benefits realization as part of measuring their success, it is the portfolios whose success mainly comes from aggregate investment performance and benefits realization.
PMBOK reference: (Table 1-2, pg. 13)

594: B
Cost Variance (CV) = Earned Value (EV) - Actual Cost (AC).
Cost Performance Index (CPI) = EV /AC.
If AC is more than EV, it will result in a negative cost variance and less than one CPI. Therefore, the project will be over budget.
PMBOK reference: (Table 7-1, pg. 267)

595: C
The project manager is using the "good guy, bad guy" technique where he is presenting his boss as the bad guy and himself as the good guy to pressure the seller in accepting his terms.
PMBOK reference: (12.2.2.5, pg. 488)

596: D
Management's mandate results in more strategic projects being initiated. Improvement in project management practice has the least impact on taking on strategic projects. Resources are managed by project managers not the project management office. Training sessions may improve project managers' capability to manage resources but do not transfer the responsibility from one to another. Stage gate reviews have to be scheduled whether project manager's performance has improved or not. The results

have no impact on this. Since the training, coaching and mentoring is one of the functions of the project management office, these results confirm that PMO has been able to deliver on one of their responsibilities. This is a result that should please the PMO manager.
PMBOK reference: (2.4.4.3, pg. 48)

597: C
The problem is with the new surprise issues not with issue management. Same way, poor risk response is not the problem, not having a risk response is. Lip service could be a reason but would be a weak choice. The best choice is that the project team is less experienced and is unable to identify and analyze all the risks and create a response plan for significant risks.
PMBOK reference: (11.2.2.1, pg. 414)

598: B
Sprint is a timeboxed iteration to perform project work; it is not a type of meeting. Iteration planning, scrum daily standup, and retrospective meetings are all performed as part of an agile project.
PMBOK reference: (4.3.2.3, pg. 95)

599: C
Prequalified sellers list is prepared or acquired in the Plan Procurement Management process and is used in the Conduct Procurement process. The list contains names of sellers who are qualified to do the work and are invited during this process to bid for the contract.
PMBOK reference: (12.2.1.6, pg. 486)

600: C

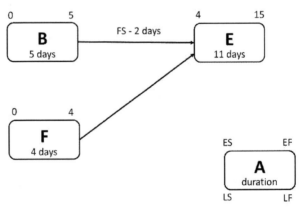

Early finish of activity B is 5 but activity E can start 2 days before activity B finishes, i.e. 5-2 is 3. Activity E, which is also dependent on activity F, is actually starting on 4 which means activity F must be finishing on 4. Since activity F early start is 0, the duration of activity F must be 4 to result in the early finish of 4.

PMBOK reference: (6.3.2.3, pg. 192 and 6.5.2.2, pg. 210)

Daud Nasir, PMP

8 – AN ADDITIONAL OFFER

This book contains 600 sample PMP questions with answers and explanations. Enhance your learning experience by obtaining access to these same tests as web-based simulated tests. You receive the following benefits:
1) Practice these tests in a simulated environment like the real exam
2) Duration of each test is 4 hours like the real exam
3) Questions can be marked for review like the real exam
4) Continuous 4 hours exam with no time stop like the real exam
5) Option to get the report showing your areas of strengths and weaknesses

You can get access to these tests by visiting the website
https://getxinstitute.com/product/pmp-exam-sample-tests/

Please use the following Amazon Book Customers Special Code for 50% off: AMZPMPQABK

ABOUT THE AUTHOR

Daud Nasir (PMP, LSSBB, Cert. Agile PM, ITIL-Foundation) is an accomplished leader and a seasoned professional in the project management and process improvement domains.

Daud has worked with small to large organizations, including, Hewlett Packard, Procter & Gamble, and General Motors and had excellent exposure to all levels of maturity in the project management and process maturity. This rich experience has helped him to become a highly effective coach and trainer, where he draws examples from various industries, functions, and situations to explain complex concepts. It provides an exceptional learning experience for mentees and trainees.

Daud is a passionate instructor and teaches courses in PMP exam preparation besides several other courses in areas like project management, Microsoft Project, Lean Six Sigma, change management, business analysis, and others.

He founded GetxSolution, now operating as GetxInstitute, a Toronto based company with a goal to improve organizational and individual performance through training courses and workshops that make a real difference in the life of the attendees.

As an active Project Management Institute Volunteer, Daud had the opportunity to contribute to The Guide to the Project Management Body of Knowledge (PMBOK®) 5th and 6th Editions as a Subject Matter Expert. Over the years, he has been an evaluator of several awards presented by PMI for excellence in various areas of project management. He also contributed to numerous standards and guides published by PMI.

Connect with Daud now,
LinkedIn: http://ca.linkedin.com/in/daudnasir/
Twitter: http://twitter.com/daudgetx
Institute website: http://www.getxinstitute.com

Made in the USA
Lexington, KY
01 September 2019